The Brother Hubbard Cookbook

A friend in the kitchen /// Garrett Fitzgerald /// Gill Books

Gill Books
Hume Avenue
Park West
Dublin 12
www.gillbooks.ie

Gill Books is an imprint of M.H. Gill & Co.

978 07171 6991 7

Edited by Kristin Jensen
Designed by Graham Thew
Photography © Leo Byrne, www.leobyrnephotography.com
Styled by Orla Neligan of Cornershop Productions, www.cornershopproductions.com
Assisted by Jane Flanagan

PROPS
Meadows & Byrne: Dublin, Cork, Galway, Clare, Tipperary.
T: (01) 280 4554/(021) 434 4100; E: info@meadowsandbyrne.ie;
W: www.meadowsandbyrne.com

Marks & Spencer: Unit 1–28, Dundrum Town Centre, Dublin 16.
T: (01) 299 1300; W: www.marksandspencer.ie

Article Dublin: Powerscourt Townhouse, South William Street, Dublin 2.
T: (01) 679 9268; E: items@articledublin.com; W: www.articledublin.com

Dunnes Stores: 46–50 South Great Georges Street, Dublin 2.
T: 1890 253 185; W: www.dunnesstores.com

Harold's Bazaar: 208 Harold's Cross Road, Dublin 6W.
T: 087 722 8789

Historic Interiors: Oberstown, Lusk, Co Dublin.
T: (01) 843 7174; E: killian@historicinteriors.net

TK Maxx: The Park, Carrickmines, Dublin 18.
T: (01) 207 4798; W: www.tkmaxx.ie

Golden Biscotti ceramics.
W: http://goldenbiscotti.bigcartel.com

The Patio Centre: The Hill Centre, Johnstown Road, Glenageary, Cabinteely, Dublin.18.
T: (01) 235 0714; W: thepatiocentre.com

Industry Design: 41 A/B Drury Street, Dublin 2.
T: (01) 613 9111; W: industrydesign.ie

Fired Earth: 19 Great Lower Georges Street, Co. Dublin.
T: (01) 663 6160; W: www.firedearth.com

Urban Outfitters: Cecilia Street, Dublin 2.
T: (01) 670 6202; www.urbanoutfitters.com

Indexed by Eileen O'Neill
Printed by BZ Graf, Poland

This book is typeset in 9.5 on 13.5pt Caecilia Light.

The paper used in this book comes from the wood pulp of managed forests. For every tree felled, at least one tree is planted, thereby renewing natural resources.

A CIP catalogue record for this book is available from the British Library.

5 4 3 2

Dedicated with thanks to those in my life who've inspired and helped me to have a wonderful adventure in food:

» *my teachers, Darina and Rory,*
» *my friends Michelle and Andrea, from whom I've learned so much,*
» *my friend and colleague, Eamon, an amazing chef with whom collaboration is such fun*
» *all the team at Brother Hubbard, so full of creativity, energy and passion,*
» *my parents for all their love and support,*
» *and finally, to my James, who puts up with me, eats the food I cook without complaint (even my disasters) and cleans up all my messes!*

GARRETT FITZGERALD left his office-based career to follow his dream: to immerse himself in the creative adventures to be enjoyed with food. That journey started off with three wonderful months in Darina Allen's Ballymaloe Cookery School. Next, he and his partner James travelled the world, exploring the flavours of local food throughout. They spent a year in Melbourne, working in a charming little bakery and in a café, both businesses dedicated to purity, creativity and quality. Deciding to focus on the relatively undiscovered yet vibrant, healthy food of the Middle East, Garrett journeyed for several months through its streets, souks and bazaars, eating with locals and learning the secrets of their food and its part in their lives. Bringing that experience back home, on a wing and a prayer, Brother Hubbard opened on Dublin's Capel Street in 2012, during the darkest hours of the recession. What once was a small fledgling café has since become so much more, with a team dedicated to bringing the best of breakfast, brunch, lunch, dinner and baking to its community of customers. A second café opened in September 2016 to continue that culinary journey.

CONTENTS

❀ ANY TIME OF THE DAY ////

Introduction

Brother Hubbard quietly opened its doors in March 2012 at the height of a dreadful recession that terrified us all (especially anyone foolhardy enough to try to open a business). Our intention was clear from the outset: to provide simple, pure, interesting food, made entirely from scratch; to share our love of food that was somewhat different to what was available elsewhere; and to provide an invitation to others, customers and staff alike, to join us on this adventure with food.

Four busy years on, we've had so much fun along the way. The recipes between these pages represent the kind of food we love to cook, inspired by our adventures and our heroes, the food that we've learned, discovered, created and invented, and the dishes our customers tell us they love the most. We've written our recipes in a certain way, encouraging you to enjoy both the cooking process and the end result. After all, cooking food should not just be functional; it should also be fun, with the possibility for adventure.

Our food is designed to offer nourishment and pleasure, and above all, you should feel better for having had it.[1] That is not an experience that happens as often as any of us would like. We try to make pure food that is healthy and full of freshness, providing a feel-good quality without compromising on enjoyment. We don't sermonise and we don't ask you to change your lifestyle.

---

1 With a few exceptions, most notably some recipes in the Treats section of this book, which might be better categorised as pure indulgence!

We genuinely feel that this is food you might enjoy, and you might just happen to feel better after having eaten it. What could be lovelier than that?

We feel passionately about cooking and we hope that by reading and using this book, we can share this passion with you, our reader. We sincerely hope you use this book, for it is absolutely designed to be used. It is not intended to be just a pretty cookbook sitting immaculately on a shelf, filled with luscious pictures. Use it! Often! Scribble in the margins, spill some soup on its pages, dab it joyfully with beetroot-stained fingers, stick pages together with careless splatter, have sesame seeds tumble out when you open it, with stray herbs as unintended bookmarks. A well-loved cookbook is one that looks like it has taken the most punishment, and that is how we will measure the success of this book: by how it is used.

THE ADVENTURE LEADING TO BROTHER HUBBARD

There we were, the two of us, cosy in our nice careers back in the heady days of the Celtic Tiger. We enjoyed our jobs, enjoyed our lives. But it wasn't quite enough. Too often we found ourselves daydreaming about doing something else, something we could be intensely passionate about. I felt I was never going to write a book[2] or paint an amazing canvas, but I knew I loved cooking and I thought I might just have a chance at being half-decent at it.

An evening course in bread-baking boosted my confidence levels, while a random chat with one of my classmates told me first-hand of her cookery school

---

2 Or so I thought – imagine my surprise at this development!

experiences. Returning to Dublin one bleak January morning after a few weeks of bliss in Argentina made us realise that we had to do something to change things. Having just turned 30, I was beginning to fully appreciate that life isn't a rehearsal. If I wanted things to change, I had to make it happen myself.

However, realising you need to change is one thing; actually changing is another. An article a few weeks later in the *Guardian* about the psychology of regret really spelled it out for us: we tend to regret mostly the things we don't do – not doing them doesn't allow us to move on, whereas doing them gives us progress and momentum. That was our 'eureka!' moment. Within a few weeks, I had reserved my place in the Ballymaloe Cookery School, and together, myself and James jumped off the cliff (so to speak), packed in our jobs and hit out for adventure.

And what a time that was. Innocently thinking it might be more of a foodie holiday, it was an intense learning experience, where each day was so valuable. Immersed in all things food, it was non-stop. Our very first class taught us perhaps the most important recipe of all: holding up fresh compost in our hands and being told that this is where it all comes from, understanding the importance of nature and the purity of the food we consume. That was the first of many, many recipes given to us over the course of that unforgettable autumn, surrounded by nature's harvest, by people obsessed with learning and discovering, by amazing artisan producers and by egg-laying hens in the midst of a cookery school on an organic farm, run by the most passionate, most energetic, most enigmatic of cooks, Darina Allen.

After Ballymaloe, we headed off for two years: the first year was to see the world, the second to get experience

in food. After a year of nomadically wandering around markets and stalls all across India, Nepal and South-East Asia, we arrived in Melbourne, famous for its casual dining and coffee scene. I found myself working with two amazing women in two amazing, small, owner-run businesses: one a little artisan bakery run by the dedicated Andrea, and the other a neighbourhood café run by the charismatic Michelle. Both businesses were committed to quality, creativity and doing their best for their customers. What an important experience that turned out to be. You will see the influence of that wonderful time throughout this book.

At the end of my time in Melbourne, I had firmly made up my mind that Middle Eastern cuisine was the type of food I loved and felt particularly passionate about – vivid, fresh, vegetarian-friendly, unsuspectingly healthy and full of texture, colour, history and more than a little intrigue. Some years earlier, I had also become more than a little influenced by the style and ingenuity of Yotam Ottolenghi. I had also discovered the writings of Claudia Roden as well as Sam and Sam Clark. I now had to experience the real thing.

So off I went for four months to discover the authentic flavours and histories of that food in Lebanon, Turkey, Syria,[3] Jordan, Israel and Palestine. Such wonderful food and such remarkable people. I talked my way into a few restaurant kitchens, couch-surfed with some locals to join them as they ate, took the odd local cookery class. It felt like a privilege to be there, to be allowed to participate in their food culture: to eat as they did, with them, and understand their approach to and the history of their food.

---

3 Though I loved all of the places I visited in the Middle East, Syria was my absolute favourite country. I feel privileged to have been able to witness it as it was, just before the troubles that have so devastated its people and its cultural history.

With that adventure over and my savings almost gone, it was time to return home. We had left Ireland in the heady days of the Celtic Tiger, only to return to economic devastation. What to do?

We looked around and saw that some people were still eating out, seeking a better, more value-driven experience, willing to pay for simple quality and creativity, something different and less indulgent, being more careful with the €5 notes than perhaps they had ever been with their €50 ones a few years earlier. That was precisely the space we wanted to occupy: casual, accessible food, humble and absolutely affordable. It was time to be brave.

It wasn't easy. We really didn't know how to begin. It seemed impossible then, with all the economic difficulties around us. Should we wait for the world to eventually change, or should we just power on ahead and change things ourselves to make things work for us?

Still inspired by that article about regret in the *Guardian* we'd read some years earlier, we decided to take the plunge. Important support from our (perhaps reluctant and worried) parents in the form of loans, a cute café space on Dublin's Capel Street[4] and a willingness to do whatever it took got us started.

We opened selling just cakes and coffee. Determined as we were to get things right, we thought we would start simply-yet-focused and take it from there. Thankfully, the response was encouraging, to say the least. Aside from people enjoying what we were offering, they were

---

4 Good heavens, it did feel brave. Even at the height of the boom, the northside was, sadly and inexplicably, relatively overlooked.

very supportive and congratulatory of us opening in the most desperate of economic situations.

A few months later, we added our lunch menu. Nine months later, we could serve you breakfast. A further nine months on, brunch. A further nine months after that (are you sensing a pattern?), we expanded into the space next door. And then our southside sibling café followed. Then our evening menu. And now, this book.

It has been so much fun. We are humbled. We started with just the two of us and two staff, but today we are bigger and busier than we ever could have dreamed of. We have a wonderful team around us of colleagues and comrades as well as so many loyal customers.

And thankfully, it still remains fun and full of adventure, particularly when it comes to our menu. We hope our book reflects that and that it brings about numerous adventures of the culinary kind for you too.

OUR APPROACH TO FOOD

Located on the northside's Capel Street but now also southside on Harrington Street, we open seven days a week, serving breakfast, brunch, lunch, treats and dinner. It certainly keeps us busy!

The approach to the food was to offer something new, creative, different and interesting, focused on quality and value. We decided to anchor our food (though not exclusively) in the culture of Middle Eastern cuisine, a cuisine full of fresh, healthy food (often vegetarian-friendly) that remained relatively undiscovered beyond very specific evening eateries.

We describe our food as deceptively vegetarian,[5] but also deceptively Middle Eastern. We have a modern approach to that cuisine: browsing our menu, it won't feel pigeonholed the way a place specialising in a particular type of food often can.

We've deliberately avoided the classics, so ubiquitous and available everywhere, such as the 'full Irish', eggs Benedict or generic mayonnaise-drenched coleslaw. These can no doubt be wonderful dishes and absolutely have their place, but we decided to avoid them, to do something different, forcing us to be that little bit more creative.

We still sometimes lose customers because they can't have a big fry-up or a bottle of Coca-Cola with their lunch; but we feel we've gained so many more customers because we are providing something different, something we've created and something we've made. Effectively, everything we give you (except for certain types of bread), we've made ourselves. That means our food can be purer, fresher and more creative. And we would like to think it's better, and better for you, as a result.

Aside from that, we've tried to create a place that's welcoming and where, as a customer, you will feel cared for. In certain respects, it should try to feel like having people over for food – you want them to feel that they are being looked after. We want you to enjoy the food, the experience and the personality of the whole offering. That's what got me cooking at home originally, and it's what sustains our approach today.

---

5 It's certainly not exclusively vegetarian, but often to the extent that meat-eaters won't realise it's a vegetarian dish, nor will they feel alienated by vegetarian food, as sometimes we can, God love us!

Suzy likes a dash of extra dressing on her salad. Fiona is very particular about our omelette, which she adores. The Judge like his toast lightly done every morning. Maria will reliably get the Superpower Bar, day after day, with her flat white. John likes his coffee that bit stronger. Peter prefers filter coffee. Paul will have the soup every time he's in; he doesn't even need to know what it is when he orders it – he trusts us, he says. That girl is back and she brought her granny this time. Those people on table 10 came here because their friends recommended us and told them to be sure to order the pancakes and the three salad plate.

All of that is what makes our day, day after day. Providing interesting food to our lovely customers, looking after them, hopefully making them happy and making something we can be proud of, together.

And so, over time, what started out as a simple café has ended up being so much more: a community of the most enthusiastic people dedicated to doing the best they can day after day, with a spring in their step, for our wonderful customers, who provide us with so much encouragement.

We hope that this book helps you to do likewise – to cook something you can be proud of and that you will enjoy, and that those you cook it for will also enjoy.

And maybe, along the way, you will learn something and you will certainly feel better because you did it yourself, and because it was even just that little bit better for you.

A FEW MORE WORDS ABOUT OUR FOOD

Our food is heavily influenced by MIDDLE EASTERN cuisine, though not exclusively so. Having first discovered a modern take on that style of food from Yotam Ottolenghi after visiting his first café only a little while after it opened, I gradually became more and more intrigued by this cuisine that's so full of flavour and texture, so vibrant, so healthy. I even spent several months 'inspecting' that part of the world in order to soak up its flavours and the way people eat there. Our food is not tied exclusively to that region, but it's a pretty big influence in what we do, with that eastern Mediterranean area being home to such diverse yet connected food traditions in Turkey, Lebanon, Syria, Israel, Greece, Morocco and parts of southern Spain. That's not to say that Irish food doesn't play a part – where would our café be without our version of the traditional Irish scone or porridge (not to mention the potato!)?

We are HERBY. Oh so herby. In most cooking, in my humble view, herbs are simply underused and overlooked. We have a heavy hand with herbs, and with good reason: they add so much flavour, vibrancy, texture, freshness and colour to so many dishes. And they're good for you! So don't be afraid to use a heavy hand too and grow your own if you can. You will notice that we have our favourites – I don't know how many times we mention parsley, coriander and mint or rave on about how fantastic lovage is – but do play around with whatever you love.[6] A lot of the time, any soft, fresh herb will work, though often better in combination with at least one other herb. If you've a penchant for dill, go crazy with the dill! The same goes for chives or whatever

---

6 And please do use the stalks of the soft herbs if you can, chopped very finely. It's such a shame to throw them out, as they are full of flavour and nutrition.

takes your fancy, though consider what might work best with the dish in question.

We are also very LEMONY. Oh my gosh, but how I do love lemon. For me, it's as critical as seasoning: it is a seasoning! Acidity is such an overlooked element to seasoning and finishing a dish. Lemon provides the much-needed acidity, but also a vigour and freshness that can be important too. Use it often, but sparingly. And more often than not, we try to use the zest too. What a shame to throw an unzested lemon into your compost bin, all that flavour and brightness gone forever.

We are SPICY. But not in a 'hot, hot, hot' way. Gentle, fragrant spices have a much bigger part to play in our food than fiery spices (which also have their place). So when we say spicy, we mean full of fragrance and flavour and not necessarily 'hot'. Throughout the book you'll see a lot of cumin and coriander, but caraway makes a frequent appearance too, as does allspice, cinnamon and sweet paprika.

We are very VEGETARIAN, but not exclusively so. We try to be 'deceptively vegetarian' – the dishes often happen to be vegetarian, rather than intentionally so, if that makes sense. We design a lot of our dishes so that they work perfectly just as they are, but if you are so inclined, you can add some meat in. Not only does vegetarian food oftentimes feel healthier, but it's also considered to be much better for our environment.

Our food is PURE. We like to make things from scratch and we encourage you to do the same. You will typically end up with a far better outcome than anything you can buy ready-made, you will be prouder of it and it will definitely be more interesting – perhaps a little like in the Mexican film *Like Water for Chocolate*,[7] where the food might come to capture and embody a little of your character, making it deeply personal.

Finally, we are THOUGHTFUL. And we want you to be too. Think about the dish, what you are doing and why you are doing it, and learn from it. Think about how you or your guests are going to eat it – the look, texture and mouthfeel as well as the flavour. Take the time at the appropriate stages to taste the food and adjust it as necessary. After all the work that goes into preparing a dish, we often forget to taste it before serving to make sure it's what it should be and is the best that it can be.[8] In pretty much every recipe, we tell you to taste it, think about it, adjust it to get it just right. Using great ingredients is one thing, as is using a great recipe, but it needs you and your thoughtfulness to bring it all together – to make it uniquely yours. No one will ever have created a dish that is precisely like the one you have before you, your very own creation, so take the time to think about it, be in control of it and ultimately, be proud of it. Use our guidance, but learn, develop and create your own style the more you cook. That's how it should be. And therein lies the adventure.

---

7 In *Como Agua para Chocolate*, the food created by the lead character captures the emotions she is feeling as she makes that food, only for those same emotions to be experienced by those who eat her food.

8 And when you think it's just right, reach for a lemon for that extra last squeeze. Of this, I am very guilty.

HOW WE'VE STRUCTURED THIS BOOK

The book is broadly structured as follows:

» *The beginning of the day: Breakfast*
Something to have any morning with little fuss or
fanfare, just simple enjoyment.

» *The middle of the day: Brunch, lunch and supper*
Slightly more substantial dishes that are suitable for
brunch, lunch or supper, depending on your mood and
inclination.

» *The late of the day: Mains and sides*
Definitely dinner, a main meal with a few
recommended side dishes, but do browse the salad
section in particular for more ideas for accompaniments.

» *Any time of the day: Treats and drinks*
Need we say more?

» *Supporting recipes and techniques*
Additional base recipes for elements to dishes that
come up again and again as well as guidance for some
basic techniques that will be common to a lot of our
recipes.

» *Ingredients we use*
An introduction to some key ingredients we use and
how to use them. These tend to be classic Middle
Eastern ingredients that are now widely available in
Ireland.

Now, a lot of our dishes could actually form part of any
meal at any time of the day, so I recommend keeping an
open mind. Browse the entire book before making any
cooking commitments! One person's brunch might well
be another person's breakfast, supper or dinner.

A WORD ABOUT OUR RECIPES

I am a cook, not a chef, and these recipes are written for cooks. I am fortunate enough to have been able to go to cookery school and now to work with food, day after day, but I am still very much a cook. We've written the recipes keeping in mind what it's like to approach a recipe for the first time, with relatively little experience, so we've done our best to write these recipes so that you are given an awful lot of guidance. In doing so, we want you to have all the support you need to be confident about what you are doing and therefore for the recipe to come out the way it should. These recipes are ultimately intended to be casual, accessible and unfussy.

A lot of the time, cooking is imprecise and is dependent on so many variables – your ingredients, your equipment, your experience, your personality and what you like, your confidence. Thus, please use these recipes in the main as guidance. We want you to make a dish your own. We want you to discover and learn and to apply your judgement so that ultimately, you've created something that you can be proud of and that you and those eating your food will enjoy.

I learned this lesson in my early days in Ballymaloe. Every day, with 50 students in the class, we would be cooking the same recipe with the same ingredients, using the same sets of equipment, yet without fail, we would get 50 different outcomes. That's a fact that should be celebrated, in my opinion. And even if something goes wrong, learn from it – write the lesson in the margin beside the recipe and promise yourself to try it again. It will turn out better the next time and you will have learned something, implicitly making you a better, more confident cook.

None of the recipes are bafflingly complex, but we also don't mince our words in order to give you all the detail and confidence you need to achieve an interesting outcome. As a result, some recipes might seem long, or even, dare I say, long-winded. However, look closer and you will see that none of the recipes really contain so much hard work, but rather, thoughtful guidance, descriptive accounts of what to do and why you do it as well as tips to help you along your way. The recipes may take longer to read, but that doesn't necessarily mean they take longer to prepare – just better prepared!

As a home cook who once dreamed of devoting myself entirely to cooking, I found the greatest weakness in my cooking was a lack of confidence or ability to judge if what I was doing was the correct way to do it. If the recipe said take the cake out of the oven after 30 minutes, the cake would come out, regardless of how under- or overcooked it was, as that's what the recipe said. Such was my fear of deviating from the script and using my own judgement! I was often left frustrated by recipes that didn't give adequate guidance, causing me to wing it unnecessarily. I learned a lot during these exasperating moments, but it was often needlessly stressful (particularly when dinner guests were just minutes away from arriving). So in writing our recipes, we've tried to get the balance right: thoughtful and instructive, but at the same time reflecting a more natural way of cooking.

Some of the recipes may seem repetitive, but that's just the nature of the way people use cookbooks. People rarely read them cover to cover, but rather hop and stagger along from recipe to recipe, like a drunken bee gathering its nectar.

At the end of most recipes, we've included some tips and tricks. Oftentimes, these are pointers for further using these recipes, what to do when things go wrong or how to adapt them in ways that might suit you. We also encourage smarter habits – doubling up on this sauce or that dressing – to make life easier for you the next time or to provide a head start or shortcut for another recipe that may call for a similar element.

We genuinely hope that you will enjoy cooking our recipes. We hope that you will cook them again and again, and that you will eventually develop your own way of doing things as your confidence grows. There is an iterative element to developing as a cook – you will always learn something by revisiting a recipe. Write in the margins, make use of your discoveries and learn from your mistakes for the next time you cook that dish. Opening a used cookbook should almost feel like reading over your old diary: an account of what you did, how it went and what you learned.

Now roll up the sleeves, put on that apron, preheat your oven and get ready for some adventures …

※ The Beginning of the Day

BREAKFAST

The most important meal of the day, so they say. Too often, I'm guilty of running out to work without having one – the irony being that we serve so many to our customers each day.

Like most of the food in this book, breakfast should be a meal that makes you feel better after having eaten it. You should get up from the table sated and with a spring in your step. While that should be true of any meal, it would seem particularly important for the first meal of your day.

Over the next few pages, we've set out a number of recipes and breakfast ideas for you to try and enjoy. Several of them are recipes you can have day after day by making a bigger batch and adding different elements to it each day. We've also included a few recipes for morning baked treats.

All these breakfast recipes are intended to be weekday recipes. Looking at our brunch section in the next part of the book, however, you might feel that many of the recipes there are just as suitable as a midweek breakfast. I would go so far as to say that the two chapters could be read in conjunction with each other and you can plan your menu from there. Food should be enjoyed, and you get to decide when you enjoy it!

※ Bircher muesli

For years, I didn't love porridge (now I do – an almost life-changing development, to be honest), so bircher muesli was a great alternative – it's incredibly easy, tasty, filling and quite healthy. It's the perfect dish to have as a breakfast or a mini-bowl to serve as part of a brunch. It also travels well, so pot it up and bring it to work or have it on the go. The base of soaked oats holds well, so you can make extra to keep in the fridge and then keep the ingredients for serving with it each morning separate.

It was developed in Switzerland many moons ago by a doctor who was ahead of his time in terms of his approach to nutrition, advocating as he did a diet built around eating lots of raw fruit and vegetables (and all of this before the discovery of vitamins!).

Dr Bircher-Benner's muesli is essentially a raw oat dish, where the rolled oats are soaked rather than cooked (as they would be for a proper porridge). By soaking them, you get them lovely and soft, particularly if you use something acidic like apple juice, which breaks the oat down slightly and gently while also imbuing it with a delicious fruity flavour. We then add all sorts of elements to this base mix to bring about all manner of wonderful combinations and textures.

As with so many of our recipes, please do use these as a starting point to go off and develop your own variations, perhaps secretly paying thanks to Dr Bircher-Benner for his delicious discovery.

※ Spring-summer bircher muesli

Though suitable all year round, bircher muesli is the ideal summer breakfast to replace porridge – we often refer to it as summer porridge in the café. This version uses more or less the same technique as the autumn-winter recipe that follows, but with the addition of coconut and summery fruits to make it the perfect summer breakfast pot. Again, please do experiment. Some finely grated fresh ginger would work well here, as would any number of other fruits, toasted nuts and seeds.

SERVES 4–6

- 300g organic rolled oats (porridge oats)
- 300ml best-quality fresh apple juice
- 200ml coconut milk
- 2 tbsp coconut flakes
- 2 tsp honey
- zest and juice of 1 lime
- 4 tbsp Greek yogurt or crème fraîche
- 150g mango, diced (optional)
- ½ pomegranate, seeds only (optional) (see page 354)
- 3 passionfruit, seeds only
- 20g fresh mint

Ideally you should soak the oats the night before, but even an hour or two in advance is fine. Place the oats in a bowl, then add the apple juice and two-thirds of the coconut milk. Stir well, cover and refrigerate overnight or for a few hours at least.

To toast your coconut flakes (and make sure they are flakes, not dusty desiccated coconut, as this makes all the difference), heat a dry frying pan over a medium heat for 2 minutes. Add the coconut flakes and continue to heat, tossing every 10–15 seconds until they are nicely toasted (2–3 minutes in total) and the edges have taken on a nice light brown colour. Transfer to a bowl, otherwise the coconut flakes might burn from the residual heat in the pan.

When ready to serve, uncover the oats and add the honey, lime zest and juice. Now stir well – the mix should have a soft, loose, porridge-like consistency. If you feel that the mix is too thick, add an extra dash of apple juice (or even a little water) and coconut milk to loosen it. If you feel it needs a little more sweetness, add more honey and stir well. Similarly, add more lime if needed to give it that fresh kick. Play around with it until you are happy that it tastes delicious. >>

To build your dish, place a cup of oats in each serving bowl. Place a spoonful of yogurt on top, then sprinkle with the toasted coconut flakes, followed by the diced mango and the pomegranate seeds, if using. Finish with a spoonful of passionfruit seeds, some torn fresh mint leaves and a drizzle of the remaining coconut milk.

The oat base will hold perfectly in the fridge for 2–3 days. Just taste it every time you use it, as the flavours and texture will evolve. Each time, it might need more apple juice or some of the reserved coconut milk (for flavour and/or texture) or more lime or honey (for flavour).

※ Autumn-winter bircher muesli

This is our autumn-winter version. As always, I encourage you to experiment with different combinations, following the basic method below. For example, orange juice works well instead of apple, or try a different mix of spices – maybe a tiny bit of ground cloves and extra ginger or even diced crystallised ginger at Christmas.

SERVES 4

- 300g organic rolled oats (porridge oats)
- 80g mixed dried fruit (such as sultanas, currants, dried cranberries)
- 400ml best-quality fresh apple juice
- 100ml water
- 1 level tsp ground cinnamon
- 1 level tsp ground ginger
- ½ level tsp ground cardamom
- 1–2 tbsp honey (or more, to taste)
- zest and juice of 1 lemon
- 1–2 apples
- 1 x 300ml tub of thick Greek yogurt or crème fraîche
- 1 banana or a small handful of grapes (optional)
- 50g toasted nuts, roughly chopped (see page 352)
- 1 pomegranate, seeds only (optional) (see page 354)

Ideally, you should soak the oats the night before, but even an hour or two in advance is fine. Place the oats in a bowl with the dried fruit, then add the apple juice, water and spices. Stir well, cover and refrigerate overnight or for a few hours at least.

When ready to serve, uncover the oats and add the honey. Now stir well – the mix should have a soft, loose consistency. If you feel that the mix is too thick, add an extra dash of apple juice (or even a little water) to loosen it. If you feel it needs a little more spice or sweetness, add more spices and/or a little more honey and stir well. It should ultimately have the consistency of a soft, creamy rice pudding. If you fancy, zest your lemon and add it at this stage.

When ready to serve, grate the apple on the biggest part of a box grater or slice it very thinly, tossing well in a squeeze of lemon juice. Add half of this to the bircher muesli and mix well.

To build your dish, place a cup of oats in each serving bowl. Top with the remaining apple divided amongst the dishes. Place a spoonful of yogurt on top, followed by the banana or grapes, if using. Finish by sprinkling over the nuts and the pomegranate seeds, if using.

The oat base will hold perfectly in the fridge for 2–3 days. Just taste it every time you use it, as the flavours and texture will evolve. It might need more apple juice (for flavour and/or texture) or more lime or honey (for flavour).

TIPS AND TRICKS

» Some chopped stem ginger would be lovely here too, or you could serve this with a spoonful of our berry and rose compote (page 343) on top.

※ Granola

Granola is a bit controversial, in my opinion. It enjoys this reputation in most people's minds as being healthy, and while it does have a lot of virtue going for it, with all those wonderful grains, seeds and nuts, it can often have a lot of sugar and oil too. We've tried to create a recipe to get the balance right, but it still sits on the somewhat indulgent end of the spectrum nonetheless.

MAKES 15 PORTIONS

- 500g rolled oats
- 125g sunflower seeds
- 125g pumpkin seeds
- 100g whole almonds
- 60g sesame seeds
- 1 tsp ground cinnamon
- ½ tsp salt
- 200g honey
- 175g muscovado sugar
- 100ml sunflower oil
- 100ml water
- 1 tsp vanilla extract
- 20g coconut flakes
- 20g currants
- 20g golden sultanas
- 20g dried cranberries

Preheat your oven to 160°C. Put the oats, seeds, almonds, cinnamon and salt in a large bowl.

Combine the honey, sugar, oil, water and vanilla in a pot and slowly heat to dissolve the sugar.

Add the wet ingredients to the dry and mix together thoroughly. Place in a shallow roasting tray or tin and bake in the oven for 40 minutes. After 40 minutes, use a metal spoon to stir the granola well to stop it from sticking to the tin. Return to the oven and repeat, stirring every 20 minutes over the course of 2 more hours.

When the time is up, give it one final mix to break up any clusters, then turn off the oven and leave the granola in the warm oven to dry out. As it cools, the granola will harden and crisp up to the desired texture and crunch. >>

Meanwhile, to toast your coconut flakes (and make sure they are flakes, not dusty desiccated coconut, as this makes all the difference), heat a dry frying pan over a medium heat for 2 minutes. Add the coconut flakes and continue to heat, tossing every 10–15 seconds until they are nicely toasted (2–3 minutes in total) and the edges have taken on a nice light brown colour. Transfer to a bowl, otherwise the coconut flakes might burn from the residual heat in the pan.

Finish the granola by adding the dried fruits and the lightly toasted coconut flakes. This makes a nice big batch, and if kept in an airtight container it will last for a few weeks.

TIPS AND TRICKS

» We serve this in the café with a generous amount of thick Greek yogurt and some berries or berry and rose compote (page 343), finished with some torn fresh mint. You could also sprinkle it over porridge or bircher muesli.

※ Hot oat porridge (and how to serve it)

We have found that a lot of people are very particular about certain things, and that a lot of these things tend to be what could be considered the basics, the staples: their tea, their scones, their soup – and their porridge!

There is a lot of grim porridge out there, that bad, lumpy mess that is difficult to eat and would nearly put anyone off porridge for life. But following the simple steps below should result in a satisfying outcome.

Porridge should be warm and comforting with a texture akin to a softish rice pudding. And it should be delicious to eat virtually untouched. Though I am guilty of adding lots of extras to my porridge, I think the best way to eat it is with a little cream and some dark brown sugar sprinkled over it. We have some further serving suggestions below.

- 1 part rolled porridge oats (organic if possible)
- 2 parts water
- a good pinch of salt per medium pot of porridge
- 1 part milk

First, plan ahead! Soak the porridge in the water for several hours, but ideally overnight. Just add the water and salt to the oats right in the pot you will be cooking the porridge in. Cover and leave out as is for several hours. Soaking the oats in advance results in a quicker cooking time and a better, softer, more flavourful porridge.

After soaking, add the milk. Put the pot on a low to medium heat, cover and bring to a very gentle simmer. Take the lid off and stir with a wooden spoon from time to time. It should simmer for approximately 10 minutes. Test it by tasting a little spoonful – it should have a nice soft mouthfeel, but it should still have some texture to it too. Serve it in a warm bowl.

TIPS AND TRICKS

Here are a number of serving suggestions for your porridge:
- » *Classic:* Pouring cream and a really lovely, rich, dark brown sugar (muscovado is ideal) or some honey.
- » *Virtuous:* Lightly toasted seeds (pumpkin, sunflower, sesame), some chopped crystallised ginger and some dried fruit.
- » *Berry:* Fresh berries, such as blueberries or raspberries, or the berry and rose compote on page 343. >>

» *Fruity:* Banana and toasted nuts is a common combo, or try something a little different by roasting apple or pear wedges sprinkled generously with sugar in a 180°C oven for 15 minutes or so, until baked through but not falling apart. Or just make extra poached pears from the pear frangipane cake recipe on page 297 or extra rhubarb from the foolish mess recipe on page 299.

» *Indulgent:* Make a honey-whiskey syrup by bringing 50g honey and 25g muscovado sugar to the boil with 25ml water and a capful (or more) of whiskey. Simmer until the sauce reduces by about a third. Taste and add more whiskey as you see fit. Drizzle over your porridge along with a splash of cream. This is a particular treat on a cold winter morning, and in my book is completely justifiable in December! This will make more syrup than you need, so keep it in the fridge and warm it up as needed.

VARIATIONS ON THE PORRIDGE

» Add a handful of chia seeds to the pot when soaking the oats and cook as per the recipe above.

» Make it dairy free by replacing the milk with coconut milk or the same quantity of water, or half coconut milk, half water.

» Add a handful or two of dried fruit when soaking the oats to get the fruits good and plump.

» For extra oaty goodness (I adore the flavour of oats), lightly toast some porridge oats (straight from the packet) on a preheated dry frying pan set over a medium heat for 4 minutes or so, until the oats take on a light golden brown colour. Sprinkle these over the porridge as you serve it or stir them through just before serving to really up the oaty flavour to hitherto unknown levels!

※ Brother Hubbard fruit salad with pearl barley and coconut porridge

I've included this not just because it's delicious and easy, but as part of my determined plan to get people eating pearl barley once more! This 'porridge' will work equally well as a healthy breakfast, a starter course to a brunch or as a tasty pudding course. It's incredibly satisfying and refreshing but also substantial, so it will set you up for the day (just note that it's eaten cold as opposed to hot).

The porridge itself will hold happily in the fridge for 3–4 days, so you can keep returning to it for breakfast over a few mornings – just be sure to taste it each time and adjust the lime, coconut milk and honey, as the flavours might evolve somewhat. A little grated fresh ginger, added to taste, would be another worthwhile addition here.

SERVES 6–8

- 300g pearl barley
- 1 x 400ml tin of coconut milk
- juice of 2–3 limes
- 2–4 tbsp runny honey
- 75g red quinoa (or sunflower seeds or roughly chopped nuts)
- 30g coconut flakes
- 2–3 oranges
- 3 apples or pears (or a mix)
- 50g fresh mint
- 1 small punnet of fresh blueberries

This first step should be done well ahead of time. Cook the pearl barley by covering it with two and a half times its volume of water and bringing to a gentle simmer in a pan set over a medium heat. Cook for approximately 40 minutes, stirring occasionally, until the pearl barley is nice and tender while still retaining a bouncy texture (just beyond al dente). Once cooked, strain and rinse under cold water, shaking really well to remove any excess water. Place in a bowl and add about three-quarters of the coconut milk (keeping the rest in a bowl in the fridge), the juice of 1 lime and 2 tablespoons of runny honey. Stir well, cover and put in the fridge for 2–3 hours, or even better, overnight.

Toast the quinoa by placing a clean, dry frying pan over a medium heat until it's good and hot. Throw the quinoa into the pan and shake it over the heat for 1–2 minutes, until it's toasted (do the same if using nuts or seeds instead). Tip into a bowl immediately afterwards so that it doesn't toast too much. >>

Using the same pan, gently toast the coconut flakes for 2–3 minutes, until they turn a light golden colour, then remove from the pan.

Peel the oranges, removing as much of the pith as possible, and cut into 1cm-thick slices. Core the apples or pears and cut into bite-sized wedges. In a large bowl, toss the oranges, apples and pears in 2 tablespoons of honey and the juice of half a lime.

Take the pearl barley porridge out of the fridge and taste it, adding more coconut milk, lime juice or honey if needed. The aim is that you end up with something akin to a rice pudding – a nice saucy porridge with a hit of coconut, honey and lime together with that soothing texture.

To serve, place some orange slices and apple or pear wedges on individual plates or bowls, tearing the fresh mint leaves over each layer. Place a big spoonful of the pearl barley porridge on top of each portion, then top with a good sprinkling of the fresh blueberries (no one will blame you for being generous!), some more mint and a good sprinkle of the toasted red quinoa (or nuts or seeds, or all of these!) and the toasted coconut flakes. Finish with a final drizzle of honey and any juice from the apple/pear marinade.

※ Yogurt, tahini, honey and nuts

This dish was inspired by a breakfast that I had in Lebanon one morning, which had a very sweet honey and tahini mixed into some labneh with fruit. Once you've tasted this, you might well crave it every so often, either for breakfast or even as a little pick-me-up later in the day. Experiment with the fruits you use here, though personally I feel banana works best.

Aside from it being wonderfully delicious and comforting, this really couldn't be easier to prepare. Use the best of each ingredient in this recipe – as there is no cooking, the better the quality of the ingredients, the better the outcome.

Finally, please do try to serve this in wide dishes or bowls. You want the ingredients spread out to make sure you can get a little of everything with each spoonful you take. It's one of those dishes where the way that it's eaten really matters – you want each spoon to have a little of each ingredient, separate, so each element is distinctive in terms of mouthfeel and taste when you eat it.

INGREDIENTS PER PERSON

- 3–4 heaped tbsp thick Greek yogurt
- ½ banana per person, chopped (or equivalent of other fruit, such as apple or melon)
- ½ tbsp tahini
- ½ tbsp honey
- small handful of nuts, toasted and chopped (see page 352)
- ½ handful pomegranate seeds (optional) (see page 354)
- a few fresh mint leaves

Place generous spoonfuls of the yogurt into an individual wide-bottomed bowl and add the chopped banana. Drizzle the tahini over the yogurt in a circular motion. Follow by drizzling over the honey, loosely tracing the path of the tahini.

To finish, scatter the chopped nuts over the dish, then the pomegranate seeds, if using. Finally, tear some fresh mint over it and serve.

» As you will see, we're big fans of toasted coconut flakes, which would be a worthwhile addition to this dish. See page 23 for instructions on how to toast them.

» Try merging this recipe with the spring-summer bircher muesli on page 23, using some soaked oats as the base on which to build the rest of this dish, giving it more texture and substance.

» A drizzle of pomegranate molasses over the finished dish can add another interesting note, as can a handful of fresh berries or some chopped pear or apple.

※ Semolina pancakes (beghrir)

I first came across a version of these in Julio in Melbourne, where I spent many a Saturday making as many as I could manage, such was their demand. I originally thought they were a Moroccan specialty, but on my travels in the Middle East, I came across various incarnations of these wonderful, fluffy delights along the way. I even spent a long time one evening being mesmerised by a group of men making giant quantities of these in an open-air market in Aleppo, Syria.

These pancakes are so versatile and match well with sweet fillings as well as savoury. We were thrilled and honoured when the wonderful Donal Skehan created his own version inspired by ours. A few serving suggestions are listed at the end of the recipe.

As these are yeast based, they are handled in a slightly different way than more traditional pancakes. They are wonderful eaten immediately, hot from the pan, but they will still be delicious later on the same day, warm or at room temperature. They actually hold up very well to being reheated the next day if stored in the fridge (see the tips and tricks below) or can even be frozen for use another time.

These are the basic pancakes that you can use to build your dish – we've some suggestions on the next pages.

MAKES ABOUT 8 PANCAKES

- 250ml milk
- 250ml water
- 2 eggs
- 10g dried fast action yeast
- ½ tsp salt
- 250g fine semolina (the finest grade, almost flour-like)
- sunflower or Irish rapeseed oil, for cooking

Put the milk and water into a pot set over a medium heat. Heat this for a few minutes, stirring – you want to get it to the point that it should be just a little warmer than your body temperature. Remove from the heat and pour into a large bowl.

Crack the eggs into the bowl, then add the yeast and salt. Whisk well. Still using the whisk, whisk in the semolina – a good energetic go will do it. The mix will get a little thicker. Cover the bowl with cling film and set aside to rest in a warm place, such as beside your oven or in a cosy corner of your kitchen. After a while, you will see the batter bubble up as the yeast works its magic. The batter should be ready after 20–30 minutes, once it's good and frothy with lots of bubbles.

Place a non-stick medium frying pan (ideally 15–18cm diameter) on a medium-high heat and let it get fully heated. When it's hot, add a tiny splash of oil and swirl it around the pan, then turn the heat down to medium.

Gently stir the pancake batter with a medium ladle, then add one ladleful to the pan or enough of the batter to cover the pan with 3–4mm depth of batter, swirling gently so the surface is fully covered. Cook for 1–2 minutes. You will see bubbles form in the batter and then it will set as the wet texture on the surface gradually disappears towards the centre of the pancake. When it's set, lift it up and flip it over to sear for a few moments – this side should almost be undercooked. Give the pan a shake so the pancake moves from side to side. Take off the heat and remove the pancake onto a plate. Keep covered with a cloth while you cook the remaining pancakes, stacking the cooked ones together under the cloth so they stay warm.

TIPS AND TRICKS

» These are best eaten fresh from the pan, but they can be stored in the fridge for 2 days and reheated and they will still come out perfect. To reheat, either cover and microwave them or else put them on a baking tray sealed tightly with tin foil and heat in a medium oven. They do need to be heated the full way through to be at their best. You can tell when they're done when the firmed-up centre returns to a nice soft texture.
» These can be served for breakfast, brunch or even as mini pancakes for dessert! Simply make them smaller and then serve, say, three per person, drizzled with honey, nuts and maybe some vanilla ice cream. See the recipes on pages 40–42 for more ideas.

❋ Sweet beghrir pancakes with rose mascarpone, berry and rose compote and fresh mint

A real delight on the plate – the tang of the mascarpone works beautifully against the sweet burst of the berries!

SERVES 4

- 1 batch of beghrir pancakes (page 38)
- ½ batch of berry and rose compote (page 343)
- 1–2 sprigs of fresh mint
- a few tablespoons of praline (page 341) (optional) or toasted chopped nuts (see page 352)

For the rose mascarpone cream:
- 1 x 250g tub of mascarpone
- approx. 2 dessertspoons honey
- ½–1 tsp rosewater or orange blossom water or the seeds from 1 vanilla pod

Make the pancakes as per the master recipe on page 38 and warm up the berry compote.

To make the mascarpone cream, put the mascarpone into a bowl and gently stir in enough honey to give the mix a light sweetness and ½ teaspoon of rosewater. Stir well and taste, adding more of either ingredient if desired. However, this should not be overly sweet, as you want the creaminess and acidity of the mascarpone to cut through the warm berry compote.

When ready to build the plates, place the warm pancakes on a warm plate, overlapping in the middle (like a Venn diagram). Divide the mascarpone across the plates, placing a dollop on the centre of each pancake (2 dollops per plate). Divide the compote across the plates, placing a large spoonful of the warm compote around the mascarpone. Tear some mint leaves over and serve immediately with some praline sprinkled over, if using, or even just some toasted chopped nuts.

TIPS AND TRICKS

Here are some more sweet serving suggestions:
- » Honey, Greek yogurt or mascarpone, toasted nuts, pomegranate seeds
- » Baked fruit, crumbled nutty meringue (page 299), vanilla ice cream
- » Ricotta with berries and honey folded through, fresh summer fruits, mint

The Beginning of the Day / 41

❋ Savoury beghrir pancakes with smoked salmon, feta and warm peppers

As the filling here is quite substantial, we only serve one pancake per person. This uses our versatile tomato and pepper sauce on page 321.

SERVES 4

- ½ batch of beghrir pancakes (page 38)
- 1 batch of tomato and pepper sauce (page 321)
- 8 slices of smoked salmon
- 50g feta cheese
- 250g baby spinach leaves
- lemon wedges, to serve
- dressed salad leaves, to serve

Make the pancakes as per the master recipe on page 38 and warm up the tomato and pepper sauce.

When ready to build the plates, place a warm pancake on each warmed plate. Sprinkle a handful of baby spinach across one half of the pancake, then top with a few generous spoonfuls of the sauce, followed by 2 slices of smoked salmon and some crumbled feta. Fold the 'naked' half over the top, allowing the filling to peek out. Serve with a wedge of lemon and some dressed salad leaves on the side.

TIPS AND TRICKS

Here are some other serving suggestions, using 1 pancake per person, served in the same way as above:
- » Moroccan zalouk (page 100) with baby spinach and feta yogurt (page 55) or smoked aubergine yogurt (page 338)
- » Mushrooms with thyme in a creamy sauce and wilted spinach
- » Roast tomato, sautéed asparagus and crumbled goats' cheese

※ Baklava French toast

This is a thoroughly delicious and somewhat indulgent breakfast – a particular treat for a Sunday morning, perhaps? Looking for inspiration from the Middle East, we wanted to add something a bit special from the region, so we got the idea of using a baklava-style filling. You get the wonderful texture of the French toast, the juicy flesh of the roasted fruit and the crunchy, nutty sweetness of the baklava filling, all counter-balanced by the mascarpone. Try to use muscovado sugar if you can, as it has such a depth of flavour, but any brown sugar will do.

SERVES 2

- 2 red dessert apples or pears (or a mix of both), cored and cut into 4–6 wedges
- 100g muscovado sugar
- 75g walnuts, roughly chopped
- 1 tsp ground cinnamon
- 15g butter, melted
- sunflower or rapeseed oil
- 2 eggs
- 100ml cream
- seeds from ½ vanilla pod or 1 tsp vanilla extract
- 4 thick slices of day-old bread (brioche or a light sourdough are ideal)
- 4 dessertspoons mascarpone
- a few sprigs of fresh mint
- a handful of pomegranate seeds (page 354) (optional)

Preheat your oven to 220°C. Line a baking tray with non-stick baking paper.

First, roast the apples or pears. Toss the wedges in a bowl with 50g of the muscovado sugar. Turn the fruit out onto the lined baking tray and pop in the oven. Check after 15 minutes – the wedges should be nicely soft but still holding their shape. Roast for longer if need be, then put to one side (we serve the fruit warm as opposed to piping hot out of the oven). There will be a lovely caramel around the fruit that you'll want to drizzle over the finished dish.

Next, make the baklava by mixing the walnuts with the remaining 50g of muscovado sugar and the cinnamon in a bowl. Pour over the melted butter, stir to combine and put to one side.

Now place your frying pan over a medium heat and add a little oil. While that's heating up, crack your eggs into a bowl and whisk really well with the cream and vanilla. Pour this into a wide pan or bowl so that you can dip the bread in it easily. >>

Dip each slice of bread into the egg mix. Be patient, as you want the egg to fully soak in but not to the extent that the bread will fall apart. I recommend letting it sit in the egg mix for 20–30 seconds, then turn the bread over and repeat on the other side.

Lift out the bread, shaking off the excess egg, and put it in the hot frying pan. Fry, shaking it loose after the first 15–20 seconds, and cook for 2–4 minutes, until it's decently browned underneath. Turn over and repeat with the other side. The bread should be lightly browned and the egg mix cooked through but not overcooked. If you think it needs more time, turn down the heat to low and let it sit until you feel it's done (check by squeezing the bread or even cutting through to the centre and seeing if it's still too wet in the middle). If cooking more than one portion, place the cooked French toast in a low oven to keep warm and repeat with the other portions. An alternative would be to cook the toast off quickly on both sides in the frying pan – repeating for all of the slices, essentially sealing them – and then place the bread on a lined baking tray and finish in the oven for about 10 minutes at 180°C, until cooked through.

Now, build your plate. Place 2 slices of French toast on each warm plate or in a wide bowl. Put 2 dessertspoons of the mascarpone on top, then crumble over 2 dessertspoons of the baklava. Divide the roasted fruit wedges over the toast. Finish by drizzling some of the caramel from the baking tray over the toast and scattering over some torn fresh mint and pomegranate seeds, if using.

TIPS AND TRICKS

» This dish can look a bit beige/brown, so spruce it up by scattering some fresh raspberries or pomegranate seeds over it. Or to get really fancy, try soaking your fruit in the berry and rose compote on page 343 before roasting it.
» I should note that this is strictly a sweet French toast – I'm not sure that crispy bacon would work well alongside the baklava and mascarpone. However, if you fancy, leave them out and just serve the plain French toast with the apples and some bacon.

※ Bacon and cheese sandwich with tomato and apple ketchup

You really need to get the best-quality bread possible for this recipe, as it is evident in every bite. A nice sourdough or a super-fresh, great-quality bread roll would be amazing. If you don't have time to make the ketchup, leave it out. There are times when I feel this sandwich works best with just the butter. And see how we recommend cooking the bacon – it really isn't any more trouble than frying it and it makes all the difference to the flavour.

INGREDIENTS PER PERSON

- 2 bacon rashers
- small handful of mixed salad leaves
- 3–4 slices good Cheddar cheese (we recommend Hegarty's)
- oil, for frying
- 1 fried egg (optional)
- 2 slices of bread or 1 bread roll, halved
- enough butter to smear over the bread
- tomato and apple ketchup (page 333) (optional)
- salt and freshly ground black pepper

Heat a griddle pan on a medium-high heat for about 10 minutes, then add the bacon. Leave to cook on each side for about 3 minutes, undisturbed, until char marks have fully imprinted on each side and the bacon is fully cooked. Trim off the fat/rind before serving if you fancy.

While the bacon is cooking, wash and dry your salad leaves and evenly slice the cheese. If you're planning on adding an egg to your sandwich, now is the time to heat some oil in a pan set over a medium heat and fry an egg until the egg white is just cooked and the yolk is still runny.

Next, lightly toast the bread. A simple way to get a nice even toast is to place the bread in the oven for about 8 minutes at 180°C or under a hot grill with a watchful eye.

When the bread has been toasted, butter one side quickly and spread the other with some tomato and apple ketchup. Top the base with the cheese, then the bacon and the egg. Finally, top with some of the mixed leaves, a twist of salt and pepper and the final piece of bread. Cut in half through the egg and serve immediately. >>

» We chargrill our bacon on a griddle pan to give it an extra element of flavour. But if you don't have a chargrill or griddle pan at home, don't despair. There are plenty of other ways to cook bacon: you can pan-fry, roast or grill it.

» For something extra special, grill the cheese on top of the bread until it's nice and melty!

※ Greek legend omelette

Follow our simple instructions to make the tastiest protein-packed, Greek-inspired omelette. It's great for after the gym but is pretty much ideal at any time of the day. The stuff of legend!

SERVES 1

- 1 ripe tomato
- good-quality olive oil
- salt and freshly ground black pepper
- 3 eggs
- 1–2 tbsp milk or cream
- 2 slices of good-quality bread, toasted
- 3–4 Kalamata olives, pitted and sliced
- 30–40g feta cheese, crumbled
- 50g baby spinach leaves
- knob of butter, softened
- chopped fresh herbs, to garnish
- pinch of sumac, to garnish (optional)
- pinch of za'atar, to garnish (optional)

Place a 18–20cm frying pan over a medium-high heat. While that's heating up, dice the tomato into medium-sized cubes. Add a splash of oil to the pan, then the tomato and a little seasoning. Shake the pan and let the tomato cook for about 5 minutes, stirring every so often. You're aiming for the tomato to be heated through and softened but not falling apart (but don't worry if this happens). Once the tomato is cooked, pop it into a bowl.

Wipe your pan with some kitchen paper and put it back on a high heat. When fully heated, add another dash of oil, swirling it around. Whisk the eggs in a bowl with the milk or cream, some pepper and a tiny pinch of salt (not too much salt, as the feta is quite salty). Get your plate warming up too at this time and toast your bread.

Tip the beaten eggs into the pan. The mixture should set immediately at the edges. After 10–15 seconds, gently push the cooked portions from the edges to the centre of the pan, allowing the uncooked eggs to run over to reach the hot pan surface. Continue cooking, tilting and gently moving the cooked portions as needed. When no visible runny liquid egg remains and the exposed upside of the omelette is setting but still glistening, add the warm tomato, sliced olives and crumbled feta cheese to one half of the omelette, then top with the spinach. Gently fold the other side of the omelette over the top. >>

Spread your hot toast with a drizzle of olive oil. Carefully fold the omelette in half again, then slide it out of the pan and onto the toast. Garnish with some fresh herbs and a good sprinkle of sumac and za'atar if you fancy.

TIPS AND TRICKS

» We recommend making your own homemade tomato paste as above, but a few sliced sun-dried tomatoes work well or even just smearing the toast with some sun-dried tomato pesto.
» Why not turn the omelette into a frittata? Simply double the ingredients and mix everything except the tomato sauce together in a bowl. Add to a hot pan and cook for 2–3 minutes, then place in an oven preheated to 180°C for 10–15 minutes, until the centre is just set and the frittata has nicely risen. Serve in wedges on toast with the tomato sauce dolloped over it with a simple side salad for a more substantial breakfast, brunch, lunch or supper. The frittata will be delicious when cool too and it would work extremely well as a sandwich filling, hot or cold.

❊ Michelle's Middle Eastern breakfast plate

I first came across this dish while working in Julio in Melbourne, where my friend Michelle had it on her menu following on from her travels in Turkey. When I was travelling in the Middle East myself subsequently, this is what I would have had most mornings before going off to visit the souks and the various ancient wonders. Some might find it odd to have cucumber and olives first thing in the morning, but please do try it! It is wonderfully refreshing and light yet substantial, and it is still the breakfast I eat most often during the spring and summer. I promise that you will feel good after having it.

This is so simple to put together and to make in bigger quantities for entertaining. And despite its name, it would work equally well with a glass of white wine for a light summer supper. As with all recipes, the better the quality of your ingredients, the better the outcome.

SERVES 4

- 4 free-range, organic eggs
- 1 cucumber
- 2–3 ripe plum tomatoes
- 16–24 Kalamata olives, pitted
- olive oil
- salt and freshly ground black pepper
- 1 x 200g block of feta cheese
- pinch of za'atar, to garnish
- hummus (pages 155–159)
- pinch of sumac, to garnish
- 4 sprigs of fresh mint
- 4–8 pitta breads or homemade flatbreads (page 322), warmed

To hard-boil the eggs, place them in a pot of cold water and bring to the boil. Boil for 7 minutes, then transfer to a bowl of cold water.

Cut the cucumber in half lengthways, then cut each half diagonally into large bite-sized chunks. Cut the ripe plum tomatoes into wedges. Place the cucumber chunks, tomato wedges and olives in a bowl and toss in a little oil and some seasoning.

Break the feta into larger chunks and place on large individual plates or one big platter to share, then sprinkle with a pinch of za'atar. Add a few big spoonfuls of hummus to the plate and sprinkle over a pinch of sumac. >>

Build the plate by arranging the cucumbers, tomatoes, olives and mint sprigs around the feta and hummus so that it looks like a lovely platter of freshness, colour and flavour. Add the hardboiled eggs to the plate. We serve the eggs unpeeled, as having to peel the egg at the table adds a degree of authenticity and ceremony to the experience, but you can peel the eggs and cut them in half lengthways if you prefer.

Serve with some warmed pitta bread or flatbread on the side. When eating, mix and match the flavours and textures – have morsels of the bread dipped in the hummus with a little cucumber, mint, feta and any other ingredient. No two mouthfuls will taste the same!

TIPS AND TRICKS

» We usually sprinkle some sumac over the hummus and a little za'atar over the feta, but you could also use a little ground cumin or good paprika, a drizzle of lemon juice or a really great olive oil (or all of the above) instead.
» If you fancy, you can serve slices of smoked salmon, cold cuts or even some pan-fried chorizo on the side to make it more substantial.
» Fresh radishes cut into chunks is another optional extra that you could add to the plate.

❋ Turkish eggs menemen

A vibrant, beautiful dish, this is ideal as a brunch or supper. This is perhaps our single most popular dish on our menu. I first came across a version of it when working in Julio in Melbourne and then was lucky enough to visit Istanbul to try the authentic version as the locals eat it. This version is our own take on it. It really is a taste sensation, with the spinach and herbs adding so much freshness and vibrancy to counterbalance the richness of the eggs.

SERVES 2 HUNGRY PEOPLE

- 1 batch of tomato and pepper sauce (page 321)
- 4 eggs
- 50ml cream
- salt and freshly ground black pepper
- olive oil
- 4 slices of good bread
- knob of butter, softened
- 2 small handfuls of baby spinach leaves
- 6–8 Kalamata olives, pitted and sliced (optional)

For the onion chilli herb mix:
- ½ small or medium red onion
- 1 medium red chilli
- 20g fresh mint
- 20g fresh parsley
- 10g fresh dill or coriander

For the feta yogurt:
- 50g feta cheese
- 100g plain yogurt

First make the sauce as per the recipe on page 321, then remove the sauce from the heat and set aside – it's best added to the dish when it's quite warm but not boiling.

While the sauce is simmering away, cut the red onion into the finest dice you can manage – ideally about the size of the head of a match! Cut the top off the chilli, remove the seeds with a teaspoon and then dice the chilli very finely too, similar in size to the onion. Finely chop the stems of the herbs (except the mint), then give the leafy bits a medium chop. Mix the onion, chilli and herbs together and set aside.

Make the feta yogurt by crumbling the feta into the yogurt and adding some black pepper (you don't need salt because the feta is already quite salty). >>

Now you're ready for the final steps. Crack the eggs into a bowl with the cream. Whisk well and add a little salt and pepper. Heat a frying pan over a medium-high heat. When it's good and hot, add a dash of olive oil. You should be warming your plates and toasting your bread at this point too. Pour in the eggs and let them sit for about 20 seconds before stirring to scramble them. This dish is to be cooked very quickly, so keep scrambling. When they are nearly fully cooked but the egg is still glistening, add the tomato and pepper sauce, mixing well, and scramble further for another 20–30 seconds.

To serve, spread the toast with some butter or a drizzle of olive oil and put on each warm plate with a small handful of baby spinach leaves on top. Divide the scrambled eggs between each plate. Top with a dessertspoon of the feta yogurt, scatter over the sliced olives, if using, and finish with a few spoons of the onion chilli herb mix.

TIPS AND TRICKS

» This is an ideal vegetarian breakfast, brunch, lunch or supper dish, but you can add smoked salmon or pan-fried chorizo on the side to make it a more substantial meal (the chorizo goes particularly well).

Scrolls

These babies are the best, especially eaten while still warm from the oven to go with a cup of coffee. But they're great any time of the day and we've a few ideas about what to do with any leftovers. My dear friends in Loafer Bread, Melbourne, made these a specialty. We drew inspiration from their recipe to create our own version with our own delightfully soft, brioche-style bun. We've suggested two sweet fillings below, but see page 75 for a savoury version.

MAKES 10–12 SCROLLS

- 125ml tepid water
- 360g strong white flour/bread flour
- 1 egg
- 30g caster sugar
- 10g dried fast action yeast
- 70ml sunflower oil

For a cinnamon and walnut filling (option 1):

- 100g walnuts, roughly chopped
- 60g Demerara sugar
- 30g muscovado sugar
- ½ tsp ground cinnamon
- 25g butter

For a chocolate and hazelnut filling (option 2):

- 80g dark chocolate
- 75g butter
- 30g icing sugar
- 20g cocoa powder
- 20g hazelnuts, roasted and crushed
- 2 tsp caster sugar

For the sugar syrup glaze:

- 150g caster sugar
- 75ml water

Measure out the tepid water and make sure it isn't too hot or too cold. The best way to judge it is to stick your finger in – the water should feel just a little bit warmer than your finger. This means it's a nice warm temperature for your yeast to get active. Put to one side while you get the next step ready.

If you don't have a food mixer with a dough hook attachment, see page 349 for our technique for making dough by hand. It's a little more work, but far more satisfying and so much fun. If you do have a mixer, place the flour, egg, sugar and yeast in the bowl. Add all of the oil and one-third of the water and put the machine on a low setting. You are just bringing the dough together gently and trying to avoid the flour going everywhere!

When the dough is forming well and a good bit of the dry ingredients have been incorporated, add half the remaining water. Continue kneading on low for another few minutes. The dough should be forming a ball now. Most or all of the dry ingredients should be incorporated and it should be starting to come away from the sides of the bowl. You need to use your judgement here as to how much of the remaining water to add, so turn the mixer up to a medium speed and leave it on for a few minutes, doing its thing. After about 5 minutes, check the dough – it should be a nice springy mass, forming a ball of sorts. If this hasn't happened, you may need to add a little more liquid. Alternatively, if the mix isn't coming together into a cohesive, smooth, shiny dough, you may need to add a little more flour.

The best way to know if your dough is adequately kneaded is to take a little bit of it (the size of sugar cube) in your hands and start spreading it out thinly between your fingers, trying to form a thin sheet. If you can get it so that it's thin enough to let some light through before it starts tearing, it's ready. If this isn't happening, more kneading in the machine is required until this can happen.

Once your dough is made, cover the bowl with cling film or a clean damp tea towel and leave in a warm place to rise for 30 minutes (beside your preheating oven or on the stove is often a good spot). The dough is ready when it has doubled in size. Alternatively, if you're making this in advance, you can leave the dough to slow prove in the fridge overnight before following the next steps.

While the dough is proving, make the filling:
» To make the cinnamon and walnut filling, mix the walnuts, sugars and cinnamon together in a bowl. Melt the butter in a small pot and pour it over the walnut mix. Stir well to combine.
» To make the chocolate and hazelnut filling, melt the chocolate and butter together in a bowl set over a pan of simmering water, making sure the bottom of the bowl doesn't touch the water. Once melted, add everything else to the bowl and mix to combine.

When the dough is ready, line a baking tray with non-stick baking paper and dust your counter with a little flour. Take the dough out of the bowl and flatten it down with your hands in a rough rectangle shape (long

side towards you), then roll the dough out into a rectangle approximately 45cm long by 35cm wide. Don't be afraid to readjust the shape of the dough using your hands so that you get a rough rectangular shape. A tip when rolling dough is to roll it evenly at all times. The dough should have a uniform thickness, but too often people jam the rolling pin into the middle of the dough and go hell for leather, rolling and tearing at the dough.

Spread the filling over the dough, leaving a 2cm 'frame' of uncovered dough around the edges. At the long edge nearest you, form a little extra bit of filling in a row – this will be the heart of your scroll, so it's a nice surprise to have a burst of filling when you bite in. Bring the dough over this mound of filling, pressing down slightly. Then just roll the dough into one long Swiss roll, but not too tightly – a loose enough roll is ideal here to get the best shape ultimately. Roll right up to the end. Pat the ends of the scroll dough with your hands so the middle bits aren't sticking out.

Using a large knife, cut the roll into slices 3cm thick. As you move towards the end, adjust the size of the scrolls a bit so that you use up all the dough rather than being left with one last slice that's too big or too small. Place these slices on the lined baking tray, leaving 3cm between the scrolls. Cover with a clean damp cloth or lightly with cling film (they need space to rise as the yeast does its thing). Again, leave in a warm place for up to 30 minutes, until they are about doubled in size. Check them after 10 minutes or so, as this doubling will be determined by how warm your environment is.

Meanwhile, preheat your oven to 190°C. Make your sugar syrup by boiling the sugar and water together in a small pot until the sugar has dissolved.

When you're ready to cook, place a large roasting tin in the bottom of the oven and fill it up halfway with water. This will add some humidity to the oven and will give the finished scrolls a lighter, softer texture. Place the scrolls in the oven and bake for 18–22 minutes. The scrolls are done when they have a lovely light brown colour. Check after 18 minutes and adjust the cooking time by 10% either way, depending on how they are cooking.

Take the scrolls out of the oven and brush with the sugar syrup while they're still hot, then repeat after 2 minutes (don't worry if there's a little puddle of syrup on the tray). Leave to cool somewhat, but try to eat them while they're still comfortingly warm, though cooled to room temperature is delicious too.

» If all of these somehow don't get eaten on the day, then simply cover them with tin foil and bake the next day in an oven set at 150°C for 15–20 minutes, until fully warmed through, to bring them back to life. They would need to be eaten warm for best results after they have been reheated.

» If you have 6–8 scrolls left over, they work wonderfully as the basis for a bread and butter pudding. You'll need a deep baking dish that's large enough to hold the scrolls (a lasagne-style dish is great for this). Rub a little soft butter over the base and sides of the dish. Chop the scrolls up roughly into big chunks and add to the dish in an even jumble tumble layer. Whisk 4 eggs in a large bowl, then add 600ml milk, 400ml cream and 150g caster sugar and mix well to dissolve the sugar. Pour over the scrolls in the dish and allow to soak for about 15 minutes. You can add some additional ingredients here, such as white or dark chocolate drops, dried fruit or a dash of whiskey or Baileys. Just before placing into the oven, mix 2 tablespoons Demerara sugar with ½ teaspoon ground cinnamon and sprinkle this mix generously over the top of the pudding. Bake in the oven at 180°C for 45 minutes – you'll know it's done when the top has crisped up nicely and the egg custard is fully set.

✤ Scones

When we first opened, we had no idea how important scones were to people – or how particular people are about them. Growing up, we weren't a very 'scone-y' household. One famous failed attempt by my dear mother resulted in all of us refusing to eat them, only for some to be given to the dog, who promptly got sick. Thankfully, I don't seem to have inherited that defective scone-making gene!

Our recipe is based on a Ballymaloe classic that we've tweaked over time. These are very pure – a few simple ingredients, lightly handled, and so much better than any of those mass-produced ones in a convenience store. And as with so much of the food we make, it is a joy to make these yourself.

MAKES 12–15 SCONES

- 750g plain flour
- 150g wholemeal flour
- 50g caster sugar
- 30g baking powder
- 110g butter, softened
- 3 eggs, beaten
- 400ml milk
- Demerara sugar, for sprinkling on top (optional)
- oats and seeds, for sprinkling on top (optional)
- orange blossom butter (page 66), to serve

Optional extras:
- 100g dried fruit and 100g crystallised ginger, chopped
- 50g oats, toasted on a dry frying pan until golden, and 50g dried cranberries

Preheat your oven to 220°C. Line a baking tray with non-stick baking paper or a silicone mat.

Place the flours, caster sugar and baking powder in a large bowl. Mix well (a whisk works well here), then rub in the butter until it's well dispersed throughout the flour, crumbling it through.

Whisk together the eggs and milk. Make a well in the centre of the dry ingredients and pour two-thirds of the wet mix into the well you've created. Mix quickly and lightly with a wooden spoon or your hand (keep one hand free and clean!), adding more of the liquid if the dough isn't coming together. You may end up having some of the liquid left (if so, you can use it for dipping the scones in later). At this stage you can add in the optional extras, if using. Try to avoid overmixing – work the dough gently until everything has just come together. You should end up with a dough that's still reasonably wet, by which I mean it should be a wet mass that's just coming together, maybe with a little glisten off of it but no liquid run-off per se. They do say that at this stage a wet scone is a good scone, as a wetter dough will encourage a better rise out of the scone while it's baking.

Flour a work surface well and lift your dough out onto it. Put some flour on your hands and pat the dough out into a rectangular shape, patting in the sides so it's one solid patty of dough. Sprinkle a little flour on top and roll to about 3cm thick, tapping in the sides so that it stays a nice, tight shape. Stamp out your scones using a 6cm round scone cutter. Alternatively, use a dough cutter or a large knife to cut into 6cm x 6cm squares or similar-sized triangles.

We dip our scones in sugar like they do in Ballymaloe to give them a sweet, crunchy topping. To do this, brush a little milk over the top of each scone (or if you've any milk-egg mix left over, use that), then dip each scone into a shallow plate of Demerara sugar. Alternatively, you could mix some oats and seeds together and dip the scones in this as a healthier option. When dipped, place the scones on the lined baking tray.

Place in the oven and bake for 25–30 minutes, until they've turned a nice golden brown and they feel quite light. The bottom will be lightly browned and crusted and they will sound hollow when tapped lightly.

Serve with butter, jam, whipped cream or any combination of these. In Brother Hubbard, we serve them with our orange blossom butter. It's so easy to make and it takes the scones to another level altogether, so it really is worth just that little bit of extra effort. See the next page for the recipe.

TIPS AND TRICKS

» Any leftover scones can be stored in the bread bin and reheated the next day in a medium oven (160°C) for 10 minutes. Make sure they are heated fully through so they come right back to life.
» Alternatively, they can be frozen. When you want to use them, allow them to defrost and reheat as above.

❀ Orange blossom butter

Our proud invention, this is a beautiful, fragrant, sweet butter to spread over your scone as an extra treat. It turns a plain block of butter into something magical. I dreamed it up while trying to put a mildly Middle Eastern twist on something as classically Irish as a scone. Orange blossom water is a classic Middle Eastern ingredient and it works superbly here.

MAKES 250G

- zest of 1 orange
- 1 tbsp orange juice
- 250g butter (salted or unsalted, depending on your preference), softened
- 40g icing sugar
- 1 tsp orange blossom water

Add the orange zest and juice to the softened butter, then add the icing sugar and orange blossom water and mix well with a wooden spoon or in a free-standing mixer with the paddle attachment. Taste and ensure it's to your liking. It should have a decent orangey angle to it, so add more zest, juice, sugar or orange blossom water as needed.

Scrape the butter onto a large piece of parchment paper and mould the butter into a long log. Roll up tight in the parchment and refrigerate until hard.

Slice as needed, but ideally let it come to room temperature before attempting to smear it over a scone so that it spreads well.

TIPS AND TRICKS

» We use salted butter in the café, as we feel it contrasts well with the sweetness of the butter and orange, but feel free to use unsalted and have a sweeter product.
» Make double or more and freeze it, wrapped well in the parchment paper and also tightly in cling film. When defrosted it might weep a little, but it will be perfectly fine to use.
» On Pancake Tuesday (or any pancake day, for that matter – see page 38 for our pancake recipe), we serve our pancakes with a pat of this butter on top, a sprinkle of sugar and lemon or orange wedges to squeeze over the pancakes. Yum!

❈ The Middle of the Day

BRUNCH, LUNCH AND SUPPER

The highlight of the week for many, brunch could be considered the king of late breakfasts, something that ticks perhaps the desire for breakfast but the timing of lunch. However, for me, it's actually a meal that you can have at almost any time. It can be a more substantial breakfast, it can be a lighter lunch or it can be an evening supper – pretty much all the recipes in this section work in that respect. So keep an open mind as to when you might want to enjoy this food. There's no wrong answer.

When we started offering brunch on our menu on a Saturday, it was an almost instant success, so much so that it's now available all day, every day, happily sitting alongside our breakfast and lunch menus during the week. I feel this is a fair reflection of people's lives now. Not everything needs to be shoehorned into a weekend anymore – that's surely a good thing!

We've grouped a lot of different dishes together in this section – some are more obviously brunch, others more lunchy, and perhaps all could be suitable as a light supper – so peruse the chapter and decide what you would like, and when you would like it!

❋ Shakshuka baked eggs

I first discovered this amazing dish via my food hero, Yotam Ottolenghi, who published a recipe for it in his weekly column in the *Guardian*. Having made it a few times, I fell in love with it, so much so that following further research as to where Mr Ottolenghi got his inspiration, I travelled to the old town of Jaffa in Israel and visited Dr Shakshuka, a lovely little restaurant famous for doing a variety of different shakshuka dishes. I even managed to talk my way into their kitchen, where I got to cook a few shakshukas alongside their chefs! This recipe varies slightly from how I saw it being done to reflect the reality of cooking at home, but it's no less delicious.

SERVES 4

- extra virgin olive oil
- 3 mixed peppers, deseeded and cut into 1cm-thick slices
- 2 x 400g tins of chopped tomatoes or 8 ripe tomatoes, cut into 1cm cubes
- 1–2 dessertspoons harissa (page 325 or use shop-bought)
- 2 tsp caraway seeds
- 1 tsp paprika
- 1 tsp ground cumin
- 1 tsp caster sugar
- salt and freshly ground black pepper
- 150–200g feta cheese, crumbled
- 8 eggs
- 4 slices of good bread, toasted just before serving
- knob of butter, softened
- 50g fresh herbs (parsley mixed with mint, dill and/or coriander), chopped

Heat a dessertspoon of oil in a saucepan set over a medium heat. Add the peppers and cook for 10 minutes or so, until soft but not falling apart. Add the tomatoes and cook for a further 5–8 minutes, until the tomato is softened (if using ripe tomatoes) and you have a chunky-style sauce. If you're using tinned tomatoes, you might need to cook it for 5 minutes longer so the sauce reduces.

Add the harissa, spices, sugar and some salt and pepper, stirring it in well, and cook for a further 2 minutes. Now taste the sauce, adding more spice, harissa, salt, pepper or even an extra pinch of sugar if it needs it. It should be a wonderfully rich and flavourful sauce with a bit of a spicy hit and it should also be very thick, almost like a stew, so keep simmering if you need to reduce it a bit further. >>

Meanwhile, preheat your oven to 180°C. Get 4 individual ovenproof bowls ready. Place a good tablespoon of crumbled feta in the bottom of each bowl, then divide the sauce evenly across each of the bowls, leaving a 1cm gap at the top so it doesn't boil over in the oven. Alternatively, if you're serving a lot of people at once, you could just as easily do this in one big batch in a larger flat dish, like a lasagne tray. The depth of the sauce in the bowl or tray should be 3–4cm.

Using a large spoon, make an indentation for each egg, so that means 2 indentations per bowl. Crack an egg into each well and sprinkle a little freshly ground black pepper over each, then crumble the remaining feta around the eggs.

Pop the dish(es) into the oven and bake for 8–12 minutes, until the eggs are cooked to your liking. This can be a little tricky – you want to cook them until each egg is just right, but it's no harm to take it out of the oven a little earlier and let it sit so the eggs continue cooking while you bring it to the table.

To serve, put a slice of toast (spread with some butter or a drizzle of olive oil) on each plate to serve alongside the shakshuka. Scatter a generous amount of fresh herbs over each dish, but try not to hide the feta and eggs too much in doing so, as the rich red of the sauce and the colours of the peppers, the white of the feta and eggs and the vibrant green of the fresh herbs should all be visible.

TIPS AND TRICKS

» This is an ideal vegetarian breakfast, brunch, lunch or supper dish, but carnivores can add pan-fried chorizo on the side to make it more substantial as a meal.
» If you fancy making our Moroccan zalouk (page 100), make extra and turn this into a baked egg dish by bringing the dish together and cooking it as described above, but using the zalouk instead of the roast pepper sauce.

✳ Savoury something

This is actually a savoury version of the sweet scrolls we do (see page 59). When we had this on our menu we couldn't come up with a name for it, so we just called it 'savoury something' and invited our customers to name it. Shamefully, no one came up with a better name, so the interim name stuck!

These are great to have with a bowl of soup or just a simple salad for a lighter lunch, and they are also ideal for a lunchbox. You can make mini versions of these for nibbles or even as a starter for an evening meal. These are best eaten warm from the oven or later that day, but they actually reheat quite well so they would still be delicious the next day too, once they are reheated thoroughly from the fridge.

We use the same brioche-style dough as for the sweet scrolls. Even though it's a sweet dough, it works really well here with the strong savoury elements of the feta and olives, especially if you add 2 teaspoons of toasted caraway or cumin seeds to the dough while it's being mixed.

MAKES 10–12 SCROLLS

- 1 batch of scroll dough (page 59)
- olive oil
- 1 red onion, finely chopped
- 3 garlic cloves, finely chopped
- 1 tsp ground cumin
- 1 tsp ground coriander
- pinch of dried chilli flakes
- 1 x 400g tin of chopped tomatoes
- squeeze of lemon
- pinch of caster sugar
- salt and freshly ground black pepper
- 150g feta cheese, well drained and rinsed
- 30g Kalamata olives, pitted and roughly chopped
- baby spinach leaves or fresh basil (optional)
- 1 egg
- sesame seeds, lightly toasted, to garnish (optional)

After you have made the scroll dough following the recipe on page 59, make the sauce while the dough is proving. Heat some oil in a pot set over a low heat. Add the onion and garlic and sweat off with the lid on and a layer of baking or greaseproof paper placed directly on the surface of the vegetables to seal in the steam. Stir occasionally – the onions will be done after about 20 minutes, when they are fully softened but not browned. >>

Turn up the heat and add the cumin, coriander and chilli flakes, stirring and cooking for 1 minute. Add the tin of tomatoes and bring to a simmer for 8–10 minutes with the lid off to thicken the sauce. Remove from the heat and place to one side to cool. Taste and season the sauce with a squeeze of lemon juice and a sprinkle of sugar as well as some salt and pepper. The sauce should be quite thick, almost lumpy, so keep reducing it if needs be. Put to one side to cool.

Once your scroll dough is ready, line a baking tray with non-stick baking paper and roll out the dough into a rectangle as per the instructions on 60. Smear over the cooled thick tomato sauce evenly but generously, leaving a 3cm margin clear around the top and bottom edges of the dough. Crumble the feta evenly over the sauce – you want it neither too finely crumbled nor too chunky. Distribute the chopped olives over the dough, then scatter over the spinach, if using.

Now you can roll up the dough. Taking the longest edge that's nearest you, roll it over towards the top of the dough (away from you). Keep rolling into one long Swiss roll, but not too tightly – a loose enough roll is ideal here to get the best shape. Roll right up to the end. Pat the ends of the roll in dough with your hands so the middle bits aren't sticking out.

Using a dough cutter or a large, sharp knife, cut the roll into slices 3cm thick. As you move towards the end, adjust the size of the scrolls a bit so that you use up all the dough rather than being left with one last slice that's too big or too small. Place these slices on the lined baking tray, leaving 3cm between the scrolls (they need space to rise as the yeast does its work). Cover with a damp cloth and leave in a warm place for up to 30 minutes, until they have doubled in size.

While this is happening, preheat your oven to 190°C. Once the scrolls have proved sufficiently, gently beat the egg with a little water to form an egg wash and brush this over the tops and sides of the scrolls. This will give them a nice glaze and even colour when they are baked.

Place in the hot oven and bake for 20–22 minutes. The scrolls are done when they have a lovely light brown colour – check after 18 minutes and adjust the cooking time by 10% either way depending on how they are cooking. Take them out of the oven and let them cool a little. Brush each one with a little olive oil if you fancy and sprinkle with toasted sesame seeds if you like. >>

» Make multiple batches of the sauce filling and freeze it for the next time you would like to make this dish.
» Try topping the scrolls with some grated sharp Cheddar or some other cheese 5 minutes before they are ready to come out of the oven.
» Try alternative fillings using the same base sauce, such as:
  • Roasted aubergine cubes and spinach
  • Green pesto, cubed mozzarella and very thinly sliced tomato
  • 200g chopped chorizo lightly fried and drained of its oil with baby spinach leaves
  • 250g pulled pork drained of its sauce, as it may get too runny, with 50g finely sliced kale (thick stalks removed first)
  • 150g mushrooms, sliced and pan-fried in some butter and oil with 4–5 chopped fresh sage leaves and 3 chopped garlic cloves, spread over the dough with some sliced spring onions

❋ Beetroot and preserved lemon fritters with eggs and smoked salmon

This is a stunning brunch dish. It looks quite beautiful and the flavours are fantastic, with the earthiness of the beetroot paired against the zing of preserved lemon. We serve this as our brunch menu special sometimes with poached eggs, savoury yogurt, dressed baby spinach leaves and smoked salmon. However, the fritters themselves would work equally as well in smaller sizes with the yogurt as a starter or nibble for a mezze plate. They are pretty delicious served at room temperature too rather than hot-hot – see the tips and tricks section for more advice.

SERVES 2

○ a simple vinaigrette (make half the quantity of the dressing on page 190 and omit the oregano)
○ 2 tbsp Greek yogurt
○ olive oil
○ salt and freshly ground black pepper
○ 50g fresh dill, coriander, flat-leaf parsley and/or lovage
○ 1 medium beetroot (approx. 250–300g)
○ 30g preserved lemons (page 331 or shop-bought), very finely diced
○ 1 tsp cumin seeds, toasted and lightly crushed (or ½ tsp cumin seeds, ½ tsp caraway seeds) (see page 352)
○ 6 eggs
○ 60g plain flour
○ sunflower oil, for shallow frying
○ 2 handfuls of baby spinach leaves
○ 2–4 slices of smoked salmon

First make your vinaigrette dressing as per the recipe on page 190.

Make a savoury yogurt by adding a dash of olive oil and a little seasoning to the yogurt. If you fancy, a little minced garlic or some lemon zest would work well here too, as would ½ teaspoon of ground cumin (or all of these for a really great, savoury concoction!).

Prepare your herbs by pulling the leaves off the fresh herbs and chopping the stalks finely. Chop the leaves roughly.

You may want to wear gloves for this next bit! Top and tail the beetroot, then peel it and rinse under cold running water. Now grate into a bowl using the largest holes on your box grater – it should come out in ribbons 5mm–1cm wide. Alternatively, use the relevant grating blade on your food processor. Place in a large bowl. >>

Add all except 1 teaspoon of the diced preserved lemon to the bowl along with the chopped herb stalks, about half of the fresh herb leaves and the cumin seeds.

To make the batter to bind the fritter together, whisk 2 of the eggs and add to the bowl together with the flour, just a little salt and some pepper. Mix it all up until everything is incorporated into one relatively loose mix.

It's critical to test this for flavour, so heat a little sunflower oil over a medium heat in a non-stick frying pan. Fry off a little of the mix for 1–2 minutes on each side, then place on a piece of kitchen paper to drain and let it cool for a moment. It should have a punchy beetrooty-lemon-cumin vibe going on with a nice balance of seasoning. If it doesn't, adjust accordingly and retest to ensure it's just right – spend a few moments on this to make sure it's delicious.

When you're happy with the mix, it's time to get cooking! A quick word of advice, though: if you're making this dish for several people, I recommend that you have your oven on a medium heat (180°C) so that when the fritters are cooked, you can keep them warm while you finish the other elements of the dish. I'd also get a pan of water simmering for poaching your eggs now (see page 358 for our technique on how to poach eggs).

Add enough sunflower oil to cover the bottom of your non-stick frying pan with 5mm of oil. Bring up to temperature on a medium heat. To test if it's hot enough, add a tiny bit of the batter – it should sizzle when added.

Place a large spoonful of the batter (about 2 tablespoons per fritter) in the pan, flattening it out into one large patty about 1.5cm deep. Do this until there are several in the pan, leaving a nice gap between each. Fry for 2–3 minutes, until the bottom is light golden. Turn over and cook on the other side for 1–2 minutes more, until it's golden brown too. Remove from the pan and briefly place on a plate lined with kitchen paper to soak up any of the excess oil. Pop in a dish and place in the warm oven, uncovered, while you cook the remaining fritters in batches.

Poach your eggs (see the method on page 358). If you're serving a lot of people, I recommend pre-poaching and flashing them in boiling water when the other elements of the dish are ready.

Time to plate up! Toss the baby spinach in a little of the dressing in a big bowl. Divide between your plates, then place 2–3 fritters on top. Add 2 poached eggs on top of that, along with 1–2 slices of smoked salmon and a spoonful of the savoury yogurt. Finish with a generous sprinkle of the remaining fresh herbs and the little bit of diced preserved lemon.

TIPS AND TRICKS

» If you don't have any preserved lemons to hand, capers would work well here as an alternative.

» Pre-poaching the eggs would really help here, otherwise it can become quite the juggling act. It doesn't compromise the quality of the dish, but eases the pressure immensely when it comes to serving.

» Roast tomato halves served on the plate with the other elements would bulk this up nicely, especially if you're leaving the salmon out.

» To make these more of a nibble or starter, simply make smaller versions of the fritters and serve on a Baby Gem lettuce leaf with the yogurt and herbs on top and a little salmon if you fancy. Pick it up and eat with the leaf underneath so you get the wonderful fresh crunch of the lettuce against the fritter.

» Carrot would work equally well here, as would celeriac – just use it instead of (or mixed with) the beetroot, using exactly the same method.

❈ Breakfast of champignons: roast mushrooms and tomatoes with blue cheese, eggs and oats

This is one of our most popular brunch dishes. It ticks a similar box to a fry-up, but you will feel so much better after having had this instead of an indulgent fry (which absolutely has its place, but perhaps only occasionally).

We are quite fond of the pun in this recipe's name. James has practically taken up punning as a full-time hobby, so happily we managed to create a dish that allowed us to bring together our love of mushrooms and our love of puns. The oat walnut crumble here adds another layer of texture to this dish to counterbalance the juicy flesh of the mushrooms. The intensity of the blue cheese is toned down by making it into a sauce, but feel free to just crumble it on top if you prefer.

SERVES 4

- 8 large flatcap or Portobello mushrooms (approx. 2 per person, or more if your mushrooms are on the small side)
- extra virgin olive oil
- 2 garlic cloves, minced
- 6 sprigs of fresh thyme
- salt and freshly ground black pepper
- 4 ripe tomatoes, halved
- 1 tbsp blue cheese (Cashel Blue is great)
- 4 tbsp crème fraîche
- 100g rolled oats or porridge oats
- 100g walnuts, roughly chopped
- 8 eggs
- 100g caramelised onions (page 346) mixed with 1 tbsp olive oil
- 4 large slices of sourdough bread, toasted
- 4 small handfuls of baby spinach leaves
- torn fresh parsley, to garnish
- finely chopped fresh chives, to garnish

Preheat your oven to 180°C. Get your mushrooms ready by giving them a thorough wash and draining well. Don't listen to people who tell you not to wash them – the science indicates that in terms of flavour it doesn't matter if they've been washed, so it certainly won't do them any harm. And to be honest, as lovely as they are, I really would prefer to eat them washed given that they grow in damp, earthy conditions.

Place the mushrooms on a baking tray and drizzle with olive oil. Toss with the garlic, half the thyme and some salt and pepper, then add the tomatoes to the tray too. Place in the oven and bake for 20 minutes or so. Check their doneness by squeezing the mushroom stalks – they should be soft and juicy, as opposed to how an uncooked mushroom stalk feels (the tomatoes will be done by this stage too). There will be a lot of juice from the mushrooms. If you fancy, drain it off into a small pan and simmer until reduced by three-quarters so it becomes an intensely flavoured sauce to drizzle over the dish. Alternatively, drain it off and keep to add to a soup or stock or another sauce or to use if you're making the roast mushroom and quinoa dish on page 197.

While the mushrooms are roasting, make the blue cheese sauce by crumbling the blue cheese into the crème fraîche, mixing well and adding some freshly ground black pepper (it shouldn't need any salt because the cheese is already so salty) and a good dash of olive oil. Alternatively, blend for a smoother result.

Make the toasted oat and walnut crumble by adding the oats to a hot, dry frying pan set over a medium-high heat and toasting for about 2 minutes, stirring halfway through. They should turn a very light brown. Add the chopped walnuts and toast for another minute, then remove the mix from the pan into a bowl so that it doesn't toast too much in the residual heat of the pan. Add the leaves from the remaining sprigs of thyme.

When ready to serve, poach your eggs (see page 358 for our method – pre-poaching and flashing to order makes the most sense).

To build your dish, smear 2 teaspoons of the caramelised onions over your freshly toasted bread and place the toast on a plate. Top with a handful of baby spinach leaves, then divide the roasted mushrooms and tomatoes between the plates (with a drizzle of the reduced sauce over them if you fancy). Place 2 poached eggs on top with a generous spoonful of the blue cheese sauce. Finally, sprinkle a generous amount of the oat and walnut crumble directly over the eggs. Garnish with some torn parsley and finely chopped chives.

TIPS AND TRICKS

» Roast off extra mushrooms and make my absolute favourite soup, the mushroom and Jerusalem artichoke soup on page 146, or for the roast mushroom and quinoa salad on page 197.
» Bulk this up with some smoked salmon or pan-fried chorizo.

✳ Brother's baked beans

A wonderfully warming and substantial breakfast, either as an element
to the meal or its key foundation. These can work perfectly as a lunch
or supper too if you are so inclined. We make ours on the spicier end of
the spectrum – that doesn't equate to hot, just full of flavour.

SERVES 2–4

- olive oil
- 1 medium onion, medium dice
- 2 celery stalks, medium dice
- 1 tsp smoked paprika
- 1 tsp sweet paprika
- 1 tsp caster sugar
- 1 tsp toasted ground caraway seeds (optional)
- ½ tsp ground cinnamon
- 1 x 400g tin of chopped tomatoes
- 150ml water
- 1 x 400g tin of kidney beans, drained and rinsed (or soak
  and cook 200g dried kidney beans – see page 359)
- 1 x 400g tin of butter beans, drained and rinsed (or soak
  and cook 200g dried butter beans)
- salt and freshly ground black pepper
- squeeze of lemon (optional)

Preheat your oven to 180°C. First let's make the sauce. Heat a little olive
oil in a large pot set over a medium heat. Sweat the onion and celery as
per the method on page 345, then add your spices and sugar and cook
for 2–3 minutes more.

Add the tomatoes and water to the pot and bring to a simmer. Cook
for a further 10 minutes before adding the beans and transferring to a
suitable ovenproof dish – a large baking dish like the one you'd use for
lasagne is ideal.

Place in the oven and cook for 25–30 minutes, uncovered. The beans are
ready when the sauce is rich, reduced and bubbling around the sides.
If you feel the sauce has reduced too much, add a dash of boiling water
and stir it up.

Remove from the oven and taste, adjusting the seasoning with some
salt and pepper and perhaps some more spices or even a little sugar if
needed. A little dash of lemon is often no harm too.

» We like to use kidney beans and butter beans, but you can use any mix you like. If you would prefer to use dried beans rather than tinned, you'll need 400g dried beans, soaked overnight and cooked according to the instructions on page 359.

» Ever the fan of an easier life in the kitchen, bulk this recipe up – any leftover beans will keep in the fridge for 3 days or so, but they also freeze perfectly to be used another time.

» Serve these as a side to go with a full fry-up or just have as the main event with some toast and perhaps a fried or poached egg on top.

» We serve our classic beans in the café with a fried egg on top with some feta yogurt (page 55) and some chopped fresh herbs scattered over. To make it more substantial, folks often add some pan-friend chorizo to this, which works perfectly.

» To make this into a baked eggs dish, try making the dish a little more saucy by adding double the quantity of tomato and when the initial bake is done, make indentations in the beans into which you can crack an egg – use as many eggs as there are people to serve. Cover the dish with tin foil and put back in the oven for another 6–10 minutes, until the whites of the egg are set but the yolk remains runny (unless you like a firm yolk). Sprinkle some chopped herbs on top and maybe a few spoons of feta yogurt (page 55) and serve at the table.

» Stir in 1–2 tablespoons of harissa (page 325) before the beans go into the oven to get an even more flavourful bean experience. In this case, I would really recommend a good dash of lemon stirred into the dish at the end before serving.

❈ Croque monsieur

A French classic, this has become a much-abused recipe over the years. This hot ham and cheese sandwich really comes into its own when you go to the trouble of using great ingredients and make the classic version, which requires a proper cheese sauce. But don't be intimidated; it's easy and so worth the effort. I know this looks like a long, involved recipe, but rest assured it isn't! Plus it's one of those 'wow' dishes to serve for friends as a brunch.

You can assemble the croques in advance and then bake them off when you're ready. Serve with a simple side salad and a glass of white wine for a stress-free brunch, lunch or supper, particularly for a group of people. You can even have them ready in the fridge, assembled but unbaked – they will keep perfectly for 2–3 days in the fridge, then bake as needed, adding 5 minutes to the baking time.

MAKES 4 SANDWICHES

For the cheese sauce:
○ 500ml milk
○ 2 bay leaves
○ decent pinch of grated nutmeg
○ 25g butter
○ 25g plain flour
○ 75g Parmesan, finely grated
○ 75g best-quality Cheddar cheese, grated (Hegarty's Farmhouse Cheddar is superb)
○ 50g blue cheese (optional)
○ 1–2 tsp Dijon mustard
○ salt and freshly ground black pepper

To assemble:
○ 8 slices of sourdough bread
○ enough butter for 8 slices of bread, softened
○ 200–300g home-baked ham or ham hock, shredded (see page 360 for our recipe for ham hock)
○ 150g best-quality Cheddar cheese

Preheat your oven to 180°C. To make the sauce, heat the milk in a saucepan with the bay leaves and a pinch of grated nutmeg. Bring to the boil, but be careful not to allow it to boil over, which can easily happen. Once the milk has boiled, remove it from the heat immediately and allow it to sit and infuse. Remove the bay leaves before using.

Meanwhile, melt the butter slowly in a pan or pot (one large enough that it will hold the addition of all the milk and cheese too) set over a low heat. Add the flour to the melted butter and stir well with a wooden spoon. The mixture will come together as an almost dough-like consistency, but just keep it on a low heat and keep stirring for 3–5 minutes. You are cooking the flour, and this roux paste will then be used to thicken the cheese sauce.

When the roux is cooked and with the heat still on medium-low, gradually add the infused milk a little at a time, beating well between additions. If you add the milk all at once, the mixture will curdle and the roux won't combine properly, resulting in lumps. Stir constantly and watch as the sauce thickens. Continue until all the milk has been incorporated.

At this point, when the sauce is smooth and has thickened nicely, remove the pan from the heat and add the cheeses, stirring until all the cheese has melted and is well combined. Finally, add the Dijon mustard, starting with 1 teaspoon. Stir well and taste, adding seasoning, more mustard or even more cheese if you feel it needs it. You should end up with a sauce that's quite strong in flavour (I also like mine quite mustardy, but use your own judgement!). You can either use this straight away, or you can cover it with a layer of baking paper or cling film pressed directly on top of the sauce to stop a skin from forming, then let it cool and refrigerate until needed.

When you're ready to assemble the croques, toast the bread slices, then butter one side. Put a thick layer of cheese sauce over one slice of bread, then add the ham and top with grated cheese. Place another slice of bread on top and spread a thick layer of the cheese sauce on top of the top slice of sourdough, covering the slice fully. Place on a baking tray lined with non-stick baking paper and repeat for all the sandwiches.

To finish the croques, place the tray in the oven for 15–20 minutes or so to melt the cheeses and heat the bread through. Check that it's fully heated and leave in for longer if needed. I often bake the tops next to the bases so the centre gets really well heated and a little toasted.

To really impress, we like to finish the croque under a hot grill for a few minutes to give it the characteristic caramelised brown finish. Just simply remove from the oven and place directly under the grill (or flash with a kitchen blowtorch if you have one). >>

» To transform this dish into something even more special, called a croque madame, simply fry an egg to your liking and top each croque with it before serving.

» This is a rich, sumptuous dish, so we try to counteract that by adding a small leafy side salad and maybe some pickles to zing it up.

» We could have written an entire chapter on alternative versions of this classic sandwich, but we'll limit ourselves here to just a few. For example, replace the ham hock with our chorizo jam (page 327) to make a croque señor! Or make it vegetarian by replacing the ham with some roasted peppers and maybe some baby spinach and/or some roasted tomato halves. Or you could use roasted Portobello mushrooms as the filling (or even just some sautéed sliced mushrooms) and replace the Parmesan in the sauce with some Cashel Blue cheese.

Eamon's chorizo rarebit

Possibly one the most popular dishes on a Sunday, Eamon's recipe really brings together these rich flavours to make for a joyously indulgent brunch or supper.

A word to the wise: you may well want to scale up this recipe multiple times. This chorizo jam will work well as snack to have on toast, but especially our flatbread on page 322. You can also make a version of our croque monsieur (see page 88) using this instead of the ham hock for an even more decadent cousin of this rarebit recipe.

If you don't have time to make the homemade hot sauce on page 330, use your favourite brand from the supermarket or skip it altogether.

SERVES 4

- 4 slices of good sourdough bread
- 300g chorizo jam (page 327)
- 4 small handfuls of baby spinach leaves
- 4 eggs
- hot sauce (page 330 or shop-bought) (optional)
- 50g pickled red onions (page 336)
- chopped fresh herbs, to garnish
- side salad, to serve

For the cheese sauce:

- 150g crème fraîche
- 100g Cheddar cheese, grated
- 2 egg yolks
- 1 tbsp Dijon or prepared English mustard

Preheat your oven to 180°C. To make the easy cheese sauce, simply place everything in a bowl and mix together until well incorporated.

Toast the slices of bread, then spread with a generous amount of the chorizo jam. Cover the jam with a handful of baby spinach, then spoon over some cheese sauce to cover. Place the bread on a lined tray and bake in the oven for 15 minutes, until the cheese sauce is bubbling and turning brown. This may take a little longer, depending on your oven.

When the rarebits are just a few minutes away from coming out of the oven, quickly fry the eggs. Take the rarebits out of the oven and place each one directly onto a serving plate. Top each one with a fried egg, then drizzle over a little hot sauce. Finally, scatter on some pickled red onions and fresh herbs and serve with a side salad, perhaps topped with some toasted seeds.

❁ Roast aubergine, three ways

We love, love, love aubergine. I think it's a wonder ingredient that's underappreciated in terms of its versatility. It provides a real depth of flavour and presence in any meal, especially a vegetarian dish.

We've set out three ways of enjoying roast aubergine on pages 95–99. Serve these as the main element to a lunch, dinner or supper accompanied by one or several of our other side salads and some fresh crusty bread.

SERVES 4

- 2 large aubergines
- 70–80ml extra virgin olive oil
- salt and freshly ground black pepper

Preheat your oven to 180°C. Line a baking tray with tin foil.

Wash the aubergines, then cut in half from top to tail, ideally leaving the stalk intact. Score the aubergine in a criss-cross pattern through the white flesh using a small sharp knife, going deep but without piercing the skin at the bottom.

Brush well with the oil, going over each half several times as the aubergine absorbs the oil, and season with salt and pepper. Place on the lined baking tray and bake in the oven for about 30 minutes, until the aubergines are softened all the way through. The best part to check is around the stalk end, making sure that area is tender all the way through. If not, return them to the oven and cook for 10 minutes longer.

Now it's time to load them up! See the next pages for ideas on how to make a feast out of this humble aubergine. And please look at the recipe for warm chunky lamb for hummus on page 166 – at the end of that recipe, I suggest how to marry that dish to this roasted aubergine delight. Oh my!

❧ Harissa baked aubergines with saffron yogurt, roasted cashews and apricots

Cashew and apricots work brilliantly together and the saffron yogurt adds a whole level of sophistication to this wonderful party.

SERVES 4

- 2 tbsp harissa (page 325 or shop-bought)
- olive oil
- 4 roasted aubergine halves (see the master recipe on page 94)
- 100g cashews
- 1–2 saffron stamens
- 2 tbsp warm water
- 4 tbsp natural yogurt
- zest of ½ lemon
- 1 garlic clove, crushed
- salt and freshly ground black pepper
- 50g dried apricots, diced
- 10g fresh coriander sprigs

Mix the harissa with a dash of olive oil so it forms a looser paste. Before cooking the aubergine halves initially, after you've made the criss-cross incisions and after brushing with the oil, brush the halves with the harissa and season well with salt and pepper, then roast as per the master recipe on page 94.

To toast the cashews, place them on a baking tray and roast in the oven for about 8 minutes, until golden brown. Alternatively, heat a dry frying pan over a medium heat, add the cashews and toast for several minutes, tossing regularly so they don't burn.

When you're ready to serve, make the saffron yogurt. Soak the saffron stamens in the warm water and leave to infuse for 5 minutes. Strain the liquid into the yogurt, then add the lemon zest, garlic and some salt and pepper, gently folding everything together (over-stirring will cause this sauce to get too runny, so only fold until everything is just brought together).

To serve, place the harissa aubergine halves on the serving plates and drizzle with the saffron yogurt. Gently crush some cashews in your hands and scatter them over the top with the diced apricots. Garnish with fresh coriander sprigs and maybe a final light drizzle of olive oil.

Harissa baked aubergines with saffron yoghurt, roasted cashews and apricots

Roast aubergines with feta, peas, tomatoes and pomegranate

Roast aubergines with green tahini, goats' cheese and spring onions

❋ Roast aubergines with green tahini, goats' cheese and spring onion

This is Eamon's creation and it works wonderfully, capturing a lovely array of Middle Eastern flavours on a pillow of soft, juicy aubergine.

SERVES 4

- 4 roasted aubergine halves (see the master recipe on page 94)
- 2 tbsp tahini
- 30g fresh parsley
- 10g fresh mint
- 5 spring onions, finely sliced at an angle
- 100g goats' cheese (crumbly is best – St Tola is our favourite)
- juice of 1/2 lemon
- salt and freshly ground black pepper
- 4 tbsp dukkah (page 337), optional

First, roast your aubergine halves as per the master recipe on page 94 and put to one side (it is best that they are at room temperature rather than piping hot when you are assembling the dish).

To make the green tahini, place the tahini, parsley, mint (reserving some for garnish) and lemon juice into a food processor and blitz until smooth. The consistency will be quite thick, similar to a thick peanut butter, so add a little hot water, a tablespoon at a time, and continue to blitz until you have reached a smooth and slightly more pourable consistency.

To serve, place each aubergine on a board. Top each of the halves with a good drizzle of the green tahini, scatter with the spring onions and crumbled goats' cheese, and garnish with the reserved mint, tearing it over the servings.

If using dukkah, which is recommended as it adds a nice crunch and fragrance to proceedings, sprinkle over the finished dish.

TIPS AND TRICKS

» To make this dish even more impressive, turn the goats' cheese into dukkah 'croquettes' by rolling it into round or pill shapes about the size of a date or a prune. Then roll each ball in a bowl containing the dukkah, pressing well so the dukkah sticks to all sides of each ball. Aim for 2–3 balls per aubergine half. When putting on top of the finished dish, break the 'croquettes' in half so you expose the lovely white of the cheese as well as the dukkah exterior.

Roast aubergines with feta, peas, tomatoes and pomegranate

Lots of sweet pops here with the peas, tomatoes and pomegranate – all of which is set off by that wonderful salty, creamy feta.

SERVES 4

- 4 roasted aubergine halves (see the master recipe on page 94)
- 10 cherry tomatoes, halved
- 1 tsp dried mint
- 1 tsp caster sugar
- 100g frozen peas
- 100g feta cheese
- olive oil
- 1 small bunch of fresh dill, chopped
- salt and freshly ground black pepper
- dressed baby salad leaves, to serve
- seeds of ½ pomegranate (see page 354 for our easy way to do this)

Roast the aubergines as per the master recipe on page 94.

When the aubergines comes out of the oven, reduce the temperature to 150°C. Arrange the halved cherry tomatoes on a baking tray in a single layer, cut side up. Sprinkle with the dried mint and sugar, then cook in the oven for 30 minutes, until golden and caramelised.

Meanwhile, bring a large pot of water to the boil with a pinch of salt and sugar. Add the peas and bring back to the boil. Once the water is boiling again, quickly drain the peas and refresh in cold water. Drain well.

Add half the peas to a large bowl and roughly smash with a large spoon. Crumble in the feta cheese and add the rest of the peas, half of the roasted tomato halves, a good dash of oil and most of the dill. Mix gently and season to taste with salt and pepper, but be careful with the salt because the feta cheese is already salty.

Place the aubergine halves on a bed of dressed salad on a large serving platter. Spoon over the feta-pea mix, dot with the remaining cherry tomatoes and sprinkle the pomegranate seeds over. Garnish with the remaining dill and a drizzle of olive oil.

TIPS AND TRICKS

» A simple lemon and olive oil dressing or balsamic dressing – something acidic – would work best here for dressing the salad leaves.

❈ Moroccan zalouk

It was the name that got me interested in this dish – it just sounded so exotic. I like to say it in a deep voice, stretching the last syllable in the hammiest way possible. Happily, it's also a wonderful dish! It's particularly satisfying on a cold day. It's one of those dishes that will taste different every time you make it – a fact to be celebrated, in my opinion.

I managed to pop over to Marrakesh last year and sampled this with my friend Jusef, who took me around the ancient, dusty streets on the search for some pottery, stopping off here and there to eat as the locals do on one of his amazing food tours.

Interestingly, the Moroccans themselves eat zalouk at room temperature as a 'cooked' salad. We serve it piping hot but it would work equally well warm as part of a lunch or supper, particularly if served with our flatbread (page 322).

See the tips and tricks for further uses of the aubergine and chickpea sauce.

SERVES 4

- 2 aubergines
- olive oil
- salt and freshly ground black pepper
- 4 celery sticks, diced
- 1 onion, diced
- 3 garlic cloves, sliced
- 2 tsp ground cumin
- 2 tsp ground coriander
- 1 tsp ground cinnamon
- 1 tsp paprika
- 6 ripe tomatoes, diced, or 1 x 400g tin of chopped tomatoes
- 250g cooked chickpeas or 1 x 400 tin of chickpeas, drained and rinsed
- pinch of caster sugar
- squeeze of fresh lemon juice
- 8 eggs
- 4 slices of bread, toast, pitta bread or flatbread (page 322)
- 4 handfuls of baby spinach
- 4 heaped tbsp Greek yogurt (or better still, our smoked aubergine yogurt on page 338)
- 50g fresh coriander, roughly chopped, stalks and all
- pinch of sumac (optional)

Preheat your oven to 180°C. Line a baking tray with non-stick baking paper.

Wash your aubergines and cut the stalks off, then cut the aubergines in half from top to tail. Cut each half into slices 2–3cm thick, then cut across those slices to make 2cm cubes. Put on the lined tray and toss well in olive oil with a little seasoning. Roast for 15–20 minutes, tossing midway through cooking, until the aubergines are well browned and cooked through. The cubes should be completely soft but still holding their shape.

Meanwhile, prepare the base sauce by heating a little oil in a medium saucepan set over a medium-low heat. Add the celery, onion and garlic, put some baking parchment over the surface of the vegetables, then put a lid on the pot. Cook until the onion is soft, which should take 15 minutes or so over a medium-low heat, stirring every 5 minutes. Add the spices and cook for 2 minutes more, stirring well.

Add the fresh or tinned tomatoes and bring to a simmer. Continue to simmer for 10 minutes, uncovered, until the sauce has reduced by about 20% or so – you want it to be thick.

Add the chickpeas and continue to simmer for another 10 minutes. Taste and adjust the spices and seasoning with salt, pepper, sugar and a squeeze of lemon, as you see fit. It should be a really tasty, rich sauce – not spicy hot, but rather spicy in a 'full of flavour' sense. Add the aubergines, remove from the heat and set aside.

Now poach your eggs (see the method on page 358) and get your toast or pitta bread ready.

To serve, place a handful of spinach leaves in each wide bowl and then spoon the sauce on top, dividing it evenly between the bowls. Place 2 poached eggs per bowl on top of the sauce and put a generous spoonful of the yogurt on top of these. Finally, scatter a decent amount of chopped coriander over the dish. A good pinch of sumac on top is also a wonderful addition. Serve the warm bread on the side of the bowl.

» Another way of presenting this is to roast the aubergine simply halved, as in the master recipe on page 94. Then make the sauce as above, omitting the diced aubergine step, of course! To build the dish, place the warm roast aubergine half on a bed of spinach, spoon over the chickpea and tomato sauce and then finish building as per the recipe. This looks wonderful and presents in a more substantial manner.

» The aubergine-chickpea-tomato sauce is wonderfully versatile. I recommend making multiples of the recipe and freezing it or storing in the fridge. This would be lovely served as a filling to an omelette or even as an interesting (if non-traditional) sauce for pasta or with rice or bulghur wheat as a nice supper.

» See also our recipe for shakshuka on page 72 – at the end of the recipe, I suggest making shakshuka using this aubergine chickpea sauce as a versatile and interesting twist.

» While not absolutely traditional, a spoon of harissa stirred through the sauce may cause some delight if you are so inclined.

» If you make extra, adding some additional tomato, stock or even hot water and blending would turn the base sauce into a really delicious soup. Serve piping hot, tasting and adjusting the seasoning, with the aubergine yoghurt dolloped on top along with some fresh herbs.

❋ Warm roast butternut squash and spiced chickpea salad

This is a most satisfying salad and perfect for a brunch or supper.

SERVES 4

- 1 butternut squash (or 1 large summer squash when in season)
- olive oil
- flaky sea salt such as Irish Atlantic Sea Salt and freshly ground black pepper
- 1 tsp ground cinnamon (optional)
- 400–500g cooked chickpeas (see page 359) or 1 x400g tin of chickpeas, drained and rinsed
- 1 tsp paprika (sweet or smoked paprika is ideal, but if using hot paprika, reduce to ½ tsp)
- 1 tsp coriander seeds, toasted and coarsely ground (see page 352)
- ½ tsp cumin seeds, toasted and coarsely ground
- 4–8 eggs (1–2 eggs per person)
- 200–250g salad leaves (a mixture of colours and textures is perfect)
- 2 red onions, halved and cut into thin slices 1mm thick
- 100g mixed soft herbs (parsley, coriander, lovage), roughly chopped
- smoked aubergine yogurt (page 338)

For the lemon and cumin dressing:
- juice of 1–2 lemons
- 50ml extra virgin olive oil
- 1–2 garlic cloves, crushed
- ½ tsp cumin seeds, toasted and coarsely ground

Preheat your oven to 200°C. While the oven is heating up, prepare the squash by scrubbing the outside of it well under cold running water, then trim off the top and tail, cut the squash in half lengthways, scoop out the seeds with a large spoon and then cut into large 4cm wedges, leaving the skin on. We roast and eat this with the skin on because not only is it less work, but we feel that it adds a better texture and more nutrition to the dish.

Place the squash in a roasting tin and toss with a drizzle of oil, a sprinkle of seasoning and the ground cinnamon, if using. Pop into the oven, tossing every 10–15 minutes, until the squash is fully cooked through. Test it by piercing with a knife to ensure it's tender and ideally the edges will be a little browned and caramelised. This could take anywhere from 20 to 40 minutes, depending on the squash.

Meanwhile, pour enough oil in a roasting tin to just cover its base. Put it on the next shelf in your oven for 4 minutes to heat up. Toss the drained chickpeas into the hot oil in the roasting tin along with the paprika, coriander seeds, cumin seeds and a good pinch of salt and pepper. Roast in the oven for a total of 30 minutes, tossing at 10-minute intervals. Taste and adjust the spices and seasoning as needed.

While the squash and chickpeas are roasting, make the lemon and cumin dressing by whisking the lemon juice into the extra virgin olive oil with the garlic, cumin and some salt and pepper. When well mixed, dip a salad leaf into the dressing and taste it, then adjust any of the ingredients until you're happy with the outcome.

Poach your eggs using the technique on page 358. A good tip here is to pre-poach them and flash them in boiling water when the other elements of the dish are ready.

Now it's time to bring everything together! Place your salad leaves in a large bowl with the sliced red onions and half of the herbs, then drizzle with half of the dressing and divide between 4 wide bowls or plates. Spoon the warm roasted chickpeas over this and drizzle a little more of the dressing over. Add chunks of the roasted squash, then top with 1 or 2 poached eggs per person. Finally, spoon the smoked aubergine yogurt on top and sprinkle with the remaining fresh herbs.

TIPS AND TRICKS

» Follow the neon pickled onion recipe on page 336 to add a little bite and extra colour by putting it over the top of the finished dish or simply put the red onion slices in a bowl, toss them in the lemon juice and let them sit – this will turn the red onion a lovely bright red colour and give it a delicious tang. It will keep in the fridge for several days like this.

❋ Smoked salmon with fennel, beetroot tartare and poached egg

A firm favourite on our Sunday brunch menu whenever it appears, this is a wonderfully light dish that is full of flavour.

SERVES 4

- 4 free-range eggs
- 200g baby salad leaves, tossed with a lemon, cider vinegar or balsamic vinegar dressing
- about 400g best-quality smoked salmon
- ½ cucumber, sliced
- turmeric pickled fennel (page 335) (optional but worth it!)
- 4 slices of sourdough bread
- 1 lemon, cut into wedges

For the beetroot tartare:

- 2 medium beetroot
- 4 gherkins
- 2 tbsp capers
- 20g fresh dill, finely chopped
- squeeze of lemon

For the gherkin crème:

- 2 gherkins
- 10g fresh parsley
- 4 tbsp crème fraîche
- 1 tbsp lemon juice
- 2 tsp capers

To make the beetroot tartare, I recommend cooking your own, but you can use cooked beetroot from a supermarket if you're in a hurry. To cook the beetroot, see our method on page 357.

When cooled, peel the beetroot and dice it into even, small squares about the same size as the whole capers. Do the same with the gherkins. Rinse the capers and give them a rough chop. Place the diced beetroot, gherkins and capers in a bowl, then add the dill and a squeeze of lemon and mix well. Add a splash of brine from the caper jar and set aside.

While the beetroot are roasting, you can pre-poach your eggs (see the technique on page 358), then flash them in boiling water when the other elements of the dish are ready.

Now for the gherkin crème: this is easy if you have a small food processor or stick blender. Just add all the ingredients except the crème fraîche and blitz briefly to a chunky consistency. If you don't have a processor, simply finely chop the gherkins, capers and parsley by hand. Place in a bowl and fold together gently with the crème fraîche and lemon juice and mix well. Taste and adjust the seasoning if needed.

This dish is best served in a wide bowl. To plate, lay a bed of mixed dressed salad leaves in the base of the bowl, then arrange some smoked salmon on top. Arrange the cucumber and fennel around the salmon together with a mound of the beetroot tartare. Top with 1–2 poached eggs per person and serve with some toasted sourdough and a lemon wedge on the side. If you have some sumac, a little sprinkle on top would be lovely.

✺ Danielle's coca-style flatbread

A coca is best described as a southern Spanish-style baked flatbread, perhaps a distant cousin of the Italian focaccia. We serve this with a side of one of our salads and/or a bowl of soup for a substantial lunch, dinner or supper. We took these off the menu once for a few days because we were under a bit of pressure with a few other projects. Shortly afterwards, the emails started, such was the worry of some of our regulars that these beauties had disappeared forever. (Epilogue: they came back with a vengeance shortly after and were more popular than ever!)

While I had originally developed the recipe for cocas, it was Danielle, our wonderful, tireless chief baker, who really made these her own, coming up with all sorts of wonderful new combinations week after week. We've set out the base recipe below, and on the following pages you'll see recipes for some topping combinations that we recommend. But please do explore your own – treat it as a slightly more lavish pizza if you want! Though very much inspired by the authentic Spanish coca, we've moved quite a way away from this to make it our own distictive dish.

Don't be alarmed by the number of stages to this recipe. It's fun to make, but you will need a little bit of time. You will also need a baking tray or sheet approximately 21cm x 31cm for all the following coca recipes. These are ideal for lunch or supper if you're having a group of people over, served with a few salads or some soup on the side.

MAKES ENOUGH COCA FOR 8 SLICES

- 180g strong white flour
- 75g semolina, plus extra for dusting the tray
- 1½ tsp dried fast action yeast
- 1 tsp salt
- 150ml warm water
- 50ml extra virgin olive oil

If making the dough by hand, place all the dry ingredients in a mixing bowl and mix well. In a separate jug, combine the tepid water with the olive oil and give it a quick stir. Now bring everything together so you can knead your dough – see the technique on page 349.

If using a standalone mixer fitted with a dough hook attachment, add the dry ingredients to the mixer bowl, then add three-quarters of the liquid mix. Start kneading on the lowest setting, until the liquid and dry ingredients form a dough ball, then turn up the speed to medium. If after several minutes of mixing you feel the dough isn't soft enough, add some of the remaining liquid. Knead the dough for a total of 10 minutes, either by hand or in the mixer.

In either method, the dough is ready when you take a little piece of it in your hand and stretch it out to try to make a thin membrane with it. Once you can see if form a very thin skin that lets the light through without tearing too much, the dough is ready.

Once your dough is made, rub a little oil over the inside of a large bowl (just a little – perhaps ½ tablespoon at most). Place the dough ball in the base, turning it over in the bowl to coat it in the oil. Finally, cover the bowl tightly with cling film so no air can get in and set it aside to prove, ideally in a warm place (perhaps near your oven, which you should now preheat to 180°C), until doubled in size. This should take about 30–45 minutes, but it depends on how warm your kitchen is.

When the dough is ready, punch the gas out of it while it's still in the bowl, then take it out and transfer it to a lightly floured work surface. Flatten it with your hands to make it into a rectangle about the size of an A4 sheet of paper, then roll it out with a rolling pin so that it fits the approximate dimensions of your baking tray or sheet (which should ideally be 21cm x 31cm). The dough should end up being about 1.5cm thick, but don't worry about being too precise.

Dust the baking tray with a generous handful of semolina or fine polenta. Lift up the rectangular sheet of dough and place it in the tray, gently adjusting the dough with your hands so it sits well in the tray.

Now you're ready to finish it with any of the toppings on pages 110–114.

❧ Coca with beetroot, goats' cheese, walnuts and spring onions

Of all the variations you can make with the coca, this is one of our absolute favourites. We caramelise an onion and smear that over the top of the coca before loading the other ingredients on top.

MAKES 8 SLICES

- 1 batch of coca dough (page 108)
- 2 medium beetroot
- olive oil
- salt and freshly ground black pepper
- 2 large red onions, finely diced
- 1 bunch of spring onions
- 50g walnuts, roughly chopped
- 50g goats' cheese

First make the dough as per the master recipe on page 108.

Preheat your oven to 180°C. Wash, top, tail and peel the fresh beetroot, then cut into bite-sized chunks. Toss in a little oil and seasoning and roast in the oven for 30–45 minutes (or more), until the pieces are fully tender all the way through.

Heat a drizzle of oil in a pot set over a medium heat, then add the red onions and cook for 20–25 minutes with the lid off, until it starts to turn brown as the natural sugars begin to caramelise. Once an even brown colour has been reached, remove from the heat and allow to cool.

Meanwhile, prepare the spring onions by removing any bruised or old outer skins and washing well. Shake dry and slice into long, thin slices at an angle.

When the dough is ready, bring the whole dish together for the final bake-off. Spread the dough out on the baking tray as described in the master recipe on page 109. Spoon the cooled caramelised onion over the dough and spread it out evenly. Top with the roasted beetroot and leave the dough to rest for another 15–20 minutes to allow the dough to rise a little again.

Bake in the oven for 30 minutes, but check it after 15 minutes – if it's getting too browned, reduce the oven temperature to 160°C. After the 30 minutes are up, turn down the heat to 150°C and cook for 10 minutes more. Remove it from the oven when the sides are nicely browned and puffed up. Finish the dish by crumbling over the walnuts and goats' cheese and arranging the sliced spring onions on top. Serve warm from the oven with a fresh side salad or a cup of soup.

Coca with fennel, peppers, courgette, ricotta and zhoug

This was one of the first cocas we did and is still perhaps my favourite.

MAKES 8 SLICES

- 1 batch of coca dough (page 108)
- zhoug (page 340)
- 2 medium-large fennel bulbs, topped and tailed
- 2 red peppers, cut in half from top to tail, then each half cut into 5mm strips
- 1 courgette, cut into bite-sized wedges
- extra virgin olive oil
- salt and freshly ground black pepper
- 200–300g ricotta cheese
- 50g mixed fresh herbs (coriander, parsley), roughly chopped
- juice of ½ lemon

Preheat your oven to 180°C. First make the dough as per the master recipe on page 108 and make the zhoug.

While the dough is proving, prepare the other ingredients. Cut the fennel bulbs in half from top to tail, then cut each half into 4–6 wedges. Prepare the other vegetables as described in the ingredients list. Toss the fennel wedges, pepper strips and courgette wedges together in a little olive oil and seasoning and place in a roasting tin. Roast in the oven for 10–12 minutes, until the vegetables have softened but still retain some texture.

Now bring the whole dish together for the final bake-off. Spread the dough out on the baking tray as described in the master recipe on page 109. Smear half of the zhoug all over the top of the dough, then top with the lightly roasted vegetables, dispersing them evenly. Leave to rest for 15–20 minutes or so, until the dough has risen a little again.

Bake in the oven for 30 minutes, but check it after 15 minutes – if it's getting too browned, reduce the oven temperature to 160°C. After the 30 minutes are up, turn down the heat to 150°C and cook for 10 minutes more. Remove it from the oven when the sides are nicely browned and puffed up.

Finish the dish by dotting dessertspoon-sized lumps of the ricotta evenly over the coca. Drizzle the remaining zhoug over the top, then scatter over the fresh herbs. A final squeeze of lemon over the coca and/or a drizzle of extra virgin olive oil just before serving is lovely too. It can be eaten after about 10 minutes of cooling or even when it's just warm or at room temperature. Bring to the table and cut into large slices for everyone to enjoy.

TIPS AND TRICKS

» Zhoug is a versatile and a wonderful accompaniment to falafel (page 266), to fold through natural yogurt as a simple sauce to go with fish or meat or even to swirl through a root vegetable soup or hummus. Add a little lemon juice to give it a fresh zing if you fancy.

✳ Coca with roast squash, red pepper, watercress and feta

Tahini works sensationally here with the chocolate, the walnuts and figs, turning this into one of the most interesting brownies you will ever encounter!

MAKES 8 SLICES

- 1 batch of coca dough (page 108)
- 1 medium butternut squash
- extra virgin olive oil
- salt and freshly ground black pepper
- 4 red peppers, deseeded and cut in half lengthways
- 2 garlic cloves, minced
- 1 dessertspoon harissa (page 325) (optional)
- 150g feta cheese
- 50g watercress or rocket
- squeeze of lemon

Preheat your oven to 185°C. First make the dough as per the master recipe on page 108.

While the dough is proving, prepare the squash by scrubbing the outside of it well under cold running water, then trim off the top and tail, cut the squash in half lengthways and scoop out the seeds with a large spoon. Cut each piece in half crossways so that you are left with 4 quarters. Now just cut them into even-sized wedges – about 6 per quarter. We roast and eat this with the skin on because not only is it less work, but we feel that it adds a better texture and more nutrition to the dish.

Place the wedges in a large roasting tin, drizzle with oil and season with salt and pepper. Roast in the oven for about 30 minutes, until golden and softened. Test with a knife to ensure the squash is nice and soft all the way through. You might want to cut off a piece and eat it to be absolutely sure it's tender enough.

To make the red pepper purée, place the halved peppers on a baking tray, drizzle with a little oil and some salt and pepper and roast in the hot oven along with the butternut squash for 30–40 minutes, until they are soft. Place in a food processor and blitz to a purée, then add the minced garlic and about 1 tablespoon of oil. Taste the purée, adding more seasoning or garlic until it tastes delicious. To give this a bit of a kick, add the harissa and blend it in well.

To assemble, spread the dough out on the baking tray as described in the master recipe on page 109. Spoon the red pepper purée over the dough and spread it out evenly, covering it right up to the edges. Top with the roast butternut squash pieces, making sure they are evenly dispersed. Leave the dough to rest for another 15–20 minutes to allow the dough to rise again.

Bake in the oven for 30 minutes, but check it after 15 minutes – if it's getting too browned, reduce the oven temperature to 160°C. After the 30 minutes are up, turn down the heat to 150°C and cook for 10 minutes more. Remove from the oven and finish by crumbling over some feta cheese and scattering with watercress or rocket. The final touch is a drizzle of good olive oil, a squeeze of lemon juice and some freshly cracked black pepper.

TIPS AND TRICKS

» A nice addition to this flatbread would be some thick slices of cooking chorizo dotted across the top halfway through the cooking time (or pan-fry it and pop it on top when the coca comes out of the oven).

✖ Tortilla, tortilla!

This Spanish classic of eggs, potato and onion is such wonderful food for any time of the day, any time of the year. It's something that really could have been invented in Ireland given our love for the very same ingredients. Once you nail the base recipe, you can go on all sorts of adventures with it. See below for a few ideas on how to get a lot more out of your tortilla.

I first made tortilla in Julio in Melbourne, where my mentor, Michelle, had some very strong feelings on the subject. I've inherited those and added my own along the way. Our recipe below, rather controversially and maybe unforgivably, does not fully adhere to the Spanish classic, but is delicious nonetheless.

This may seem like a lot of garlic and onions, but don't worry, you'll thank me as they bring an amazing flavour to this simple dish. A word of warning, however: there are healthier dishes out there, but this is still worth making. Offset it by serving with a salad of crisp leaves, for example (or maybe a short jog at some stage!).

Ideally you should use a 21–23cm diameter non-stick pan, but any similar-sized pan should be fine, or even two smaller ones. Just make sure your pan is ovenproof!

SERVES 8–10

- 500–750g waxy potatoes
- salt and freshly ground black pepper
- 1–2 large onions (500g)
- 2 heads of garlic
- olive oil
- 10 of the best, freshest eggs (ideally free-range and organic)

First get the potatoes cooking. Give them a good wash if needed and pop them in a pot of cold water with 1 teaspoon of salt. Cover with a lid and bring to the boil, then reduce down to a simmer and cook for about 30 minutes, depending on the size of the potatoes, until they are somewhat tender to the point of a knife but not falling apart. Drain and leave to cool.

Meanwhile, caramelise the onions and garlic, as this takes a little time. See our recommended method on page 346. >>

Peel your potatoes when they're cool enough to handle (cooler is better, as they firm up a bit better for the next step) and cut into 1cm-thick slices. Heat a little oil in a pan set over a medium-high heat. Fry off the potato slices in batches with a little seasoning. You want them to take on a nice golden brown colour on both sides, so don't overcrowd the pan.

At this point, preheat your oven to 150°C. Whisk your eggs in a large bowl until they have just broken down but aren't airy. Add the potatoes and the caramelised onion and garlic and mix gently. Test the mix by frying a little off in a hot pan with some oil – taste and adjust the seasoning according to your preference. This step is absolutely crucial to ensure you get a delicious result!

Once you're happy with the mix, get the pan you will be using for cooking the tortilla (ideally an ovenproof 21–23cm diameter non-stick pan) and put it over a high heat with enough oil to cover the base of the pan. Get it good and hot, then add all of the egg-potato-onion mix at once. Your plan is to set the outside of the tortilla as soon as possible, which avoids it sticking to the sides of the pan.

Let it cook like this for about 30 seconds or so. Check the sides by sticking in a spatula and tucking it back from the side of the pan so you can have a look at it. Once you're happy that it's getting sealed and just lightly golden, turn off the heat and place the pan in the preheated oven. Bake for 15–20 minutes, but it might need a little longer.

Check it after 15 minutes by giving it a shake – there should be a little wobble in the middle. If you think it's done, take it out of the oven but keep a tea towel around the handle at all times, as it's easy to forget that it's still hot! Stick a knife into the centre, pushing it to one side so you can peer in a little. If it's still quite runny inside, it needs more time. If it's just set or almost set, it should be fine as it will continue cooking a while longer in its residual heat. If anything, many consider an underset tortilla to be the perfect outcome, with it oozing ever so slightly in the middle when you cut it.

Leave to one side to cool a little in the pan, then take a large plate – one that's big enough to cover the top of the pan – and invert fully so that the omelette turns out onto the plate. Be brave! It feels like a bit of a risky manoeuvre, but just be sure that you've got towels in both hands, covering your wrist under the plate in case any oil slips out. The tortilla should be a nice light brown on top, but if it's too pale, you can always put it back in the pan and place it on a medium heat on the hob to give it a little more colour. If it's a little too dark, don't worry – just plate it top side up to hide it. It will still taste delicious!

I suggest waiting until it cools down before serving, as it's best served warm as opposed to piping hot, and if anything, the flavours truly shine when it's at room temperature. It certainly demands the company of a salad and maybe even some nice crusty bread.

TIPS AND TRICKS

» A lovely addition to this is to gently heat up some of the tomato and pepper sauce on page 321 and serve it as a sauce on the side or drizzled over the tortilla when serving.
» Tortilla is best eaten on the day it's cooked, but if there is some left, cover it and store in the fridge. It's not as lovely to eat straight out of the fridge, so let it come back up to room temperature before serving. It's not unheard of to heat it up in a microwave, covered (but you didn't hear that from me), or pop it into a moderate oven (180°C) to warm.
» Believe it or not, one of the best ways to eat tortilla is as a sandwich! Try it on fresh crusty bread with some crunchy leaves. A smear of mayonnaise is quite legitimate here with it, as is a slice of Serrano ham tucked underneath. Or make a pan tomaca by roughly blitzing some super ripe tomato with some crushed garlic, a dash of oil and some salt and pepper (taste and adjust the garlic and seasoning) and smearing this over the bread, then put the tortilla slice and/or ham on top.
» As you might have gathered by now, I'm a big fan of making larger batches of certain recipes to save time the next time I'm preparing a dish, so you can happily make multiples of the caramelised onion and garlic mix, though it might take somewhat longer to caramelise. Just let it cool, transfer it to an airtight tub and freeze, and you have a lot of the legwork done for the next time you want to make a tortilla. It also works wonders as an addition in so many other recipes – try stirring it through couscous or folding it through some hummus.

VARIATIONS ON THE TORTILLA THEME

My favourite tortilla is still the classic. It's a great example of a simple dish, kept simple. However, if you want to fancy it up, here are some great ideas.
» *Chorizo tortilla*: Using a hot, dry frying pan set over a high heat, quickly fry off some chunks of chorizo, cut about the size of a toffee. Add this to the eggy mix just before adding the eggs to the tortilla pan.

» *Roast pepper and feta tortilla:* Roast peppers work amazingly well here, as does crumbled feta. Cook about 3 peppers, roasted as in the recipe for on page 229, and add to the eggy mix with 100–150g of feta chunks at the same time as the potato, giving it a gentle stir to ensure it's evenly distributed.

» *Courgette tortilla:* Grate 1 or 2 medium courgettes on the big holes of your box grater. Add this to the mix at the same point as the potato along with some pebble-sized chunks of feta or lots of chopped fresh herbs and proceed from there.

» *Super green tortilla:* Make it super herby with lots and lots of mixed herbs (80–100g) such as dill, flat-leaf parsley, lovage, baby spinach leaves and even a little mint or wild garlic if it's in season. You can also throw in a few handfuls of peas (frozen peas blanched in boiling salted water for 1 minute and drained well). Some crumbled feta would work nicely with this combination too. Just add these to the eggy mix when adding the potato, then proceed as in the main recipe

❊ Merguez sausage rolls

Sausage rolls remain one of the most guilty of pleasures. They're so handy to eat on the trot or to have with a nice leafy salad as a lunch or supper. These are our take. Now, I tend to be quite the purist and insist on making everything from scratch, but homemade puff pastry has really tested my limits in the past. I happily recommend using shop-bought puff pastry for this recipe (we use Jus-Rol), where there is no great sacrifice of quality – and definitely no sacrifice of time compared to making puff pastry from scratch!

MAKES 12 SAUSAGE ROLLS

- 1 tbsp fennel seeds, toasted and finely ground
- 1 tsp cumin seeds, toasted and finely ground
- 1 tsp coriander seeds, toasted and finely ground
- 1 tsp hot paprika
- 1 tsp salt
- 1 tsp freshly ground black pepper
- 500g minced lamb (ideally from the shoulder)
- 2 garlic cloves, crushed to a paste
- 1 tbsp harissa (page 326 or shop-bought)
- 100g feta cheese
- 50g caramelised onion (page 345) (optional)
- 20g fresh mint, finely chopped
- 2 x 320g packs of ready-made puff pastry
- 1 egg, lightly beaten
- sesame seeds, to garnish
- tomato and apple ketchup (page 333), to serve

Mix the toasted and finely ground seeds with the paprika, salt and pepper (see our tips on page 352 for how to toast seeds). Place the lamb in a large bowl along with the spices, crushed garlic and harissa. Crumble in the feta (not too finely – a little lumpy is good), then gently mix in the caramelised onion, if using, and the chopped mint. Mix well to incorporate the flavours completely throughout the meat but without turning the mix too pastey. Fry off a little of the meat in a hot pan to test for the flavour and seasoning. Adjust as necessary, adding more of any element as desired. When you're happy with the flavours, refrigerate until ready to use.

At this stage, preheat your oven to 180°C and line a baking tray with non-stick baking paper.

Unroll each of the puff pastry rolls – these will each form a large rectangle. Divide each rectangle into 6 even-sized rectangles (about 11.5cm x 7.5cm each), giving a total of 12 rectangles. >>

Weigh the meat mixture, then divide into 12 even portions. Shape each portion into a small sausage-shaped roll about the length of the long side of your rectangles. Place a sausage patty onto each pastry square, placing them just underneath the midway point. Brush each pastry square all around the sausage with a little water and gently fold the excess pastry over the sausage to connect with the other side. Gently squeeze and crimp the pastry where it meets the other side to make a tight envelope with no holes. Repeat for all 12 rolls.

Once they are ready, place them flat side down on the lined baking tray. Using a very sharp knife, cut 3 small slits through the pastry on top of each roll. Brush with a little beaten egg and sprinkle with sesame seeds.

Bake in the oven for 25–30 minutes, until golden brown and bubbling. These rolls are great enjoyed hot or at room temperature served with our tomato and apple ketchup (page 333) as a dipping sauce. Serve with a light salad on the side.

TIPS AND TRICKS

» The merguez sausage is a delicious filling in these rolls, but you could also make this mix into patties to fry off and have as part of a nice breakfast or lunch.
» Ask your butcher to mince you some lamb shoulder for this recipe. It has a higher fat content, which keeps the meat moist when cooking. If you don't love lamb, beef mince would work very well here too.
» For an extra spicy or saucy kick, you can do one of the following: either mix 1 tablespoon of harissa with 1 tablespoon of water and brush this over the puff pastry squares before you place the sausagemeat filling on top or smear some of the tomato and apple ketchup over the pastry squares before you add the sausagemeat.
» Another nice addition is some baby spinach leaves laid out on top of the pastry before putting the sausagemeat filling on top.

SOUPS

Soup, soup, wonderful soup. But oh, how so many go awry! Too often, soup is served as a generic bowl of 'something' – too salted, too stock-cubed, to really taste of anything specific. Too often, it's an afterthought or just a dumping ground for leftover ingredients. But it can be so much more – a nourishing bowl of beauty that can sit proudly up against any other item as a lunch or a supper rather than being considered something lesser.

We put a lot of effort into soup in our cafés. I would go so far as to say that we put a lot of love into our soups. As you will see, I feel very strongly about soup.

Over the next few pages, we outline some points for you to consider as you try some of our recipes.

Don't take stock (unless it's homemade)
For starters, we generally don't use stock. Controversial, I know, but I
believe soup should be its own stock and that it should be made with
a generous hand when it comes to the base ingredients – your onion,
celery, garlic and the main soup ingredient. I don't think anything
should come out of a tub, a packet or a cube – in my experience, these
are by and large substandard, over-salted powders or gels that won't do
your soup much good. If you happen to have the time to make a lovely
chicken or vegetable stock yourself, by all means use it – the soup will
only be better as a result. But don't worry – be generous with the core
ingredients and all will be fine. Plus it will be better – and better for you
– than reaching for a stock cube.

It needs to be what it should be
Soup needs to taste of what it's supposed to taste of. Pea soup should
taste of peas, mushroom soup should taste of mushrooms. Again, a
generous hand is all that's required when it comes to the main 'flavour'
ingredient.

Broaden your seasoning horizons
When thinking of seasoning, go beyond the typical binary choice of salt
and pepper – think sweet and sour too. A little bit of honey or sugar
and a dash of lemon juice can often elevate a soup to a level you never
thought possible. We also view the following as our friends to add a
little extra something when finishing a soup:
» Ground cumin
» Tomato sauce or purée
» A pinch of cinnamon (a very light hand – it should add depth without
   the soup actually ending up tasting of cinnamon)
» Mushrooms
» A little dairy (cream or butter, but buttermilk is actually best!)
» Coconut milk (depending on the soup)

Just please remember one thing: you can always add more seasoning, but
it is nearly impossible to remove if you add too much! So add a little, taste
and adjust a little more, bit by bit, until you're happy with the balance.

Blitz until you can blitz no more
To get that silky smooth mouthfeel to a puréed soup, blitz it for far
longer than you might think would be necessary. The soup will be all
the better for it. Now having said that, not everyone likes a smooth
soup, but if that's what you're after, then a good, long blitz will get it
just right for you.

It's always worth getting dressed up

We dress our soups more often than not. We add all sorts of toppings – creamy ones, herb oils, toasted seeds, mixed herbs. Using these little tricks, the soup can be so much more. It can look more pleasing, taste more pleasing and have that extra dimension to its mouthfeel and texture. We've listed recommended dressings with each soup over the coming pages.

Just one minor quibble, if I may: please ask your guests not to stir the dressing into the soup! It's there for contrast. You want the smoked aubergine yogurt to stand up against the mushroom soup so it feels more like a party in your mouth. Each mouthful will taste different as a result. If we had wanted the two to be fully mixed together, we could have just stirred it in for you! I better stop now because I'm worried that I'm beginning to sound like the famous 'Soup Nazi' from *Seinfeld*.

✤ Green pea and lovage soup

Lovage is my absolute favourite herb. It adds such a savoury element to any salad or soup. We use it in our herb mixes for many of our recipes. It can be tricky to track down in a regular supermarket, but you will often come across it in a Polish shop. It works really well in this fresh, vibrant soup alongside the pea and the mint. If you can't find it, perhaps double the amount of celery in the recipe, making sure to use absolutely all of the leaves.

SERVES 3–4 AS A SUBSTANTIAL LUNCH

- 1 tbsp olive oil
- 250g onions (2–3 onions), diced
- 250g leeks (2–3 medium leeks)
- 250g celery (about ½ head, leaves and all), diced
- 6 garlic cloves, sliced
- 250g potatoes (about 4 medium potatoes), peeled and diced
- 2 litres boiling water
- 1kg frozen peas
- 100g fresh lovage
- 20g fresh mint, leaves picked from the stalks
- salt and freshly ground black pepper
- Greek yogurt, to serve

First prepare the onions, celery, garlic and potato as described above. Cut the rough end leaves off your leeks and remove the rough outer layer, then slice the leeks in half, rinse them thoroughly and cut into slices 1cm thick. Cut the stalks off the lovage and chop them finely and reserve the leaves.

Heat the oil in a large saucepan set over a medium heat. Sweat the onions, leeks, celery and garlic for about 15 minutes, until fully tender (see page 345 for our easy method). Add the potatoes and cook for a further 10 minutes, then pour in the boiling water. Bring to the boil and cook, uncovered, for about 10 minutes more, until the potato is starting to break down. Add the peas and bring back to the boil again, then remove from the heat straight away and add the lovage and mint leaves.

Blitz the soup thoroughly (this soup will benefit greatly from a long blitz here, far longer than you might think necessary) and taste, adjusting the seasoning and adding more herbs if you feel it's necessary (and give it a final long blitz if needed too). If the soup is too thick, add a little more water to get the consistency you'd like. >>

Serve in warmed bowls with a spoonful of thick Greek yogurt on top or see below for further dressing ideas.

RECOMMENDED DRESSINGS

Mixed herb and chilli 'salsa' (page 149) or roast garlic crème fraîche (page 148)

TIPS AND TRICKS

» If you fancy a touch of heat in this, a medium red chilli (with most of the seeds removed) or ½ tsp dried chilli flakes added to the base when sweating the onion works well.

❈ Roast tomato and red pepper soup

This sensual, warming soup always brings a smile to my face. It's best served with some sourdough bread, a crumble of feta and some fresh mint or basil.

SERVES 3–4 AS A SUBSTANTIAL LUNCH

For the red pepper and tomato element:
- 1kg ripe tomatoes, cut into quarters
- 2 red peppers, deseeded and roughly chopped
- 1 red onion, cut into quarters
- 1 chilli, deseeded and roughly chopped
- 6 garlic cloves, peeled and left whole
- 60ml olive oil
- 1 tbsp soft brown sugar
- 1.5 litres boiling water
- salt and freshly ground black pepper

For the soup base:
- 1 tbsp olive oil
- 250g onions (2–3 onions), diced
- 250 celery (about ½ head, leaves and all), diced
- 4 garlic cloves, roughly chopped

Preheat your oven to 180°C. Put the tomatoes, peppers, onion, chilli and garlic in a roasting tin, then drizzle with the olive oil and sprinkle with the sugar. Toss everything together and roast in the oven for 30–40 minutes, stirring often, until the vegetables are really soft and starting to turn slightly brown.

While the vegetables are roasting, prepare the base by heating the oil in a large pot set over a medium heat and sweating the onions, celery and garlic for about 15 minutes, until fully tender (see page 345 for our easy method).

When the oven-roasted vegetables are ready, add them to the base in the pot. Pour in the boiling water and simmer for 5 minutes. Working in batches, spoon the mixture into a food processor or blender and blitz until smooth (or use a hand-held blender and blitz the soup directly in the pot). Adjust the consistency, adding more liquid if needs be, then taste, adjust the seasoning and serve piping hot in a warm bowl with either of our suggested dressings.

RECOMMENDED DRESSINGS

Mixed herb and chilli 'salsa' (page 149) or roast garlic crème fraîche (page 148)

❊ Roast beetroot and tomato soup with caraway seeds

This vibrant magenta soup is incredibly tasty. Double up on the caraway seeds if you fancy – it's one of my favourite spices. Rather than this being a pure beetroot soup, we've added tomato because as much as we love beetroot – and we so do! – it can be a little too intense on its own. The tomato really helps to bring another dimension to the soup.

SERVES 6–8

- 800g beetroot
- 1 tbsp olive oil
- 250g onions (2–3 onions), diced
- ½ head of celery, diced
- 4 garlic cloves, roughly chopped
- 250g potatoes (about 4 medium potatoes), peeled and diced
- 1 x 400g tin of chopped tomatoes
- 2 litres boiling water
- 2 tsp caraway seeds
- salt and freshly ground black pepper
- pinch of soft brown sugar
- squeeze of lemon (optional)

Preheat your oven to 180°C. Cook your beetroot according to either method described on page 357.

Meanwhile, prepare your base vegetables. Heat the oil in a large saucepan set over a medium heat. Sweat the onions, celery and garlic together for about 15 minutes, until fully tender (see page 345 for our easy method). Add the diced potato and cook for another 10 minutes, uncovered, then add the roasted beetroot, chopped tomatoes, water and caraway seeds. Bring to the boil, then reduce the heat and simmer for about 10 minutes, until the potato is just cooked.

Remove from the heat and allow to cool a little before blitzing. Adjust with more liquid if needed to get the desired consistency. Season with salt, pepper and brown sugar to taste, and even a little lemon if you feel it needs it. This is a soup that responds well to blitzing, so do blitz it for about twice as long as you feel is necessary.

RECOMMENDED DRESSINGS

Yogurt and fresh herbs, roast garlic crème fraîche (page 148), fried garlic crisps (page 149), za'atar croutons (page 150) or baked kale crisps (page 150)

❊ Gently spiced parsnip soup

This is a very rewarding recipe – parsnip soup is always so comforting. Here we recommend using a special spice mix called ras el hanout. See the tips and tricks for how to make this yourself or you can buy it ready-made in most good supermarkets nowadays. Ras el hanout is Arabic for 'head of the shop' and traditionally means that the spice merchant would use their very best spices for this mix.

SERVES 4 AS A SUBSTANTIAL LUNCH

- 1 tbsp olive oil
- 250g onions (2–3 onions), diced
- 250g celery (about ½ head), diced
- 150g leeks (1–2 leeks)
- 4 garlic cloves, roughly chopped
- 1kg parsnips, peeled and diced
- 3 tsp ras el hanout (see the tips and tricks below for the recipe or use shop-bought)
- salt and freshly ground black pepper
- 1.5 litres boiling water
- squeeze of lemon (optional)

First prepare the parsnips, onions, celery and garlic as described above. Cut the rough end leaves off your leeks and remove the rough outer layer, then slice the leeks in half, rinse them thoroughly and cut into slices 1cm thick.

Heat the oil in a large saucepan set over a medium heat. Sweat the onions, celery, leeks and garlic for about 15 minutes, until fully tender (see page 345 for our easy method). Add the parsnips and continue cooking, covered, for another 10–15 minutes, until the parsnips have started to soften. Add the ras el hanout and cook for another 5–6 minutes, then season with salt and pepper.

Add the boiling water to the saucepan and bring to a simmer. Remove the pan from the heat and blitz with a hand-held blender or in a food processor until nice and smooth – you cannot over-blitz, so do stick with it. Adjust with more liquid if needed to get the desired consistency. Taste and adjust the seasoning and temperature, adding more ras el hanout, seasoning or even a little dash of lemon if you feel it needs it.

Roast garlic crème fraîche (page 148) or za'atar croutons (page 150)

TIPS AND TRICKS

» To easily make a homemade ras el hanout, simply place 2 tablespoons cumin seeds, 2 tablespoons coriander seeds, 2 tablespoons black peppercorns and the seeds from 3–4 cardamom pods in a spice grinder or pestle and mortar and grind to a fine powder. Next add 1 tablespoon ground cinnamon, 2 teaspoons ground ginger and 1 teaspoon ground turmeric and mix well. This mix will last for weeks in an airtight container.
» Replacing half the water with buttermilk would also work extremely well with this recipe, giving it a delicious tang.

❈ Roast sweet potato soup with sumac and black garlic

I need to be honest here: I don't love sweet potato. So much so that it was never on our menu – right up until I took a little trip away and a few of our chefs, determined to bring the much-loved vegetable into our kitchen, put this soup on behind my back. As it transpired, not only was it a big hit with our customers, but we happened to have a top food critic in while I was away. The verdict?

> *A cup of roast sweet potato soup is flavoured with black garlic and sumac and topped with a dollop of lemon-flavoured yogurt. These are sophisticated combinations, and there's a sense of generosity to the food, not only in terms of the portion sizes but also of the thought that goes into it. Any café can produce a sweet potato soup and put it on the lunch menu, but I can't think of another that would involve so many elements… It's evidence of a kitchen ethos committed to going the extra mile and rejecting the easy option. (Irish Independent, May 2015)*

Thank you, my cooking colleagues, point made. And yes, sweet potatoes have made an occasional appearance ever since.

SERVES 8

- 800g–1kg sweet potatoes, peeled and cut into even-sized chunks
- 1 medium red onion, cut into thick wedges
- 2 tbsp olive oil
- 1 tbsp sumac, plus extra to serve
- salt and freshly ground black pepper
- 4–6 cloves of black garlic (if available) or regular garlic (see the note in the tips and tricks)
- 1.5 litres boiling water
- Greek yogurt, to serve

For the soup base:
- 1 tbsp olive oil
- 250g onions (2–3 onions), diced
- 250g celery (about ½ head), diced

Preheat your oven to 180°C. Place the sweet potatoes and red onion in a roasting tin with the oil, sumac and seasoning and toss around until everything is well coated. If you're using regular garlic instead of black garlic, add the whole unpeeled cloves to the roasting tin now too. Cook in the oven for 20–40 minutes, depending on the vegetables, checking after 20 minutes and tossing them around every 10–15 minutes. They are done when both vegetables are fully tender and soft.

To prepare the soup base, heat the oil in a large pot set over a medium heat. Sweat the onions and celery for about 15 minutes, until fully tender (see page 345 for our easy method).

When the sweet potatoes and red onion are cooked, add them to the pot along with the roughly chopped black garlic, if using, and the boiling water. If you're using regular garlic, squeeze the cloves out of their skins into the pot at this point. Bring to a simmer, then remove from the heat and blitz the soup in batches in a food processor or blender or directly in the pot with a hand-held stick blender, adjusting the consistency as desired with more water if necessary.

Check the seasoning, adding more salt, pepper and sumac if needed, and reheat in a clean pot set over a low heat. Serve with a spoonful of Greek yogurt and a dusting of sumac.

RECOMMENDED DRESSINGS

Yogurt and fresh herbs, mixed herb and chilli 'salsa' (page 149) or roast garlic crème fraîche (page 148)

TIPS AND TRICKS

» If you can't get your hands on black garlic, there's no need to worry. Black garlic is garlic that has been roasted for a long time on a slow heat to caramelise the sugars, turning it a rich black colour. To replicate this process at home, wrap a full bulb of garlic in tin foil and roast it in the oven at 150°C for about 45 minutes. The garlic will not fully take on the characteristic black colour, but the flavour will be very similar. Otherwise simply add your whole cloves of regular garlic to the roasting tin while roasting the sweet potatoes. They will take on a nice flavour in the time it takes to soften the sweet potato.

❈ Green soup

We called this green soup because it just tasted really, well, green (and because calling it chlorophyll soup would have been a bridge too far). It's one of those soups that's really satisfying but it also makes you feel really healthy too.

This is a soup that benefits from cooking low and slow at the beginning and then finishing the soup particularly quickly at the end when you are adding the green elements. This allows you to develop a strong, complex flavour but also to keep the beautiful green colour. As a rule of thumb, never put a lid on a pot of green soup (or anything green in general, for that matter), as that's what will encourage that lovely bright green colour to transform into its murkier cousin.

SERVES 8

- 1 tbsp olive oil
- 250g onions (2–3 onions), diced
- 250g celery (about ½ head), diced
- 250g fennel (about 1 large or 2 medium bulbs)
- 250g potatoes (about 4 medium potatoes), peeled and diced
- 50–100g fresh parsley
- 4 garlic cloves, roughly chopped
- 1 tsp ground fennel seeds
- 1 tsp ground coriander
- 1.5 litres boiling water
- 250g frozen peas
- 250g kale
- 250g spinach
- salt and freshly ground black pepper
- Greek yogurt, to serve
- pinch of sumac, to serve

Prepare the onions, celery, potatoes and garlic as described above. Chop the feathery tips off the fennel and reserve for later. Slice the fennel in half lengthways and remove the tough core at the bottom and discard. Give the fennel a good wash, then cut into slices about 1cm thick. Wash your kale well, remove any thick stalks and discard, then thinly slice the kale and put to one side. Do the same for your spinach. Remove the bigger parsley stalks and chop them finely.

Heat the oil in a large pot set over a medium heat. Sweat the onions, celery, fennel, potatoes, parsley stalks and garlic for about 15 minutes, until fully tender (see page 345 for our easy method). Stir in the spices, then add the boiling water and bring to a simmer. Now is the time to add the peas, kale, spinach and parsley leaves (reserve a little of the latter for garnishing). Increase the heat to quickly bring the soup back to a simmer and cook, uncovered, for 3 minutes – no longer!

Blitz the soup well using a hand-held blender or in your food processor or blender. The soup will still have green specks of kale in it, which is an intended outcome. Adjust the consistency with more water until it's how you like it. Taste and adjust the seasoning if you feel it needs a bit of a perk.

Serve immediately, fully heated, in warmed bowls. Garnish with a swirl of yogurt, a sprinkle of sumac and the reserved parsley or try the baked kale crisps on page 150.

TIPS AND TRICKS

» A superb variation of this soup that adds decadence and class is to serve it in a low, wide, warmed bowl, crumble over some smoked mackerel and top with a soft poached egg and pea shoots or some fresh herbs. Honestly, fit for a king.
» When cutting the vegetables, the smaller, the better. This allows the vegetables to cook quicker, and in general, the quicker the soup comes together, the more nutrients and vitamins it will retain – but that's easy for a chef to say. If you don't want to spend too long chopping, don't worry about it unduly. Just let them cook a little longer instead so the heat does a lot of the work for you.

❈ Carrot and buttermilk soup

Buttermilk is sensational in a soup with root vegetables. It brings an entirely new level of depth to the experience. You could replace the carrot with parsnip or, most spectacularly of all, celeriac.

SERVES 6–8

- 1 tbsp olive oil
- 250g onions (2–3 onions), diced
- 250g celery (about ½ head), diced
- 6 garlic cloves, roughly chopped
- 1kg carrots, peeled and diced
- 1 tsp ground coriander
- 1.5 litres boiling water
- 300ml buttermilk
- salt and freshly ground black pepper
- squeeze of lemon (optional)

Heat the oil in a large pot set over a medium heat. Sweat the onions, celery and garlic for about 15 minutes, until fully tender (see page 345 for our easy method). Once the mix is softened, add the carrots and ground coriander and cook for about 10 minutes more, until the carrot is slightly softened. Cover with the boiling water and simmer for 20 minutes, uncovered, until the carrots are fully cooked. Remove from the heat and allow to cool for 5–10 minutes, then add the buttermilk.

Blitz the soup until smooth, adjusting with more liquid if needed to get the consistency you would like. Season to taste with salt and pepper, adding a touch of lemon if you feel the soup needs more brightness. Serve in warm bowls and garnish with one of the recommended soup dressings.

Greek yogurt, mixed herb and chilli 'salsa' (page 149) or brown butter (page 356)

TIPS AND TRICKS

» Buttermilk is an amazing addition to a soup. It adds a tart flavour and a creamy texture when blitzed. If you don't have buttermilk to hand, though, you can use some yogurt with a little water added or you can easily make some at home.

» To make homemade buttermilk, add 2 tablespoons of lemon juice or vinegar to 500ml of milk, stirring well. Allow it to sit at room temperature for about 10 minutes and then it's ready to use. You will see that the milk has curdled slightly and some solids will have formed. When ready to use, give it a quick stir and use all of the mixture, including the solids.

» As alluded to in the introduction, this recipe works well as a base recipe for celeriac and buttermilk soup too. Simply swap the same weight of carrots for celeriac, and try brown butter (page 356) for the dairy as it works especially well in the celeriac version of this soup.

❊ Butternut squash and coconut soup with ginger and chilli

Comforting and satisfying, this soup works well at any time of the year, but perhaps is at its best on a spring or summer day, using whatever squash is in season.

SERVES 4 AS A SUBSTANTIAL LUNCH

- 1kg butternut squash (about 1 medium or large squash)
- olive oil
- 1 tsp ground coriander
- 1 tsp ground cumin
- 250g onions (2–3 onions), diced
- 250g celery (about ½ head), diced
- 6 garlic cloves, roughly chopped
- 1 fresh red chilli, deseeded and roughly chopped, plus thin slices to garnish
- 30g fresh ginger, peeled and roughly chopped or grated
- 1 litre boiling water
- 1 x 400ml tin of coconut milk
- salt and freshly ground black pepper
- squeeze of lemon or lime (optional)
- chopped fresh coriander, to garnish

Preheat your oven to 180°C. Prepare the squash by scrubbing the outside of it well under cold running water. We roast and eat this with the skin on because not only is it less work, but we feel that it adds a better texture and more nutrition to the dish. Trim off the top and tail, cut the squash in half lengthways and scoop out the seeds with a large spoon. Put each half on the chopping board cut side down so that it doesn't roll around and cut in half again. Chop the squash into even-sized pieces (3–4cm cubes is fine) and place in a large roasting tin with a drizzle of oil and the ground coriander and cumin. Toss well to coat the squash in the oil and spices and roast in the oven for about 25 minutes, until just softened. Don't allow it to get too brown or it will discolour the soup. Just softened and very lightly browned (if at all) is best.

While that's all happening, heat about 1 tablespoon of oil in a large pot set over a medium heat. Sweat the onions, celery and garlic for about 10 minutes (see page 345 for our easy method), then add the chilli and ginger to the pot and continue sweating everything together for 5–10 minutes more, covered, but stirring every 5 minutes and keeping an eye on it to make sure the mix doesn't brown. The vegetables are ready when everything is soft.

Add the roasted squash to the pot with the boiling water and coconut milk. Bring to a simmer, then reduce the heat and cook for about 10 minutes on a low heat.

Remove from the heat and blitz in a blender or directly in the pot with a hand-held blender. Purée for twice as long as you think is necessary to get a silky smooth soup, adjusting the consistency as desired with more water and/or coconut milk if necessary.

Taste and adjust the seasoning, adding more salt and pepper or even a dash of lemon or lime if you feel it needs it. Serve in warmed bowls and garnish with some thinly sliced red chilli and chopped fresh coriander or one of the recommended dressings.

RECOMMENDED DRESSINGS

Thick coconut cream and fresh coriander or toasted coconut flakes (page 151) or try the herby red onion and chilli mix we put on top of our eggs menemen (page 55)

» *Mushroom and Jerusalem artichoke soup*
» *Moroccan harira soup*
» *Gently spiced parsnip soup*

❋ Moroccan harira soup

This soup is a traditional Moroccan staple. I was fortunate enough to pay a visit to Marrakesh not so long ago, and despite the intense heat, this seemed to be the almost universal choice for lunch there daily amongst many of the locals. We serve pretty little palm-sized Moroccan bowls of this as part of our mezze sharing platter on our evening menu. It's a true star.

SERVES 6–8

- rapeseed, sunflower or olive oil
- 1 large onion, diced
- 6 garlic cloves, roughly chopped
- 2 tsp hot smoked paprika
- 1½ tsp ground cumin
- 1 tsp ground cinnamon
- 1 tsp ground ginger
- 6–8 ripe tomatoes, chopped, or 2 x 400g tins of chopped tomatoes
- 200g dried chickpeas, soaked overnight and drained, or 1 x 400g tin of chickpeas, rinsed and drained
- 200g dried green lentils, rinsed
- 1–2 litres boiling water
- salt and freshly ground black pepper
- squeeze of lemon
- 30–50g total fresh coriander and parsley leaves, chopped, with some reserved for garnish

Heat a drizzle of oil in a heavy-based pot with a lid set over a medium heat. Add the onion and fry gently for 10–15 minutes, until softened but not coloured. Stir in the garlic and spices and cook for another few minutes. Add the tomatoes, chickpeas, lentils and enough boiling water so that it becomes a light brothy mix (it should be thin, not thick). Cover with a lid and simmer gently for 40–60 minutes if using dried soaked chickpeas, stirring regularly, until the chickpeas are completely tender. If using tinned chickpeas, cook for 20–30 minutes.

Taste the soup, adjusting the seasoning and/or spices until you're happy with the flavour. A good dash of lemon juice works wonders here too. Depending on the texture of the soup, you might want to add a little more water as well. If you feel it's lacking intensity, a few spoonfuls of tomato purée can really help (dissolve it in a little bowl of the hot soup, then add to the pot), as can a spoonful of harissa if you have that to hand and/or some of the spices.

Finish by adding the chopped herbs to the soup and pouring into warm bowls. Garnish with some of the reserved fresh coriander and parsley.

RECOMMENDED DRESSINGS

Plain Greek yogurt or smoked aubergine yogurt (page 338) and fresh herbs or the mixed herb and chilli 'salsa' (page 149)

TIPS AND TRICKS

» We cannot recommend our smoked aubergine yogurt dressing highly enough with this soup. You won't believe how well it goes alongside the herbs as a garnish.
» To make this soup into something entirely different, pan-fry some finely chopped chorizo and add to the bowls with the herb garnish when serving along with a drizzle of the oil from the pan. Serve with some flatbread or sourdough for a light lunch.

❋ Mushroom and Jerusalem artichoke soup

I think Jerusalem artichoke is one of those wonder ingredients that far too few people are familiar with, so please do give it a go. Honestly, please make this soup. It has a wonderful earthy taste while being really rich and comforting. It's my favourite winter soup. The cinnamon is added to give a really good foundation to the earthy flavours – it's not enough to make the soup taste of cinnamon, so fret not!

You can, of course, just leave out the artichoke (especially when it isn't in season), but it's really worth including it. See the tips and tricks below for advice on how to make this soup more of a classic mushroom soup. This soup is also dairy free, but you'd never guess because it's so creamy when blitzed well.

SERVES 8

- o 750g mushrooms (Portobello or mixed), washed and sliced
- o olive oil
- o 250–300g Jerusalem artichoke, washed thoroughly and sliced 1cm thick (no need to peel)
- o 250g onions (2–3 onions), diced
- o 250g celery (about ½ head), diced
- o 4 garlic cloves, roughly chopped
- o 1.5 litres boiling water
- o ½–1 tsp ground cinnamon
- o salt and freshly ground black pepper
- o squeeze of lemon (optional but highly recommended)
- o Greek yogurt, to garnish

Preheat your oven to 200°C. Place the mushrooms on a baking tray and toss in a drizzle of olive oil. Roast in the oven for about 20 minutes.

Meanwhile, heat about 1 tablespoon of oil in a large pot set over a medium heat. Sweat the artichoke, onions, celery and garlic for about 15 minutes, until fully tender (see page 345 for our easy method). When the vegetables are completely soft, add the roasted mushrooms and all the juices from the baking tray to the pot along with most of the boiling water and cinnamon. Simmer for 5 minutes, uncovered.

Whizz with a hand-held blender or in a blender or food processor until smooth. Blend for a long time for the best result. Now taste and adjust the seasoning as you see fit. Does it need more salt, pepper, lemon or even a touch more cinnamon to add some depth? Or is it too thick?

If so, add the remaining boiling water (or more) to get it to the right consistency for you.

Serve piping hot in warmed bowls with one of our recommended dressings on top or just a spoonful of Greek yogurt.

RECOMMENDED DRESSINGS

Spiced oats (page 151) or roast garlic crème fraîche (page 148)

TIPS AND TRICKS

» To convert this into a simple mushroom soup, just replace the artichoke with the same weight in mushrooms and add the leaves of a few sprigs of thyme, saving a few to sprinkle on top of the yogurt, if using, when serving.
» Lemon works well in almost everything, but a little dash of it when serving anything with mushrooms does seem to bring out the mushroom flavour all the more, so I highly recommend it for this recipe.
» This will freeze well if you want to scale up the recipe. You just might need to whizz it again before serving and adjust the seasoning, especially with another squeeze of lemon.

SOUP DRESSINGS

A soup is never fully finished without a dressing. Why? Well, we think a well-chosen dressing can add so much to the appeal of a soup. It will not only enhance the look of the soup when serving, but it will often add a really fantastic flavour and texture element to the experience too. Some soup dressings are extremely easy, while others are a bit more involved. While we love a soup with these added extras, these are the savoury 'cherry' on top of the cake (soup), so they're not absolutely necessary – particularly if you've done your job correctly and made a very tasty soup to begin with!

Roast garlic crème fraîche

This goes well with so many soups.

MAKES 150G

- 5 garlic cloves, unpeeled and left whole
- 150g crème fraîche
- juice of ½ lemon
- salt and freshly ground black pepper

To roast the garlic, follow the instructions on page 348. When it's cool enough to handle, remove the outer skins and squeeze each clove into a bowl – the garlic will just pop out. Use a fork to gently mash the roasted garlic into a purée, then add the crème fraîche and lemon juice. Mix well and season to taste with salt and pepper. This should still be super for up to 4 days if stored in an airtight container in the fridge.

Mixed herb and chilli 'salsa'

This is a staple recipe in our kitchen. We use it as a topping for the eggs menemen (page 55), one of our most sought-after breakfast dishes, but it works equally well sitting atop so many soups. It's not quite a traditional salsa, but we didn't know what else to call it and the name stuck!

MAKES ENOUGH TO GARNISH
4–6 BOWLS OF SOUP

- ¼ red onion
- ½ chilli
- 10g fresh lovage
- 10g fresh parsley
- 10g fresh dill
- 10g fresh mint

Cut your onion into the finest dice you can manage – ideally about the size of the head of a match! Similarly, cut the top off your chilli, remove the seeds with a teaspoon and then dice the chilli as finely as you can too, similar in size to the onion.

Gather all the herbs together and chop off the stalks, then slice the stalks as finely as you can (except the mint). Chop the leaves a little rougher than the stalks to give a bit of textural contrast.

Pop everything into a bowl and mix well. Ideally you should use chopped fresh herbs on the same day, but this should still be fine for up to 2 days if stored in an airtight container in the vegetable crisper of your fridge.

Fried garlic crisps

These are a delightful addition to soup for their texture as well as their flavour. Be careful, however – if overcooked, these can be extremely bitter and unpleasant! When adding to a soup, do so at the last moment before serving so their texture is at its best.

MAKES ENOUGH TO GARNISH
8–10 BOWLS OF SOUP

- 1 garlic bulb
- olive oil
- salt and freshly ground black pepper

Separate the bulb of garlic into individual cloves. Carefully peel the cloves without bashing them. Using a very sharp knife and a steady hand, slice the cloves finely into thin slices.

Heat a splash of oil in a large pan or pot over a medium heat. To test if the oil is hot enough, drop a small piece of bread into the oil – if it sizzles straight away and turns brown within a few seconds, it's ready. Carefully drop the garlic slices into the hot oil a few at a time and fry until golden brown. Remove the garlic with a slotted spoon and drain on a plate lined with kitchen paper. Repeat with the remaining garlic, then season with salt and pepper. These crisps will keep in an airtight container for 2–3 days.

Za'atar croutons

Try to get your hands on the best za'atar possible for this recipe, as it makes all the difference. These croutons add a great crunch when added just as you are serving. These are also great added to a salad, but again, add them at the last moment before serving to avoid sogginess.

MAKES ENOUGH TO GARNISH
6–8 BOWLS OF SOUP

○ 4 slices of stale bread (ideally sourdough)
○ 4 tbsp olive oil
○ 1 tbsp za'atar
○ salt and freshly ground black pepper

Preheat your oven to 180°C. Cut the bread into small squares about the size of a dice. Toss the bread in a large bowl with the olive oil, za'atar and seasoning. Place the coated bread on a large baking tray big enough to keep the bread in a single layer (use 2 trays if need be). Bake the croutons in the oven for about 20 minutes, giving them a shake about halfway through. They are ready when they have got a golden colour and are nice and crispy (they will crisp up further when cooled). Store in an airtight container for up to 2 weeks.

Baked kale crisps

As well as being great on the right soup, these add a nice texture to most salads and are a deliciously healthy snack on their own.

MAKES ENOUGH TO GARNISH
6–8 BOWLS OF SOUP

○ 100g kale
○ olive oil
○ salt and freshly ground black pepper

Preheat your oven to 180°C. Remove the tough woody stems from the kale with a small knife. Tear or cut the leaves into bite-sized pieces. Wash the kale well and drain and dry in a salad spinner.

Place the dried kale in a large bowl with a dash of oil and season with salt and pepper. Put the kale in a single layer on a large baking tray, then bake in the oven for 8–10 minutes, until crisp and charred around the edges. Remove from the oven and allow to cool – it will continue to crisp up as the kale cools. Keep in an airtight container for up to 2–3 days.

Gently spiced roast oats

These are so moreish and would happily go on top of so many salads for some extra crunch and a spicy hit. However, they work equally well sprinkled over a soup. They would also work as the oat crumble on our breakfast of champignons (page 84) and as an extra dimension for our baked beans (page 86), sprinkled over just before serving.

MAKES ENOUGH TO GARNISH
6–8 BOWLS OF SOUP

- 50g jumbo oats
- splash of olive oil
- ½ tsp smoked paprika
- ½ tsp hot paprika
- ½ tsp ground cinnamon
- salt and freshly ground black pepper

Preheat your oven to 180°C. Add all the ingredients to a large bowl and mix well. Place on a large baking tray or roasting dish and toast in the oven for 8 minutes. The oats should be lightly browned and dried out. Leave to cool and the oats will crisp up a little. Store in an airtight container for up to 2 weeks in your cupboard.

Toasted coconut flakes

This is a simple yet amazing addition to our butternut squash and coconut soup or any soup involving coconut. Toasting the coconut adds a new flavour dimension and texture, plus it smells amazing when it's in the oven. It's a great addition to granola and muesli mixes too. You're looking for the large dried coconut flakes here. Using desiccated or fresh coconut simply won't do the job.

MAKES 50–100G

- 50–100g coconut flakes

Preheat your oven to 180°C. Once the oven is hot enough, simply spread the coconut flakes out on a baking tray and toast in the oven for about 8 minutes, just until they turn a nice golden brown. You need a watchful eye, though – too long in the oven and they will turn quite dark and bitter. Eight minutes should be plenty, but if they are still not golden, give the tray a shake and return to the oven and check at 2-minute intervals until they're ready. Store in an airtight container for up to 2 weeks in your cupboard.

Alternatively, heat a dry frying pan over a medium heat for 2 minutes, then add the coconut flakes, tossing regularly until they are toasted and lightly golden at the edges. Remove from the pan immediately.

HUMMUS

More often than not, my breakfast involves hummus on toast with some fun additions. However, this is one of the best examples of something that works really well at any time of the day – on its own with bread or fresh crunchy vegetables, as part of another, bigger dish or just as a side to something. It really is the gift that keeps on giving. No fridge should ever be without a regular supply of (ideally homemade) hummus.

Here's a little story about hummus, that simple chickpea paste that's so versatile, so popular and so tasty.

There we were in Jordan. Three months into our tour of the Middle East. Three months of hummus, daily, often more than once. And we read about a little café in Amman that serves, according to our guidebook, the best hummus in all of the Middle East.

It's chickpeas, tahini, garlic, spices, oil, lemon. How much better could it be than all the other hummus we've eaten this past while, we said, rather naively. How wrong we were. The first taste of a classic version of hummus, on freshly baked flatbread, wowed us into silence. Another bowl was ordered and discussed intensely. How could these same few ingredients be so different from any of the other hummus we'd tasted?

I guess the point of the story is that there's no better example to demonstrate the wonder of cooking. Same base recipe, same ingredients, same equipment, but myriad different outcomes, often down to the variations in nature's pure ingredients and the hand, enthusiasm and creativity of the person using them. No two hummuses will ever be the same. And that's a good thing, I reckon.

I've been chasing that version of the Amman hummus ever since. I've never quite replicated it, but I've learned so much along the way, trying all the different types and styles of hummus I could imagine. As a result, I've come up with some versions that I feel are (almost) as good as the Amman hummus, in their own way.

Here are some thoughts on making the hummus that's perfect for you.

The chickpeas
We prefer to soak and cook our chickpeas ourselves (see page 359). It gives you a better outcome and would seem to be more environmentally friendly than tinned. Having said that, they do require a little more planning. Good-quality tinned chickpeas are perfectly fine if drained well and thoroughly rinsed.

Even though they are the main ingredient in hummus, the chickpeas can happily be replaced with other beans (butter beans being a particular favourite) or combined with some other bean or pulse to bring you up to the total quantity called for in the recipe. Purists would perhaps not call it a hummus, but it remains in the spirit of hummus!

The tahini
Tahini is a wonderful ingredient, available in most supermarkets nowadays. Different styles are available, from light to dark. Experiment with these if you fancy, but we tend to go for a lighter style. It often separates in its tub or jar, so do stir it up as best you can before using. A little is better than a lot, but again, this is down to your own individual preference. We use tahini in a number of recipes throughout the book (see especially the yogurt, tahini, honey and nuts on page 36 as an extra special treat), so a tub is handy to have in the cupboard, where it keeps perfectly for a good stretch, even after opening.

The seasoning
Salt, pepper, garlic, ground toasted cumin seeds and lemon juice are all critical components. We've given you guidance in the recipe, but please do start cautiously and add more until you have the perfect blend. Make it yours by tweaking these ingredients to get the flavour you want and also consider how you will be eating it and what you will be serving it with. If it's going with simple ingredients, you will want a stronger-flavoured hummus with a touch more garlic, cumin and lemon.

The other ingredients
A lot of the time we serve hummus with fresh vegetables on the side or on top as well as bread. When it comes to the tomatoes, cucumbers, radishes, herbs, etc. you use, the fresher they are, the better. Homemade flatbread (page 322) is a real winner, but warmed pitta bread is lovely too, as is a decent rustic bread, fresh or toasted.

The texture and consistency
Rough, smooth or something in between, this is entirely up to you! If you want an in-between texture, hold back a third of the chickpeas before puréeing, then blend the mix extremely well, add back the whole chickpeas and give it one final blitz so that you get a very smooth hummus with a little bit of a coarser texture going on too. We tend to purée our hummus very well – a special hummus for me has an almost mousse-like texture – and we reserve a few of the whole cooked chickpeas to put on top, which is an authentic way of serving it and it adds a nice texture to proceedings.

Hummus should really be like a paste. It should be firm and able to hold its own shape – the best way of describing it is that it should be like soft mashed potato in terms of holding its shape. Ideally use a food processor for the puréeing stage, but you can get by with a stick blender. You might not achieve an absolutely smooth hummus, but happily, this is not a requirement.

Serving hummus
Really, whatever rocks your boat (within reason!). I love it on warm flatbread or sourdough toast. Try it with our homemade flatbread (page 322), still warm from the oven. It's amazing with some crudités dipped into it (celery, carrot, cucumber sticks) to scoop it up. Or get a Baby Gem lettuce leaf, put a dollop in and eat it like that.

✺ Basic hummus

So here it is, one of the most simple recipes you can make – and yet so profoundly delicious and varied are its outcomes. I would urge you to read the introduction to this chapter to get a better sense of how to approach hummus. Having said that, there is very little that can go wrong – so just go for it if you like!

MAKES 250G

- 200–240g cooked chickpeas (see page 359) or 1 x 400g tin of chickpeas, drained and rinsed
- 1 garlic clove, minced
- juice of ½ lemon
- 2 tbsp boiling water
- 1 tbsp tahini
- 1 tbsp extra virgin olive oil
- ½ tsp salt
- pinch of ground cumin

Place all the ingredients in a food processor and blitz. Depending on your preference you can blitz it to a very smooth, light, mousse-like purée by blending for a full 10 minutes (in which case we suggest adding an extra tablespoon of water), but if you like a chunkier, more rough hummus, you can simply pulse the food processor until all the elements have combined nicely. The longer you blitz, the more mousse-like the texture will be. If you don't have a food processor a stick blender can work too, but it will take more time and will not achieve a fully smooth texture.

When the hummus has reached the consistency you're happy with, taste it and add more salt, tahini, lemon, garlic or cumin to the mix, depending on how you like it. Think carefully about this step and get it just the way you like it.

Store in the fridge, covered, for 3–4 days. Stir it up and taste it each time you use it – you may need to adjust the seasoning or add more lemon. In addition, avoid serving it cold from the fridge – the texture and flavours really are at their best when it's eaten at room temperature.

» *Beetroot hummus*
» *Roast carrot hummus*
» *Green pea hummus*
» *Flatbread*

ꕥ The variations

Follow the master recipe on page 155, adjusting as appropriate from these suggestions below.

Roast beetroot hummus

Replace a quarter to a third of the chickpeas with approximately the same weight of roasted beetroot (see page 357) and proceed as per the master recipe. A light touch of orange zest stirred in at the end works incredibly well with this hummus.

Roast red pepper hummus

Replace a quarter to a third of the chickpeas with approximately the same weight of roast red peppers and proceed as per the master recipe.

Roast carrot hummus

Replace a quarter to a third of the chickpeas with approximately the same weight of roast carrots. Peel, top and tail your carrots, chop roughly and drizzle them with oil and seasoning, then roast for 20–30 minutes in a 180°C oven, uncovered, so they roast and caramelise and become fully soft. Then proceed as per the master recipe.

Massive secret reveal! I've been asked many times what the secret to our roast carrot hummus is, and here it is: I strongly recommend adding a few pinches of ground cinnamon when blitzing – not enough that it fully tastes of cinnamon, but rather more of a background flavouring.

Roast butternut squash/roast pumpkin hummus

Proceed as for the carrot recipe, replacing the carrot with roughly chopped roasted squash or pumpkin. We tend to leave the skin on unless it's very thick or rough – it adds a lot of nutrition to the dish as well as being less work! Again, a touch of cinnamon works wonders here.

Herby hummus

Make the master recipe but add in some roughly chopped herbs (a few bunches, more or less to taste – I tend to be quite generous, though, and I chop the stalks superfine). Hold back a quarter of the herbs, getting everything to a good purée, then stir them in just before serving to give a mix of textures. Recommended herbs are flat-leaf parsley and coriander. Dill and chive also work in this mix, as would a bit of lovage.

Caramelised onion hummus

This is really delicious. See page 346 for instructions on making caramelised onions. Make the master hummus recipe, then stir in the caramelised onion to taste at the end, when the hummus is puréed, reserving a final spoonful to put on top when serving.

Baba ghanoush hummus (smoked aubergine hummus)

See page 338 for our method of making smoked aubergine. Make the aubergine paste (but omit the yogurt), adding the spices, garlic and lemon for a strong, punchy flavour. Fold this through the basic hummus without overmixing so you get bursts of the aubergine rather than a homogenous paste. Reserve some of the aubergine paste to spoon on top.

Harissa hummus

If you want a more fiery hummus, stir in or purée with a little harissa (page 325). Add it cautiously to start with, though, as you can always add more but you can't take it out! Additional lemon and lots of fresh coriander on top would work well with this.

Pea and mint hummus

Blanch 150g frozen peas in salted boiling water for 1 minute, then drain and quickly rinse under cold running water. Put half to one side, adding the other half to the hummus when puréeing. Add the last half and give it one quick final blitz – you want the remaining peas to be only lightly mashed in to give a rougher texture. Finely chop a bunch of mint leaves and stir through. Some crumbled feta and red radish wedges on top would be gorgeous when serving.

Hummus as more: build it up to a meal

Any time of the day, toast some bread (ideally a nice sourdough), spread with a generous smear of hummus and add your choice of the following toppings:

» Try a good sprinkle of our homemade dukkah on top of this (page 337), some crumbled feta cheese and some chopped herbs (any combination of each or all of the following will work well: coriander, parsley and/or mint).

» Add a boiled egg (hard or soft, warm or cold, as you wish), chopped or halved and gently seasoned.

» A small cucumber and/or fresh tomato chunks big it up even better to something more substantial.

» Some broken-up pitted Kalamata olives work sensationally here.

» Add a few halved cherry tomatoes, finely sliced red onion, broken-up Kalamata olives and some chopped soft herbs (our old friends coriander, parsley and/or mint).

» Hummus is one of the star ingredients in our Middle Eastern breakfast plate on page 52, which is one of our most popular dishes.

» One of our most popular dishes in our cafés is hummus smeared generously over toast, then piled with some dressed leaves, avocado chunks dressed with lemon, 2 warm poached eggs and a generous sprinkle of dukkah (page 337) on top, topped with a drizzle of hot sauce.

» Hummus is a key part of a mezze platter for a simple lunch or supper. Serve a bowl of your hummus with a selection from pages 272–273. It's a bit more work doing a lot of mini-dishes, but it does make for a fun hour or two in the kitchen and a sensational supper. On our evening Middle East Feast menu at Brother Hubbard, the sharing starter course includes a bowl of one of our hummus variations, sprinkled with our homemade dukkah (page 337). Alongside this, we serve small bowls of Moroccan harira soup (page 144), sweet potato falafel (page 266), roast cauliflower florets with red pepper yogurt dressing (page 173), warm za'atar flatbread (page 322) and our homemade pickles. It never fails to get a 'wow' at the table, so it's worthwhile for a special supper to share.

❊ A warming beef topping for hummus

This is a real winner – a warm, gently spiced minced beef topping sitting on hummus, ready for you to scoop up with some flatbread. Delicious and so comforting.

We are very fond of harissa, but we've given an alternative if you don't have any to hand (but take our advice, it's a handy thing to have in the kitchen). The toasted sunflower seeds give a lovely additional texture to things.

This dish is perfect as part of a mezze selection and it doesn't need to be served piping hot; warm is fine (if not actually more ideal, in my book). The hummus should be at least at room temperature, but serving it slightly warm would be even better. We are working on a fishy version of this too, but you might have to wait for the next book for that recipe!

SERVES 4 AS A SUBSTANTIAL STARTER OR A
LIGHT SUPPER SERVED WITH BREAD AND SALAD

- olive oil
- ½ medium onion, diced
- 2 celery sticks, diced
- 400g lean minced beef
- ½ tsp roughly ground cumin seeds
- ½ tsp roughly ground coriander seeds
- 3 garlic cloves, minced
- 1 tbsp harissa (page 325 or shop-bought or see the tips and tricks below)
- 50–75g sunflower seeds, toasted (see page 352)
- 2 tsp pomegranate molasses (or more to taste)
- squeeze of lemon (optional)
- salt and freshly ground black pepper
- 1 batch of hummus (page 155), to serve
- chopped fresh herbs, to garnish (optional)
- pomegranate seeds, to garnish (optional) (see page 354)
- flatbread (page 322), to serve

Add a drizzle of oil to a frying pan set over a medium heat. Sweat the onion and celery for about 15 minutes, until fully tender (see page 345 for our for easy method). When ready, remove from the pan and keep to one side.

Increase the heat in the pan to get it to medium-high, fully preheating the pan before adding the beef mince along with the cumin and coriander. Cook until all the liquid has reduced and the meat is well browned and starting to caramelise. Add the garlic and harissa (or the alternative spice mix, if using). Cook for another 5–8 minutes, until the mix is quite dry, then add the onion and celery mix back to the pan. At this stage, the beef mix will be fully cooked and nicely flavoured, but you might notice that a lot of the mix might be sticking to the pan. To counteract this and get every last ounce of flavour out of the pan, add half the sunflower seeds and take the pan off the heat, then cover the pan with a lid to allow everything to gently steam together and add a little moisture back to the dish.

When ready, taste and adjust the seasoning as you see fit. Add the pomegranate molasses to taste – it will give a sweet-sour element to the dish. The beef should be full of flavour, so do adjust the seasoning, cumin, coriander, harissa and acidity (using more pomegranate molasses and/or lemon juice) until it tastes perfect.

Spoon the (ideally warm) hummus into a large bowl, making a well in the middle. Spoon a mound of the beef mixture onto the centre of the hummus and finish with a drizzle of olive oil, the reserved sunflower seeds and a final drizzle of the pomegranate molasses as well as the herbs and/or pomegranate seeds, if using. Serve with flatbread on the side.

TIPS AND TRICKS

» For a vegetarian option, I suggest using the Moroccan zalouk (page 100), reducing the chickpea element and increasing the aubergine element accordingly.
» Another option for vegetarians would be to serve a version of our ubiquitous tomato and pepper sauce on top of the hummus (see page 321, but perhaps reduced down a bit more so it's not as saucy). Some pan-fried halloumi or crumbled feta and chopped fresh herbs would also be good additions.
» Minced lamb would work equally well here as a substitute for the beef.
» If you don't have any harissa to hand, this is a good substitute: mix together 2 teaspoons ground cumin, 2 teaspoons ground coriander, 1 teaspoon ground caraway seeds (optional) and ½ teaspoon chilli flakes or cayenne pepper, then stir this into 1 tablespoon tomato purée.

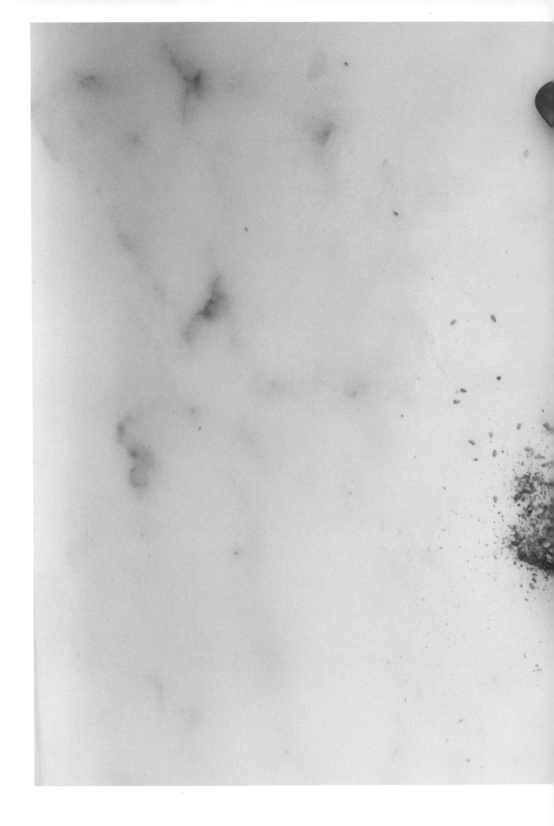

❋ Warm chunky lamb for hummus

Another winner. You could serve this as a main course by smearing
the hummus on the plate, adding this lamb on top and then perhaps
serving with a chunky side salad, some grains, some flatbread and a
glass of wine. Or as with the previous recipe, serve this as part of a
mezze selection for a light supper. Again, the hummus should be at
least at room temperature, but serving it slightly warm would be ideal.

SERVES 4 AS A SUBSTANTIAL STARTER OR A
LIGHT SUPPER SERVED WITH BREAD AND SALAD

- 400g finest-quality diced lamb
- 3 garlic cloves, minced
- ½ red chilli, finely diced (seeds removed if you prefer)
- 1 tsp sumac, plus extra for garnish
- 1 tsp za'atar (optional)
- ½ tsp ground cumin
- ½ tsp ground coriander
- olive oil
- ½ medium onion, finely diced
- 2 sticks of celery, finely diced
- 1 tbsp tomato purée
- 1 tsp honey
- 1 batch of hummus (page 155) – you may not need it all
- 20g fresh mixed soft herbs (coriander, parsley and/or
  mint), chopped
- 1 lemon, cut into wedges, to serve
- flatbread (page 322), to serve

Place the lamb in a bowl with the garlic, chilli, sumac, za'atar (if using),
cumin and coriander. Leave to marinate for at least 1 hour, though
overnight in the fridge is best.

When ready to cook, heat a little oil in a large pan set over a medium
heat. Add the onion and celery and cook slowly to caramelise the
two, stirring routinely (this should take about 15 minutes or so).
When the vegetables are softened and have taken on a bit of colour,
remove from the pan and increase the heat to high, adding another
drizzle of oil.

Add the lamb, including the marinade, to the hot pan and fry quickly
until golden brown and beginning to crisp. Don't stir too often so that
you allow the outside of the meat to caramelise. Depending on the size
of your pan, you may want to do this in batches rather than overcrowd
your pan. You want the outside to be seared but the meat itself to be
tender (I recommend serving it quite pink, but cook as suits you). When

all the lamb is cooked, add the onion and celery back to the pan along with the tomato purée and honey. Continue to cook for 2 more minutes.

To serve, put the (ideally warm) hummus in a large, wide, flat bowl and make a well in the centre. Add the lamb with all the juices and crispy bits from the pan to the well in the centre of the hummus. Top with the herbs, a drizzle of olive oil and a sprinkle of sumac. Serve with lemon wedges and some flatbread.

Alternatively, smear the hummus generously over individual plates (perhaps covering a third of the plate), spoon your lamb and its juices over this, top with the herbs and serve with some salad and grains on the plate.

TIPS AND TRICKS

» If you're in the mood, making the smoked aubergine yogurt (page 338) would work sensationally on this. Just omit the yogurt and aim for a more baba ghanoush-style sauce, adjusting the seasoning of the minced aubergine with garlic, lemon and salt and pepper, and spoon a little over the lamb.
» Another option would be to roast or pan-fry some aubergine chunks and throw this in with the lamb at the last moment before serving on top of the hummus.
» As you can probably tell, I'm in love with the combination of lamb and aubergine, so you could also use the roast aubergine master recipe on page 94 and layer the hummus and lamb on top of the warm roasted halves to make it more of a main course. I would be tempted to throw some chopped fresh coriander and pomegranate seeds over this when serving along with a final drizzle of olive oil.

SALADS

There's a famous song from *The Simpsons* that suggests 'you don't win friends with salad' – an entertaining notion, but one with which I wholeheartedly beg to differ!

From the outset in the cafés, we were determined to put as much love as possible into our salads. Happily, this seems to be very much appreciated by our customers – we get asked about our salad recipes more often than any other type of dish we do.

Salads should be something that make you feel good after having eaten them, not something you struggled to finish just because it was good for you (as may often be the case). You should eat salad because it's delicious as well as healthy. Yes, we use oils in our dressings and sometimes dairy too, but part of being healthy is about balance and nutrition rather than just being purely about the lowest-fat option.

Most of the salads on the next pages are designed to be served as part of a meal – either with meat, fish, a bowl of soup or perhaps one or two other salads to make a main meal.

Rather than it being something that is simply thrown together, a salad needs to be properly constructed, to be built. As with most of our food, we design salads that take flavour, texture and colour into account, all leading to a vibrant outcome that makes you feel better for having had it. We also design most of our salads to be are vegetarian (we've one or two exceptions included in this list) and they are often vegan too.

We are tireless in our kitchens in terms of moving forward with recipes and trying new ideas – to turn often humble ingredients into beautiful, delicious creations. We encourage you to use our salads here as a starting point and evolve them yourself.

One final note: salads are best served at room temperature, where the flavours get to shine.

So go on, give some of these recipes a go. Despite what the Simpsons sang, you might even win a few friends along the way!

✤ Pearl barley tabbouleh

This is a modern take on a classic Middle Eastern dish using an unsung, underused and underrated hero in the ingredients world: pearl barley. It's an amazing addition to this salad, as it has the most wonderful texture. The other great thing about pearl barley is that it's grown here in Ireland and has a long-standing place in traditional Irish cooking.

We've tried to do a bit more with pearl barley. You'll see it as a breakfast item in our fruit salad with pearl barley and coconut porridge (page 33). It also works incredibly well as a carby addition to soups and broths alike.

I should say that this is inspired by the classic tabbouleh rather than strictly adhering to that version. A proper tabbouleh is a very herby experience, so please do be extremely generous with your herbs here.

SERVES 4 AS A SUBSTANTIAL SIDE SALAD

- 250g pearl barley
- 50–100g fresh parsley
- 25g fresh dill
- 25g fresh mint
- 4 ripe plum tomatoes, diced
- zest and juice of 1 lemon
- 20–30ml extra virgin olive oil
- 1 tsp ground cumin
- 1 tsp ground coriander
- ½ tsp allspice
- ½ tsp ground cinnamon
- ½ tsp freshly ground black pepper
- 1 bunch of spring onions, cut into thin slices at an angle
- 50g sunflower seeds, toasted (see page 352)
- ½ pomegranate, seeds only (see page 354)

To cook the pearl barley, rinse it under cold running water and drain. Bring a large pot of water to the boil with a drizzle of oil and a pinch of salt, then add the pearl barley. Cook until it's soft but still retains some bite. This should take 20–35 minutes, depending on the barley. Drain and cool in a colander under some cold running water, then drain well again.

Finely chop the stalks of the parsley and dill. Remove the leaves from the stalks of mint and finely slice them along with the parsley leaves and dill fronds.

Place the diced tomatoes in a bowl and sprinkle in the lemon zest and juice, olive oil and spices, then add the pearl barley, herbs and spring onions. >>

Give the salad a good mix, then add the toasted sunflower seeds. Taste and adjust the seasoning, adding more salt, pepper or lemon as needed. Sprinkle over the pomegranate seeds to serve.

TIPS AND TRICKS

» A tablespoon of pomegranate molasses would be a worthwhile addition to the dressing. Just add it when you mix the spices, oil and lemon together.
» See page 260 for a warm side dish inspired by the concept of tabbouleh, again using pearl barley.
» If you prefer to lean more towards the classic version of tabbouleh, replace the pearl barley with bulghur wheat, perhaps using half the dry weight of the wheat barley. Couscous would also work here.
» To add more of a fresh crunch, some thinly sliced red onion, fennel or celery would bulk up this salad – deliciously so!

�֎ Roast cauliflower florets

This is a beautiful, reasonably substantial salad that works incredibly well alongside fish, meat, as part of a mezze or as a bigger salad offering for lunch or supper. It also holds well in the fridge (though ideally without the yogurt sauce that you dress it with when serving) so long as the dish is allowed to return to room temperature for serving.

SERVES 4 AS A SUBSTANTIAL SIDE SALAD

- 1 level dessertspoon ground turmeric
- 2 level tsp ground cumin
- 2 level tsp ground coriander
- 1 level tsp ground ginger
- ½ tsp chilli flakes
- 2–3 dessertspoons olive oil
- 1 medium-large head of cauliflower (1–1.2kg), broken into bite-sized florets
- 2 handfuls of baby spinach
- 1 small bunch of fresh parsley, leaves picked

For the red pepper yogurt dressing:
- 1 red pepper, halved and sliced into 1cm-thick strips
- olive oil
- 100g Greek yogurt
- ½ garlic clove, minced
- 1 tsp lemon juice
- salt and freshly ground black pepper

Preheat the oven to 220°C. Line a baking tray or roasting tin with non-stick baking paper.

Mix the ground spices with the oil in a small bowl. Place the cauliflower florets in a large bowl and toss well with the spiced oil. Pop onto the lined baking tray and roast in the oven for 10–12 minutes. The cauliflower should still be good and crunchy (remember, it will continue cooking in the residual heat) and it will hopefully have a slightly caramelised exterior. If it doesn't and you would like it to, take the tray out and turn the oven up to max, then flash for another few minutes to get that slightly charred look.

Get the pepper sweating for the dressing by popping the strips into a pan with a dash of oil. Cook, covered with a lid, on a medium heat for 10–15 minutes, until nice and soft. When cooled, purée the pepper using a hand blender. You could always pop these into a roasting tray and put them in the oven alongside the cauliflower for a similar amount of time – again, cook until fully soft. >>

While your cauliflower is roasting, you can get on with finishing the dressing. Place all the dressing ingredients, including the red pepper purée, in a bowl and gently fold them together. Taste and adjust the lemon, seasoning and/or garlic until you're happy with the flavour.

To assemble the salad, place your cauliflower in a wide bowl ideally, interspersing the florets with baby spinach leaves. Drizzle over the red pepper yogurt. Finish with the parsley leaves and maybe a drizzle of best-quality olive oil.

TIPS AND TRICKS

» Toasted spiced oats (page 151) work really well on this dish, as does a little scattering of our pickled onions (page 336).
» To make this more substantial for an easy lunch or supper, some smoked salmon, trout or mackerel would work well with this dish alongside some crusty bread. Grilled or fried halloumi would work well too to keep it vegetarian.
» An alternative dressing that would work well here is our green tahini dressing on page 201. However, you would be missing some colour, so think about adding some tomato wedges, cherry tomato halves, some sliced fresh or roasted red pepper or our neon pickled onions (page 336).

⁂ Middle Eastern slaw

This is one of my favourite salads and something I am very proud to have dreamed up one day when trying to figure out how to take something as classic as a slaw and put a modern, Middle Eastern twist on it. As you will see you end up with a very tasty salad that doesn't require mayonnaise or eggs. This dressing is also very versatile, so it's definitely one to experiment with in other salads.

SERVES 6–8 AS A SUBSTANTIAL SIDE SALAD

- 1 small head of red cabbage (or ¼ large head)
- 1 small head of white cabbage (or ¼ large head)
- 2 medium red onions
- 2 bulbs of fennel
- flaky salt (such as Irish Atlantic Sea Salt) and freshly ground black pepper
- 100g fresh dill, stems chopped finely and fronds roughly chopped
- 2–3 tbsp za'atar (or see the tips and tricks)

For the dressing:

- 250g crème fraîche
- 200g tahini
- 2–4 garlic cloves, minced
- juice of 2 lemons (but zest them beforehand for the salad!)
- 2–3 tbsp extra virgin olive oil

First prepare the cabbages by cutting away the thick core and removing any brown or tough outer leaves. Finely shred the cabbages into strips 3–4mm thick – this can be done by hand, on a mandolin or by putting it through the thick (3mm or so) grating disk of a food processor.

Cut the onions in half, top to tail, removing the outer skin. Trim off the top and root and cut into thin 2mm slices (again, by hand or using a mandolin or the thin slicing blade on a food processor). Repeat for the fennel bulbs.

To make your dressing, place the crème fraîche in a medium bowl, gently folding in the tahini, garlic, two-thirds of the lemon juice and the olive oil with a spatula until everything is well mixed. Taste and adjust the seasoning, adding more of any element to get it to your liking. You should end up with a dressing that is full of flavour and with the consistency of natural yogurt. Get it good and strong in terms of flavour, as it really needs to battle against the slaw vegetables to truly sing! >>

Finally, place the cabbage, red onions and fennel in a large bowl, tossing in the remaining lemon juice that you reserved from the dressing and the seasoning. Add two-thirds of the dill and all of the dressing, tossing until well mixed.

To finish, taste and adjust the seasoning, adding more lemon if necessary. Sprinkle the remaining dill on top along with the za'atar and the lemon zest when serving.

TIPS AND TRICKS

» Grated beetroot would be a very worthy addition, or any typical slaw ingredients.
» This salad would work very well with grilled lamb or in a lamb burger.
» The dressing here also works perfectly on a simple salad of cucumber and tomato wedges, but be sure to serve immediately after dressing.
» If you don't have any za'atar, use a mix of 1 tablespoon each of sesame seeds and cumin seeds, lightly toasted in a dry frying pan set over a medium heat for 2–3 minutes.
» An alternative dressing here would be to use our smoked aubergine yogurt (page 338).

❋ Jonathan's cucumber and samphire salad with lemon dressing, toasted seeds and lots of herbs

Samphire is one of those ingredients that looks sensational when cooked briefly and dressed simply. Just make sure to rinse it thoroughly, as it really does take in a lot of salt from where it grows by the sea. In fact, it's no harm to soak it in advance in lots of water while you're getting on with other things.

This is another salad intended as a side dish to marry especially well to a fishy main course, or you could add some hard-boiled egg halves and cherry tomatoes (with poached salmon, perhaps) on top to make it more substantial to serve alongside some fresh crusty bread as a light lunch or supper.

SERVES 4–6 AS A SUBSTANTIAL SIDE SALAD

- 100–200g samphire
- extra virgin olive oil
- 2–3 cucumbers
- 100g in total of each or any of the following: dill, flat-leaf parsley and/or mint, leaves roughly chopped and dill or parsley stems finely chopped
- 2 tbsp of a mixture of some or all of the following: sunflower seeds, pumpkin seeds and sesame seeds, toasted (see page 352)

For the dressing:
- zest and juice of 1 lemon
- 25ml extra virgin olive oil
- 2–3 garlic cloves, minced
- 1 tbsp cumin seeds, lightly toasted and finely ground
- flaky salt (such as Irish Atlantic Sea Salt) and freshly ground black pepper

To prepare the samphire, first give it a really good rinse under cold running water. Bring a pot of water to the boil (don't add salt, as samphire is naturally quite salty) and pop in the samphire. Simmer for 1 minute or so, then drain and cool under cold running water. Shake well to remove any excess water, then toss in a bowl with a dash of extra virgin olive oil and a few pinches of pepper and put to one side.

Top and tail the cucumbers, then cut them in half lengthways. Cut each of these halves in half again lengthways. Finally, cut each of these strips into bite-sized chunks, ideally cutting diagonally at a jaunty angle. >>

Make the dressing by whisking the lemon zest and juice into the extra virgin olive oil with the garlic, ground cumin and seasoning. When well mixed, dip a piece of cucumber into the dressing and taste it, adjusting each of the ingredients until you're happy with the outcome. Remember, the dressing needs to be punchy if it's to stand up well against the cucumber and samphire!

Mix the cucumbers and samphire together in a large bowl, adding three-quarters of the chopped herbs and toasted seeds. Dress lightly, taste and adjust the seasoning, but be very careful about adding salt due to the natural saltiness of the samphire. Sprinkle the remaining herbs and toasted seeds over the salad. Ideally, let it sit for 10 minutes for the ingredients to marinate a bit in the dressing, then serve.

TIPS AND TRICKS

» If you can't get samphire, asparagus would work delightfully here. Prepare it by breaking off the woody ends, then blanching for 1 minute in plenty of boiling salted water. Rinse under cold running water immediately, drain well and cut into 3cm lengths at a jaunty angle. Toss in olive oil and seasoning and proceed with the recipe above, simply replacing the samphire with the asparagus.
» Some red chilli, finely diced or cut into thin strips or slices, would work quite well here added in at the end.

❆ Mackerel, baby potato, pea and fennel salad with a smoked aubergine yogurt dressing

This is ideal as a substantial-yet-light summer lunch or supper served with some fresh crusty bread. Leave out the mackerel for vegetarians or to make it a side to a main course (off the barbecue!), or even just add some warm poached eggs on top with some rocket.

The smoked aubergine yogurt dressing here is a revelation. We love the Middle Eastern baba ghanoush dip and decided to try to turn it into something more versatile. This always gets such a great reaction and it's the type of dressing/sauce that will go wonderfully in so many dishes. It's is also the suggested sauce for some of our soup recipes, our Moroccan zalouk (page 100) and several other dishes scattered throughout the book, so when you make it, just double the dressing recipe here if you plan on making any of those other dishes too – it will hold for several days in the fridge.

SERVES 4 AS A SUBSTANTIAL SIDE SALAD

- olive oil
- 1kg baby potatoes, cut into bite-sized wedges
- flaky salt (such as Irish Atlantic Sea Salt) and freshly ground black pepper
- 250g fresh peas (or good-quality frozen peas)
- 1 tsp caster sugar
- 1 head of fennel, top and tail trimmed off
- juice of 1 lemon
- 4 fillets of fresh mackerel (optional)
- smoked aubergine yogurt (page 338)
- 25g fresh dill, stems chopped finely and fronds chopped roughly
- 25g fresh flat-leaf parsley, stems chopped finely and leaves chopped roughly
- 100g red radishes, topped and tailed and cut into 2mm slices or thin wedges
- ½ preserved lemon (page 331) or the rind of 1 fresh lemon, avoiding the pith and very finely sliced into small strips

Preheat the oven to 180°C. Add enough oil to barely cover the base of a roasting tin and put it in the oven to heat up. Take the roasting tin out of the oven and toss the potato wedges in the hot oil. Add a sprinkle of salt and pepper and return to the oven. Roast for approximately 30 minutes, tossing after 15 minutes or so. Check the potatoes are done by skewering with a knife to ensure they are tender all the way through. If not, continue to cook until this happens and there is a nice bit of

browning on the outside. If need be, turn the temperature up by 30°C for 5 minutes or so to ensure a golden brown finish.

Bring a small pot of water to the boil, then add the peas and sugar and cook for 1–2 minutes. Drain and rinse under cold running water until fully cooled, then drain again and shake well and put to one side.

Prepare the fennel by cutting the bulb in half from top to tail, then cutting each half into very fine slices. Use a mandolin if you have one or else take your time to try to cut each slice very finely (1mm). If you don't have the time or patience, marginally thicker slices of up to 3mm or so are fine too. Place in a bowl and toss in a dash of olive oil and the juice of half a lemon with a little seasoning.

If you're using mackerel, preheat the grill to high. Brush each fillet with olive oil and a little sprinkle of seasoning. Place skin side up under the grill for 3–5 minutes, depending on the thickness of the mackerel fillets – enough to just cook the fillet through and get it a little charred on top.

Assemble the salad by placing the warm or cooled potatoes in a large bowl and tossing with the smoked aubergine yogurt and half of the herbs. Spoon half of this onto your serving platter or bowl, then scatter over two-thirds of the fennel slices, half of the peas and half of the remaining herbs. Repeat with another layer of the potatoes and then a final layer of the fennel and the remaining herbs and peas on top. Finally, scatter over the radishes. If using, place the mackerel fillets on top along with the diced preserved lemon or sliced lemon rind strewn over. A final squeeze of lemon juice over the full dish will finish this nicely.

Gribiche potato salad

In Brother Hubbard we serve three salads every day, which form our salad plate. Whenever we have this dish on (or indeed, any potato salad), it always seems to sell out no matter how much we make. That's Ireland for you, I guess! This is not a classic version of a gribiche salad, but it's inspired by it.

SERVES 4–6 AS A SUBSTANTIAL SIDE SALAD

- 1kg baby or new potatoes, cut into bite-sized wedges
- salt and freshly ground black pepper
- extra virgin olive oil
- 1 medium bulb of fennel
- 4–6 eggs (1 per person) (optional)
- 30–50g fresh flat-leaf parsley, stems finely chopped and leaves roughly chopped
- 30–50g fresh dill, stems finely chopped and fronds roughly chopped
- 100g red chard, chopped

For the dressing:

- 3–6 large gherkins, rinsed
- 3 tbsp capers, rinsed
- 4 tbsp crème fraîche (optional)
- 2 tbsp Dijon mustard

Preheat the oven to 180°C. To roast the potatoes, toss them in a bowl with some salt, pepper and oil. Place them in a large roasting tin and cook in the oven for 30–35 minutes, until they are fully cooked through and starting to crisp up. Remove from the oven and allow to cool while you make the dressing. Alternatively, it wouldn't be the end of the world to boil your baby potatoes if you wish – cook them whole in a pot with lots of water and 1 teaspoon of salt until tender but not falling apart. Drain and leave to cool a little while you make the dressing. When cooled, cut into wedges.

To make the dressing, chop the gherkins and capers together so they are finely chopped without necessarily being minced (this is a very forgiving recipe, though, so it doesn't matter that much). Add to a bowl with the crème fraîche (if using) and Dijon mustard and mix together well.

Wash and trim the fennel of any leafy fronds and remove the woody base. Using a mandolin or the thin slicer attachment of your food processor (or a sharp knife and a steady hand!), slice the fennel as thinly as possible. >>

If you're using the eggs, cover them with water in a small saucepan, add 1 teaspoon of salt and bring to the boil. Cook for 5 minutes for soft-boiled or 9 minutes for hard-boiled eggs. Cool immediately under cold running water, then peel.

To assemble, place the potatoes in a large bowl with the sliced fennel and fresh herbs, reserving a handful of the fresh herbs to throw over the salad at the end. Add enough of the dressing to gently coat the potatoes, then fold through the red chard. Taste and check the seasoning. Add the chopped or halved eggs, if using, sprinkle the remaining herbs on top and serve immediately.

TIPS AND TRICKS

» Make this into more of a one-salad main course by adding 100g of blanched peas, some smoked fish and the chopped egg, serving in individual bowls. The above recipe would serve 4 that way.

❋ Striped cucumber and carrot salad

Here we use a light and quick pickle for the carrot, which gives it a lovely flavour while ensuring the crunch and brightness of the carrot are retained.

SERVES 4 AS A SUBSTANTIAL SIDE SALAD

- 2 cucumbers
- 2–3 garlic cloves, minced
- zest and juice of 1 lemon
- 2 tbsp sesame seeds, toasted (see page 352)
- 1 tsp cumin seeds, lightly toasted and roughly ground
- 1 tsp coriander seeds, lightly toasted and roughly ground
- 1 red pepper, deseeded and cut into 5mm strips
- 20–40g mixed soft herbs (any or all of the following: parsley, dill, lovage, coriander and/or chives)
- salt and freshly ground black pepper

For the pickled carrots:
- 2 carrots
- 200ml cider vinegar
- 200ml water
- 2 tbsp caster sugar
- 1 tsp salt
- 1 tsp yellow mustard seeds

To lightly pickle the carrots, wash them well and peel them. Using the vegetable peeler, start to peel thin strips of the carrot from top to bottom to make nicely uniform, thin ribbons. A mandolin will do this job nicely for you too. Alternatively, cut into very thin slices. Place in a small container.

Combine the vinegar, water, sugar, salt and yellow mustard seeds in a small pot and bring to the boil. Boil for about 3 minutes, then remove from the heat. Pour the hot vinegar over the prepped carrots and leave to cool to room temperature, then refrigerate for about 2 hours before using.

Using the same vegetable peeler, peel the cucumbers into long, thin slices. Place the cucumber in a large bowl with the garlic, lemon zest and juice and the sesame, cumin and coriander seeds. Add the red pepper slices and half of the mixed herbs along with a pinch of salt and mix well.

Finally, drain the pickled carrots from the liquid, add to the bowl and give it all one final mix. Taste – you should have a zingy, sweet-and-sour salad. Adjust if needed with more seasoning, sugar, lemon or garlic. Throw the remaining herbs over the salad to serve.

TIPS AND TRICKS

» Love a pickle? Then why not make a bigger batch of the carrots? These carrots will last for up to 3 weeks in the fridge and are perfect additions to cheese boards, fish dishes and all salads.
» I recommend bringing the salad together only at the last moment. Cucumber salad is not one to be left sitting around for terribly long, as the juices run out of it, meaning the dressing gets greatly diluted. The herbs won't hold up well for long in this dressing either.

❈ Greek-style cucumber salad

Such a refreshing dish, perfect alongside some poached fish, grilled meat and fresh crusty bread. This is one to make at the height of summer, when cucumbers and tomatoes are at their best.

SERVES 4 AS A SUBSTANTIAL SIDE SALAD

- 2 cucumbers
- 1 red pepper
- 1 green or yellow pepper
- 4 ripe plum tomatoes
- 1 red onion, halved and thinly sliced
- 100g feta cheese, diced into 1cm cubes
- 50g Kalamata olives, pitted and roughly chopped
- salt and freshly ground black pepper

For the dressing:
- 4 tbsp best-quality olive oil
- 2 tbsp red wine vinegar
- 2 tsp dried oregano
- 1 garlic clove, minced

Top and tail the cucumbers, then cut them in half lengthways. Cut each of these halves in half again lengthways. Finally, cut each of these strips into bite-sized chunks, ideally cutting on the diagonal at a jaunty angle.

Cut the peppers in half, removing the stalk, seeds and pith. Cut into long strips lengthways, so that you end up with slices 1cm thick. Slice the tomatoes in half lengthways, then slice each half into thin wedges, aiming to get 4–6 wedges per half.

Make the dressing by whisking together the olive oil, red wine vinegar, oregano and minced garlic.

Combine all the ingredients together in a large serving bowl. Taste and adjust the seasoning, adding more salt, pepper, vinegar or garlic as needed.

TIPS AND TRICKS

» We've proposed using dried oregano here, but if you can get your hands on fresh oregano, use that!
» Lemon juice could be swapped out for the red wine vinegar.
» Make it even better by making large croutons (page 150) and tossing them over the salad just as your serve it.
» Believe it or not, some chunks of watermelon would sit happily in this recipe alongside everything else.

❊ Cucumber and fennel salad with tahini

A real winner, dress this salad just before serving. The powerful dressing works so well against the juicy crunch of the cucumber.

SERVES 4 AS A SUBSTANTIAL SIDE SALAD

- 2 cucumbers
- 1 medium-large bulb of fennel
- 1 medium red onion, halved and sliced as finely as possible
- 20g fresh flat-leaf parsley, stalks finely chopped and leaves roughly chopped
- 20g fresh dill, stalks finely chopped and fronds roughly chopped

For the tahini dressing:
- 3 tbsp tahini
- 4 tbsp warm water
- juice of ½–1 lemon
- 1–2 garlic cloves, minced (optional)
- salt and freshly ground black pepper

Top and tail the cucumbers, then cut them in half lengthways. Cut each of these halves in half again lengthways. Finally, cut each of these strips into bite-sized chunks, ideally cutting on the diagonal at a jaunty angle.

Cut the fennel in half from top to tail, removing any herby fronds (keep them for garnish) and removing the tough woody core. Place the fennel on your chopping board cut side down and slice as finely as possible into half-moons, similar to the red onion. A mandolin works well here.

To make the dressing, place the tahini in a bowl. Using a whisk, slowly add the warm water and whisk together. You are looking to loosen the tahini to make it runny and smooth rather than thick. Add the lemon juice and whisk again until smooth. Taste and adjust the seasoning, adding more lemon or tahini if you feel the sauce needs it. If you fancy, a clove of minced garlic gives added depth of flavour here.

When you have reached the desired dressing texture and flavour, add the cucumbers, fennel, red onion and half the herbs to a large bowl, then slowly add the dressing, tossing gently. You may not need it all, so use your judgement and taste, taste, taste. Throw the remaining herbs over the salad and serve.

✤ Broccoli and green bean salad with chargrilled steak

This is ideal as a substantial-yet-light summer lunch or supper, served with a fresh crusty loaf. You can add some poached salmon or chicken instead of the steak or leave out the steak for vegetarians or to make it as a side to a main course item (off the barbeque!).

SERVES 4 AS A SUBSTANTIAL SIDE SALAD

- 1 yellow courgette, topped and tailed
- 50ml white wine vinegar or cider vinegar
- 2 red onions, halved and very finely sliced (1mm)
- juice of ½ lemon, plus extra to serve
- 800g tenderstem broccoli
- 75ml extra virgin olive oil
- flaky salt (such as Irish Atlantic Sea Salt) and freshly ground black pepper
- 400g French beans, topped and tailed
- 100g broad beans or frozen peas
- 2–3 rump steaks (250–400g)
- 3–4 garlic cloves, sliced 1mm thick
- 2–3 red chillies, deseeded and cut into 2mm strips at an angle
- 1 small bunch of fresh flat-leaf parsley, leaves picked

Cut the courgette in half across the middle, then use a vegetable peeler or small knife to cut into long, very thin slices or ribbons approximately 2mm thick. Place in a bowl and toss in the vinegar, then leave for 20–30 minutes to lightly pickle – this will end up as a very fresh pickle that retains the texture of the courgette.

Put the red onion slices in a bowl and toss them in the lemon juice. Leave to sit while you make the rest of the salad. This will give the onion a lovely bright red colour and a delicious tang.

Cut the fibrous ends off the broccoli, then cut each stem lengthways – aim to have each piece approximately the same size (bite-sized is ideal). Bring a 2 litre pot of water to the boil, then add 1 tablespoon of salt, drop all the broccoli in at once and return the pot to the boil. Cook for 1 minute, then drain into a sieve and cool the broccoli under cold running water. Once cooled, strain well and shake off any excess water. Toss in a bowl with a decent dash of the olive oil and some freshly ground black pepper to season. Set aside. Repeat for blanching the French beans. >>

Put the broad beans in a pan, cover with boiling water, return to the boil and cook for 3 minutes. Drain and refresh under cold running water. Slit each pod along its seam and run your thumb along the inside to push the beans out. If using frozen peas instead, blanch as for the broccoli.

Heat a ridged griddle pan for 7–10 minutes on a medium-high heat, until it begins to smoke. Season the beef and cook on the pan for 1–2 minutes on each side, just enough to sear the outside and get those lovely dark chargrill marks for flavour and colour. We like it quite rare, but you are welcome to cook it the way you would normally like it – for medium or well done, turn down the heat to low-medium after the initial searing on the griddle pan and continue to cook until it's cooked the way you like it. Once cooked, let the beef rest on a chopping board for 10 minutes or so, then slice into strips approximately 2–3cm wide, again making sure they are bite-sized.

Carefully wipe down the griddle pan with a dry cloth and keep it over a medium-high heat. Cook one-third of the broccoli on the hot griddle pan at a time for 1–3 minutes so that the pieces get nicely charred, then turn and repeat on the other side.

Prepare the dressing by heating the remaining oil in a frying pan set over a medium heat. Once it's good and hot, add the garlic and chilli. Remove from the heat after 1 minute to let the oil infuse for a few minutes (this dressing is designed to be drizzled over the salad while still hot).

In a large bowl or serving platter, build up layers of each ingredient (broccoli, courgette, French beans, broad beans, red onion slices, beef and parsley leaves), spooning the dressing over each layer. Extra seasoning may be required – we recommend a quick squeeze of lemon over the plate just before serving.

TIPS AND TRICKS

» The broccoli needs to retain its fresh crunch and bite, so don't be tempted to leave it in any longer in the boiling water. The same applies to the beans and peas.

✼ Rachel's mushroom and red quinoa salad

This is a delicious warm salad for an autumnal or wintry day. It is best served warm and will work as a side salad or as the hot accompaniment to a main course.

SERVES 4 AS A SUBSTANTIAL SIDE SALAD

- 250g chestnut mushrooms
- salt and freshly ground black pepper
- extra virgin olive oil
- 2 sprigs of fresh thyme, leaves picked
- 250g red quinoa
- 200ml boiling water
- 2–4 ripe tomatoes, small dice
- 1 medium or large red onion, finely sliced
- 4 tbsp mixed seeds (sunflower, sesame, pumpkin), toasted (see page 352)
- zest and juice of 1 lemon
- fresh thyme, parsley, dill, coriander and/or lovage, chopped, to garnish

For the thyme pesto:
- 50g baby spinach leaves
- 2 garlic cloves, chopped
- 3 sprigs of fresh thyme, leaves picked
- 50–100ml extra virgin olive oil

Preheat the oven to 160°C. Wash the mushrooms well and cut each one in half (if they are very large, cut them into quarters). Place them in a roasting tin, season with salt and pepper and drizzle with oil. Sprinkle over the thyme and toss it through. Cover the tray with foil and cook in the oven for 25–30 minutes, then remove the foil and cook for a further 10 minutes, uncovered. Remove the mushrooms from the tray with a slotted spoon – there should be a good amount of liquid left in the tin. This is the stock that you will cook the quinoa in.

Simply sprinkle your quinoa directly into the tin with the mushroom stock and the boiling water and mix well. Cover the tin with foil again and return to the oven for 35–40 minutes to cook the quinoa. Check the tin halfway through to make sure there is enough liquid, adding a little more hot water if needed. Remove the foil for the last 5–10 minutes to gently toast the quinoa and reduce any remaining liquid. Taste the quinoa to make sure it's cooked. If the quinoa is ready but is still retaining a lot of water, simply drain the liquid off in a colander or sieve. Or better still, reduce that drained liquid by simmering in a pot and adding back to the quinoa when it has been reduced by two-thirds.

Meanwhile, to make the thyme pesto, blitz together the spinach, garlic, thyme and some salt and pepper with enough oil to make it a nice drizzling consistency.

To assemble the salad, place the quinoa in a large bowl with the roasted mushrooms. Top with the diced tomatoes, sliced red onion and toasted seeds, mixing together lightly with the lemon zest and juice and perhaps a splash of oil. Spoon over the thyme pesto and garnish with the chopped herbs.

TIPS AND TRICKS

» Have a go at adding some gentle spices to this – a little cinnamon, nutmeg and/or ground cumin might work a charm.
» Bulk it up even further by adding a decent amount of roasted Jerusalem artichoke so it becomes quite a substantial lunch or supper, perhaps with a poached egg on top.

❋ Charred stone fruit and goats' cheese salad with pomegranate molasses

A fiesta of colour, flavour and textures, these ingredients come together as something quite beautiful on the plate. A smaller plate will work wonderfully as a starter or bigger plates as a delicious main course washed down with a chilled white wine, of course. We recommend nectarines when in season, but apricot, pear, peach or plum will work deliciously here too following the same steps.

SERVES 4 AS A SUBSTANTIAL SIDE SALAD

- 2 heads of chicory or Baby Gem
- 2 heads of radicchio
- 200g goats' cheese (soft but crumbly is good – we love St Tola)
- 50g dukkah (page 337)
- 4–6 ripe nectarines (but not over-ripe)
- 100g rocket

For the dressing:
- 50–75ml extra virgin olive oil
- juice of 1 lemon
- 1 tbsp pomegranate molasses (or see our tip below)
- flaky salt (such as Irish Atlantic Sea Salt) and freshly ground black pepper
- 1–2 tsp runny honey (optional)

Prepare the chicory and radicchio by removing any older outer leaves, then cutting each head in half, then in half again, cutting out the hard core/heart towards the bottom. Cut each quarter into thin wedges and set aside.

Form the goats' cheese into nuggets about the size of a small cherry tomato and roll in the dukkah. Repeat until all of the cheese is used up – this should give you several nuggets per person.

Heat a griddle pan over a medium-high heat for 6–8 minutes, until it's smoking hot. While that's happening, cut each nectarine in half and remove the stone, then cut each half into 3–4 wedges. Place each wedge on the hot griddle, flesh side down, for 2–3 minutes, until good char lines appear. Resist the urge to move the wedges until these form. Turn over and repeat for the other side, then remove all the wedges to a plate.

Prepare your dressing by whisking the olive oil, lemon juice and pomegranate molasses together. Taste and add seasoning to adjust. If you feel it needs some sweetness, add some honey to taste. >>

Build your plates or platter by arranging the radicchio, chicory and rocket nicely over the surface. Drizzle the dressing reasonably heavily over the leaves and finish by placing the goats' cheese nuggets and grilled nectarines on top. It's no harm to break up some of the goats' cheese nuggets in order to expose some of the lovely white cheese for contrast.

TIPS AND TRICKS

» If you prefer, a simple balsamic vinegar dressing would work perfectly here.

❋ Roast root vegetable salad with green tahini dressing

This one is always a huge success with our customers. It's completely satisfying, and for those people who want to eat salad but don't love it, it's a winner! You will certainly have some of this dressing left over, so try it on other dishes (see below for additional tips). This dish works well warm or at room temperature, but definitely not fridge-cold.

SERVES 4 AS A SUBSTANTIAL SIDE SALAD

- 300–400g carrots (4 medium or 2 large), cut into bite-sized pieces at jaunty angles
- 300–400g parsnips (4 medium or 2 large), cut into bite-sized pieces at jaunty angles
- olive oil
- 1½ tsp cumin seeds, lightly toasted and lightly crushed (see page 352)
- 1¼ tsp coriander seeds, lightly toasted and lightly crushed
- salt and freshly ground black pepper
- a few handfuls of baby spinach leaves (optional)
- 50g total fresh herbs (coriander, parsley or both), stalks finely chopped and leaves roughly chopped
- 1 bunch of spring onions, cut into slices 5mm thick

For the green tahini dressing:
- 100g tahini
- 30–50g fresh parsley
- 100–150ml warm water
- 30–40ml lemon juice
- 1 garlic clove, minced (optional)

Preheat the oven to 180°C. Toss the carrots and parsnips in a little oil with the cumin, coriander and some seasoning, then place on a large baking tray and roast in the oven for 25–30 minutes, making sure you shake the tray a few times to stop them from browning too quickly. They will be done when they are just about soft all the way through, but if you prefer more of a bite in the middle (recommended), just take them out earlier if that's the case.

Now make the green tahini dressing. If you have a small blender, simply add all the ingredients and blitz to a smooth consistency that's similar to runny yogurt. Otherwise, chop the parsley very finely and whisk with all the other dressing ingredients in a bowl. This won't be as smooth an outcome versus doing it in the blender, but it will still be fantastic. >>

Taste and adjust the seasoning as necessary. If you feel it needs it, a clove of minced garlic would work well here.

Now that everything is ready, assemble the salad. The vegetables can be warm or at room temperature; in fact, it actually works better if the vegetables are at room temperature, as otherwise the leaves and herbs will wilt. Spread out the vegetables in a large, wide bowl or plate, not stacking them too high – ideally in a single layer – with some baby spinach leaves underneath and around, if you're using them. Toss in some of the fresh herbs, reserving some for the end. You can also scatter most of the spring onions over the vegetables now, then drizzle with the tahini dressing. Be generous without drenching the vegetables in the dressing. Finish with the remaining herbs and spring onions on top.

TIPS AND TRICKS

» This works amazingly as a salad to go with fish or meat. It can also work as a hot side dish for a hot meal – I would just make it up as soon as the vegetables come out of the oven and then serve it piping hot alongside the rest of the main meal.
» This green tahini dressing works well on a simple tomato and cucumber salad, any other roast vegetable salad (like the roast cauliflower florets on page 173) or even as a dressing for a nicely grilled fish or lamb.
» Serve with a poached egg on top (page 358) to make it more substatial.

❈ Potato, preserved lemon and kale salad

Kale has become such a popular ingredient, and rightly so. It's great that its wonders have been rediscovered, but I would like to see the same thing happen to some other overlooked ingredients: pearl barley, caraway seeds and even prunes are on my hit list. Here we have a salad that is substantial, satisfying, pretty and good for you – everything a salad should be! As per usual, play around with the flavours until it's as you would like it to be.

SERVES 4–6 AS A SUBSTANTIAL SIDE SALAD

- 2 tbsp olive oil
- 1kg baby potatoes, cut into bite-sized pieces
- 2 garlic cloves, crushed
- 1 tsp ground cumin
- 1 tsp smoked paprika
- salt and freshly ground black pepper
- 200g kale
- ½ preserved lemon (page 331 or shop-bought)
- 1 red chilli, deseeded and finely diced or thinly sliced into rings
- 20g mixed fresh herbs (parsley, dill and/or mint), parsley and dill stalks finely chopped and all leaves roughly chopped
- juice of ½ lemon

Preheat the oven to 180°C. Pour the oil into a large roasting tin and place in the oven to heat through. Place the potatoes in a large bowl, then add the garlic, cumin and smoked paprika along with some seasoning and mix well. Carefully place the well-seasoned potatoes into the hot oiled tin, give it a shake and return to the oven for 25–30 minutes, shaking once midway through. The potatoes are done when they have taken on a nice brown colour and are tender all the way through.

Remove the central rib/stalk from the kale and discard it, then roll up the leaves like a cigar and slice them finely. Remove any of the flesh that's still inside the preserved lemon and discard it, then finely dice the rind.

Place the hot potatoes in a large bowl and toss with the kale, preserved lemon, chilli, mixed herbs, lemon juice, a drizzle of oil and some black pepper and mix well. Taste and season accordingly, adding more garlic, lemon juice, spices or seasoning as you see fit. You can serve this immediately, while it's still warm, but there is also no harm in letting it sit a while so the flavours mingle and the kale softens slightly.

Sadie's superfood salad sensation

We came up with this recipe one dark January morning when the residual guilt of the excesses of the festive season was still weighing us down (metaphorically and perhaps physically too!). This recipe certainly provided an antidote! We serve this salad on our brunch menu in the café, topped with a poached egg and a pinch of sumac. It also works wonderfully with some poached chicken or smoked fish.

SERVES 4

- 300g red quinoa
- 10g fresh mint
- 10g fresh dill
- 10g fresh lovage
- 80g kale
- juice of 1–2 lemons
- olive oil
- salt and freshly ground black pepper
- 1 avocado
- 85g currants
- 50g baby red chard or baby spinach leaves
- 1 red chilli, deseeded and thinly sliced at an angle (or leave the seeds in if you fancy a bit more heat in your salad!)
- 150g feta cheese, crumbled
- 10g alfalfa sprouts or pea shoots (optional but worth it!)
- 2 tbsp sunflower seeds, toasted (see page 352)

First cook the quinoa. Place the quinoa in a pot and cover with water. Place on the hob and bring to the boil, then reduce to a simmer and cook, covered, for 12–15 minutes, just until the quinoa still retains a little bite. Remove from the hob and pour into a fine mesh sieve or colander. Rinse the quinoa under cold running water until it has completely cooled.

Wash and dry the herbs and chop them finely, chopping the stalks very finely (except for the mint stems, which can be quite woody).

Remove the central rib/stalk from the kale and discard it, then roll up the leaves like a cigar and slice them finely. Toss the kale in half the lemon juice, some oil and a little seasoning in a large bowl. Let it sit while you prepare the remainder of the dish.

Run your knife lengthways around the stone in the avocado, then gently twist to separate the two halves. Remove the stone and discard it. Use a large spoon to remove the flesh from the skin, then chop it into large dice. Place in a bowl with a good squeeze of lemon juice and some seasoning.

Place the cooled red quinoa in the bowl with the kale. Add the currants, red chard, chilli and herbs and mix well. Season well and add a drizzle of oil and a good squeeze of lemon juice to taste.

Divide the salad between your serving bowls. Divide the diced avocado between the bowls, then crumble over the feta cheese and finish with the alfalfa sprouts, if using, and sunflower seeds. Serve immediately.

❀ Roast cauliflower with turmeric and tahini

A solid favourite on our salad menu, this is quite a beautiful dish and extremely tasty. It also does what all salads should: it makes you feel really good about yourself after eating it.

SERVES 3–4 AS A SUBSTANTIAL SIDE SALAD

- 1 large head of cauliflower (600–800g)
- 1 tbsp ground turmeric
- 1 tbsp fennel seeds
- salt and freshly ground black pepper
- olive oil
- 100g almonds
- 100g in total of sunflower and/or pumpkin seeds
- 100g sultanas
- 50g soft fresh herbs (dill, parsley and/or coriander), stems finely chopped and leaves roughly chopped
- juice of ½ lemon

For the lemon tahini dressing:
- 3 tbsp tahini
- juice of ½ lemon (the other half from the one used above!)
- 4 tbsp warm water

Preheat the oven to 200°C. Remove the large green leaves from the head of cauliflower. Using a small knife, gently cut the smaller florets from the larger stalk. You want to end up with lots of smaller bite-sized florets. Wash these and drain well, then toss the florets in the turmeric, fennel seeds, some seasoning and olive oil in a large bowl. Transfer to a baking tray and cook in the oven for 10–15 minutes, just until the cauliflower starts to char a little at the edges and the florets are cooked but still retain some bite. Remove from the oven, toss them around in the hot tray and allow them to cool.

To toast the almonds, simply place the whole almonds on a baking tray and pop in the oven for 8–10 minutes. Remove and allow to cool. Repeat for the sunflower and pumpkin seeds, but add some oil and seasoning to them before roasting for 6–8 minutes.

To make the lemon tahini dressing, mix the tahini with the lemon juice and some salt and pepper in a small bowl before slowly adding the warm water to loosen it to a pouring consistency. >>

To assemble, add the cooled cauliflower, toasted almonds, toasted seeds, sultanas, half the chopped herbs, a good dash of oil and a squeeze of lemon to a large bowl. Either serve in the bowl or on a platter, more spread out. To finish, drizzle with the lemon tahini dressing and garnish with the remaining chopped herbs.

TIPS AND TRICKS

» To add a little more colour to this, some pickled red onion (page 336) works wonders as well as adding a distinctive flavour to proceedings.
» Some sliced red chilli would also work here to add brightness and heat.

❋ Carrot, fennel, seed and herb salad

A great salad that comes together to make something unique and quite different from its individual components. This is very much one of those examples, with the whole being greater than the sum of the parts.

I recommend making more and leaving the extra unassembled and undressed. It will all keep in the fridge perfectly for another day. Even dressed it will hold fine, but you may need to drain off the juice that comes out of it and season and dress it again before serving the next day.

SERVES 4 AS A SUBSTANTIAL SIDE SALAD

- 2–3 large carrots (400–500g)
- 1 large or 2 medium fennel bulbs (200g or so)
- 50g fresh lovage (if available – see the tips and tricks)
- 50g fresh dill
- 100g toasted seeds – we recommend sunflower, sesame or a mix, perhaps including pumpkin and poppy seeds too (see the method on page 352)

For the dressing:
- juice of 1–2 lemons (or 2 tbsp pomegranate molasses and juice of 1 lemon)
- salt and freshly ground black pepper
- 40ml olive oil
- 40ml rapeseed or sunflower oil

Wash, peel and top and tail the carrots, then grate with a box grater or food processor to get a more chunky-style grate.

Trim any leafy fronds off the fennel (keep these for garnish) and remove the woody base. Cut in half from top to tail and rinse well. Using a mandolin or the thin slicer attachment of your food processor (or a sharp knife and a steady hand!), slice the fennel as thinly as possible.

Gently wash and dry the herbs and chop them finely. Chop the stalks separately, chopping them very finely. Do the same with any fennel fronds you've reserved.

To make the dressing, add the lemon juice (and/or the pomegranate molasses) and seasoning to a small bowl. Whisking constantly, slowly pour in the oil until it's fully incorporated and the dressing has thickened. >>

To serve, mix the carrot, fennel, herbs and toasted seeds in a large bowl. Add some dressing, mix well and taste. It may need more seasoning or more dressing.

TIPS AND TRICKS

» There are so many variations for this salad – here are a few ideas:
» Use finely sliced celery in addition to or instead of the fennel.
» Pomegranate molasses adds a wonderful element to this dressing – simply reduce the amount of lemon juice and add 1 tablespoon of pomegranate molasses instead.
» Use toasted sesame seeds (ideally black and white) instead of the sunflower seeds or toasted red quinoa (see page 352).
» Use chives, parsley, coriander and/or mint for the herb element of this salad.
» Use a combination of grated beetroot and carrot for this salad (though it will go a messy red, there are worse things that can happen!) or grated fresh parsnip.
» An interesting variation on the above dressing is to add about 1 teaspoon of orange blossom water to the dressing when whisking it all together. It gives it a lovely light orangey fragrance. Taste and carefully add more orange blossom water if you feel it needs it.
» Please don't be light-handed with the toasted seeds. They are a wonderful addition that make all the difference here.
» Lovage can be tricky to get a hold of. I often source it in any of the Polish shops that have popped up around the country. If you can't get it, celery leaf is an excellent substitute along with very finely diced celery stalk, or else just bulk up on the dill or try something like parsley or chive as an alternative to the lovage.

❖ The Late of the Day

MAINS

We've finally reached the main meal of the day. Having said that, it used to be more common to have your 'big' meal earlier in the day. I feel this is a better way to do things, but I also realise that it doesn't sit entirely well with the way we live our lives today. So with that in mind, we've set out some of our recipes for dinner here. By and large, however, the intention is that these represent our approach to having a lighter evening meal so that you hopefully still have a spring in your step late in the day while also feeling sated.

While reading this chapter and coming up with some ideas for your evening meal, feel free to combine our main dishes with any number of the side dishes – and perhaps even a salad or two from the previous section. In fact, we have a little section at the end (pages 272–273) on how to bring together a mezze, which is essentially a meal made up of a number of individual dishes that allows you to enjoy a marvellous combination of flavours, textures and colours, with the entire meal intended to be shared amongst your family, friends and guests. Honestly, nothing adds more to making a meal a fantastically enjoyable experience than sharing it!

✺ Brother Hubbard's beef koftas

Oh my! This is one very special dish. The kind of dish you will be thinking about long after you've had it, plotting when to have it next.

Koftas are simply a Middle Eastern version of meatballs. As with a lot of our dishes, these are full of herbs and flavour – please don't be shy with the fresh herbs, as they make such a meaningful difference. The sauce packs a welcome punch to make these a wonderful lunch, dinner or supper.

This recipe bulks up incredibly well if cooking for a larger group. It will take a bit more effort to hand-roll more koftas, but honestly, it's worth it. In fact, this is one of my go-to recipes for entertaining at larger gatherings.

We recommend serving these with the wedding couscous on page 270 and/or the flatbread on page 322. Any leftovers make an amazing sandwich with some baby spinach leaves in a warm pitta with a little of the sauce.

SERVES 4

- 750g lean minced beef (rib mince is good)
- 150g feta cheese, crumbled
- 50g fresh parsley, chopped
- 50g fresh mint, chopped
- 5 garlic cloves, finely minced or crushed (2 tbsp)
- 2 tsp dried mint
- 2 tsp ground cumin
- 1 tsp ground cinnamon
- 1 tsp allspice

For the tomato and roast red pepper sauce:
- olive oil
- 2 red peppers, diced into 1cm cubes
- 1 medium red onion, finely chopped
- 4 garlic cloves, thinly sliced or chopped
- 50ml apple cider vinegar
- 2 tsp ground star anise or fennel seeds
- 2 x 400g tins of chopped tomatoes
- 150ml water
- 2 tbsp tomato purée
- pinch of caster sugar
- salt and freshly ground black pepper

To serve:
- wedding couscous (page 270)
- flatbread (page 322 or shop-bought)

To make your sauce, heat a little oil in a medium-sized pot. Sweat the red peppers, red onion and garlic together, covered, until softened – 10–15 minutes on a low-medium heat should do it. You want them to be well softened without falling apart too much. Next add the cider vinegar and the ground star anise or fennel seeds (if you can't get ground star anise, use two whole ones) and simmer for about 15 minutes, keeping an eye on it to make sure the dish doesn't dry out. Add the chopped tomatoes, water, tomato purée, sugar and seasoning. Reduce to a quite thick sauce, like pasta sauce, stirring regularly to prevent it from sticking. When the sauce has reached your desired consistency, remove from the heat and taste, adjusting the sauce with sugar, vinegar or seasoning as you see fit – you want a really fragrant sauce that's full of flavour. If you've used whole star anise, take them out at this stage. Put to one side.

Preheat the oven to 180°C. To make the koftas, put all the kofta ingredients in a large bowl, reserving a quarter of the feta and a quarter of each of the fresh herbs to use later (don't add salt, as the feta will bring saltiness to it all). Mix well with your hands until everything comes together as one, but don't overmix or it will turn into a fine paste! When well combined, test the mix by frying a little bit in a pan with a little oil. Leave to cool for a moment and taste. This step is critical: decide if you need to add more pepper, garlic or spices if you feel it's needed. You can also add a little salt if you feel it's necessary. Adjust and repeat the tasting step if necessary until it's just right.

Using a kitchen scale, weigh out small 50g balls of the mixture – or just do one like this to get an approximate idea of how much you need, then shape the others to that size (about the size of a walnut in its shell). Form the balls into slightly oval shapes and place on a baking tray. If you're not cooking these right away, they can be covered with cling film and refrigerated for cooking later.

To cook the koftas, we char them on a preheated griddle pan (at maximum heat) for 1–2 minutes on each side, making sure they are well browned on a few sides. A frying pan would be fine here, though you won't get the char marks. This step sears the meat and adds additional flavour from caramelising (browning) the outside of the kofta, but see the tips and tricks for advice if you want to skip this step. Transfer to a baking dish and pour the warm sauce over. Place in the oven and cook for 20 minutes. If you have a thermometer probe, they should hit 71°C – if you've minced the meat yourself and are confident as to the quality, you may prefer them to be a little rarer.

Bring the koftas to the table in the baking dish, with the remaining feta and herbs sprinkled over, for serving alongside any accompaniments (the wedding couscous, flatbread and perhaps some salad). Otherwise, plate up the individual portions, sprinkle with the feta and herbs and serve with the accompaniments.

TIPS AND TRICKS

» This sauce will hold perfectly, so make multiple batches at once and freeze to make it so much easier to do this recipe the next time.
» The koftas work very well as part of a mezze selection and are as good warm as they are piping hot. If anything, all food tastes better warm rather than piping hot.
» A spoonful of thick Greek yogurt drizzled over the koftas and sauce when serving works wonders here, but better still would be our smoked aubergine yogurt (page 338 – it is rather mind-blowing) and maybe even a drizzle of our homemade hot sauce (page 330).
» You could make this recipe with mixed lamb instead, in which case I recommend doubling the amount of dried mint.
» Skipping the charring: If you're cooking for a lot of people, skipping this step won't have a devastating outcome! Instead, preheat your oven to 230°C and pop the koftas in a large baking dish greased with a little oil and cook in the oven for 6 minutes, giving them a shake halfway through. Take them out of the oven and drain off the juices and oil, then add the heated sauce, turn down your oven to 180°C and pop them back in for 15–20 minutes, testing as suggested in the main recipe above.

✿ Chicken tagine with fennel

A tagine is a classic Moroccan dish, essentially a meat cooked slowly in a spiced, often sweet, sauce. A trip to Marrakesh to buy some tableware for our evening menu allowed me to taste the real deal. There, I made contact with the wonderful Jusef of marrakechfoodtours.com, where I got to sample the authentic local cuisine surrounded by local diners, well away from the tourist traps – I highly recommended it. And when you come home, cook this to bring back the memories.

Tagines often have a lot of fruit in them, such is the love for the savoury-sweet combination in traditional Moroccan food. We've avoided it in this recipe, though, as it's not for everyone. But if you fancy it, add a handful of dried apricot halves before this goes in the oven. One teaspoon of ground cinnamon or a whole cinnamon stick wouldn't go astray in this dish at that point too.

SERVES 4

- 1–2 fennel bulbs
- 8 chicken thighs, bone in and skin on
- olive oil
- 1 large onion, finely diced
- 4 garlic cloves, minced
- 2 tsp coriander seeds
- 1 tsp ground turmeric
- 1 tsp fennel seeds
- 3 carrots, cut into bite-sized pieces
- ½ preserved lemon (page 331 or shop-bought), skin finely chopped
- 1 generous bunch of fresh coriander
- wedding couscous (page 270), to serve

Preheat the oven to 160°C. Chop the woody root off the fennel bulb and cut off any leafy fronds, reserving them for garnish. Cut the fennel bulb in half, then slice each half into thin wedges, rinsing well under the tap to remove any grit. Trim the chicken thighs of any extra overlapping skin or fat.

Heat a little oil in a large ovenproof pot with a lid, ideally a cast iron Dutch oven, set over a medium heat. Add the chicken thighs to the hot oil, skin side down, to brown and seal the skin. Once the thighs have been cooking for 6–8 minutes and are nicely browned, turn them over and repeat on the other side. I recommend doing this in 2 batches rather than overcrowding the pan. When cooked, remove them and put to one side.

Add the onion to the pot and cook slowly for about 10–15 minutes, until the onion starts to caramelise. Add the garlic and spices and cook for approximately 5 minutes, stirring well. Add the carrots and the chicken thighs back to the pot and pour in enough water to just cover the meat.

At this stage you can transfer the lidded pot to the oven and cook for about 1 hour. Alternatively, leave the pot on the range and reduce the heat to its lowest setting, cover with a tight-fitting lid and cook for 1 hour.

After the first hour has elapsed, gently stir the tagine and add the fennel wedges to the pot. Check how much liquid is still in the pot – if you feel like too much has evaporated or the bottom of the pot has begun to stick, add a little more water and stir well but gently. Cover again and continue to cook for another hour.

If you're cooking the tagine in the oven, check it after the 2 hours have elapsed, give it a stir and return to the oven for another 30 minutes to finish. If you have cooked the tagine on the stovetop, 2 hours should be enough. Either way, the meat should be falling off the bone and the vegetables should be nice and tender.

When you're ready to serve, taste the sauce and adjust the seasoning as desired. It may well need more seasoning or even a dash of lemon. Spoon equal servings of the tagine into large serving bowls and garnish with the chopped preserved lemon, plenty of roughly chopped fresh coriander sprigs and the reserved fennel fronds and serve with some couscous. Alternatively, garnish the pot and bring to the table to serve from that.

TIPS AND TRICKS

» I like things saucy, but if the tagine is swimming in sauce at the end of its cooking time, you might want to reduce it down. This will also intensify the flavour. To do this, drain most of the sauce away from the tagine, put it in a wide pot and boil until reduced. Taste, adjust the seasoning and add it back to the tagine pot, returning the entire pot to heat if you feel it has lost some temperature.
» When I was in Marrakesh, I had this with a big spoonful of warm caramelised onion over it. It's not something I would have thought of, but it was wonderful. See our recipe for caramelised onions on page 346 if you'd like to do the same.

❀ Aubergine imam bayildi (the sultan fainted)

This is such a superb dish and it's one of the most popular dishes on our evening menu, which is surprising, as it's vegan! I first came across this on an afternoon cookery class in Istanbul. Aside from learning to make the classic version of this dish, we were also told of the story and history behind it: the name means 'and the sultan fainted', referring to a sultan who reputedly swooned and fainted after tasting this, so amazed was he by its flavour.

This is our version of the dish, accompanied by a delightful sauce. Serve with rice or the wedding couscous on page 270 and maybe some side salad. It may seem like a lot of steps, but it's really easy and straight-forward. This dish can also be assembled and set aside for a few hours so that when you are ready to eat, you just need to pop it into the oven for 20 minutes or so.

SERVES 4

- 2 heads of roast garlic (page 348)
- olive oil
- 1–2 medium leeks
- 300g spinach
- 50g whole almonds (ideally unskinned), roughly chopped
- ½ tsp ground turmeric
- salt and freshly ground black pepper
- 2–3 large aubergines, topped and tailed
- 2–3 large courgettes, topped and tailed

For the sauce:
- 2 medium onions, finely diced
- ½ head of celery, diced into 1cm cubes
- 2 x 400g tins of chopped tomatoes
- 250g cooked chickpeas (see page 359) or 1 x 400g tin of chickpeas, drained and rinsed
- 1–2 tbsp harissa (page 325 or shop-bought or see the tips and tricks)
- squeeze of lemon (optional)

To serve:
- wedding couscous (page 270), flatbread (page 322), rice or bulghur wheat

When the roast garlic is cool enough to handle, squeeze the 'paste' from each clove into a bowl. Add a good dash of oil and mash with a fork until you have a spreadable paste. >>

While that's happening, get on with preparing the filling. Prepare your leeks by cutting off the rough green end, removing the rough outer layer and then cutting off the base. Slice along the middle from top to tail and rinse well, then cut across into 1cm strips. Add to a large pot with a good dash of oil and sweat over a medium heat with the lid on for 10–15 minutes, until the leek is soft but not melting. Turn up the heat, add the spinach and cook, uncovered, until it wilts, stirring regularly. Put to one side with the lid off.

Toss the almonds in a little oil, the turmeric and some seasoning and toast in a dry pan set over a medium heat for a few minutes, then put in a bowl and set aside.

To make the sauce, sweat the onion and celery in a medium-sized pot for 10–15 minutes, until softened (see page 345 for our easy method). Add the tomatoes, chickpeas and the harissa or spices. Let it simmer over a medium heat for 10–15 minutes, stirring occasionally. Taste and adjust the flavour, adding seasoning, lemon juice and/or more harissa or spices as needs be. You should end up with a very fragrant sauce that's full of flavour and personality (but not too full of heat).

For the main dish, preheat your oven to 180°C. Cut the aubergines and courgettes lengthways into approximately 5mm-thick slices. Place each slice on a lined baking tray (you may need to use more than one tray) and smear each slice generously with the roast garlic paste. Roast in the oven for 10–15 minutes, until the slices are cooked without falling apart. Put to one side to cool slightly.

To assemble, turn over the aubergine slices so that the garlic-brushed side is facing down. Place a strip of courgette over this. Place 2–3 tablespoons of the spinach-leek mix towards the bottom third of the slices and sprinkle with some of the almonds, then roll up into a snug but not overly tight roll. Repeat, using up all the aubergine and courgette slices and all the filling, but leave half the almonds for serving at the end.

Spread the sauce in the bottom of a shallow baking tray or a wide ovenproof pan. Sit the rolls in this sauce with an open end facing up. The dish can be made up to this stage and put to one side for a few hours or even overnight in the fridge.

To finish, put the dish back in the oven (still set at 180°C) and bake for 15–20 minutes, until thoroughly heated through.

To serve, divide the remaining almonds over each roll and bring to the table with a large spoon for serving directly from the pan or dish. Serve with wedding couscous, rice, bulghur wheat or some warm flatbread.

<u>TIPS AND TRICKS</u>

» Great fans of versatility that we are, this sauce could be bulked up and used as the basis for the zalouk on page 100 by simply adding the roast aubergine component suggested in that recipe and up to double the quantity of chickpeas listed for this recipe.
» We've kept this vegan, but some ricotta or feta at the centre of each roll with the spinach and leek filling would work quite well here. Just add 150–200g of cheese, divided up amongst the rolls.
» If you're not using harissa, use the following instead: 2 teaspoons ground cumin, 2 teaspoons ground coriander and 1 teaspoon paprika mixed with 2 tablespoons tomato purée.

✽ Middle Eastern ratatouille (turlu turlu)

Ratatouille is one of my favourite French foods, so what better way to adapt it than to put a Middle Eastern twist on it?

This is an adapted version of a classic Turkish dish called turlu turlu, a rich and rewarding recipe. It may seem like a bit of work, but it scales up incredibly well should you wish to make more and freeze it for a rainy day. Working equally well as a lunch, dinner or supper, it is fragrant and warming. Finally, see the tips and tricks for an easy way to turn this into a soup or even a baked egg recipe – we are big fans of versatility, so do make multiples of this and use it as you wish.

You'll see that there is cinnamon in this. If you don't like cinnamon, don't worry – it adds a great foundation to the flavours of the dish, but not to the extent that it actually tastes of cinnamon.

SERVES 3–4

- 2 courgettes, cut into 2cm cubes
- 1 aubergine, cut into 2cm cubes
- olive oil
- salt and freshly ground black pepper
- 2 red onions, cut into 2cm-thick wedges
- 1 head of garlic, half the cloves roughly chopped into pieces the size of a raisin and half crushed or finely chopped
- 4 ripe tomatoes, cut into 2cm cubes
- 2 red peppers, deseeded, halved and cut into 2cm-wide strips
- 1 tsp cumin seeds
- 1 tsp coriander seeds
- 1–2 tbsp harissa (page 325 or shop-bought)
- 1 tsp ground cinnamon
- 2 x 400g tins of chopped tomatoes
- squeeze of lemon (optional)
- 10g fresh parsley
- 10g fresh coriander
- 10g fresh mint
- 1 whole preserved lemon, skin only (page 331 or shop-bought)
- wedding couscous (page 270), bulghur wheat or brown rice, to serve
- 1 small tub of Greek yogurt, to serve

Preheat the oven to 180°C. First roast the vegetables. It's best to do this in separate dishes or baking trays for the different vegetables, as different vegetables will cook at different times, but you can have them all in the oven at the same time, taking them out when you feel they are done. It may seem like a lot of work to roast the vegetables separately, but you have better control over things this way and you will end up with a much better result.

Place the courgettes and aubergine in a roasting tin (these roast at the same rate) and toss liberally with olive oil and a little seasoning. Roast for 18–20 minutes, until cooked through but not too soft and still holding their shape. Do the same with your red onion wedges and the roughly chopped garlic cloves, tossing well in oil and roasting for 15–20 minutes, until cooked but still retaining their shape. Finally, do the same in a separate tray with the fresh tomatoes and the peppers. The tomatoes will break down and the peppers should be soft (but not meltingly so) after about 15 minutes.

Heat some oil in a large saucepan set over a medium heat, then add the crushed garlic. Cook for 2 minutes, stirring well, then add the cumin and coriander seeds (ground is fine, but roughly ground from whole seeds is even better!) and cook for 1 minute more. Add the harissa and cinnamon, stirring well and cooking for another minute or two before adding your tinned tomatoes, stirring so everything is well mixed.

Bring to a slow simmer, then add all the roasted vegetables. Stir everything up and leave on a low-medium heat so it remains on a low simmer. Cook for 25–30 minutes, uncovered so the sauce reduces somewhat, and stirring occasionally. Taste the sauce – you should have a reasonably thick, saucy dish that's fragrant and warming. Be brave! It should be full of flavour, so add more seasoning, harissa (ideally mixing it with a shot of hot water to loosen it and then adding it to the pot), lemon juice, any of the spices and even more crushed garlic if you feel it needs it.

Strip the leaves off the parsley and coriander, then chop the stalks finely and add them to the pot. Roughly chop the parsley and coriander leaves along with the mint leaves and put to one side. Add about three-quarters of your diced preserved lemon to the pot. Give it one final taste to make sure you're happy with it.

To serve, ladle into bowls and serve with couscous, bulghur wheat or brown rice. Garnish liberally with the chopped herbs, adding a generous dollop of thick Greek yogurt over it and the remaining diced preserved lemon. >>

» Cauliflower that's been cut into bite-sized florets and roasted off would work superbly here too.

» To convert any leftovers into a soup, simply take your leftovers from the pot, add about the same volume again of boiling water and purée into a soup (roughly or fine, as you like it). Taste and adjust the seasoning with our old friends salt, pepper, lemon and spices. Serve as above, with a spoonful of Greek yogurt and the chopped fresh herbs on top.

» This will also make a wonderful baked eggs dish for brunch. Follow the recipe on page 72 for shakshuka from the point where you are about to add the eggs, simply replacing the shakshuka base with this and bake off as you do in that recipe.

» To make this extra special, make our smoked aubergine yogurt on page 338 and use that on top instead of the Greek yogurt.

✿ Stuffed roast red peppers, three ways

Red peppers (or all peppers, for that matter) are such a versatile ingredient. You will see them pop up again and again in a lot of our savoury recipes, such is their influence on Middle Eastern and southern Mediterranean cuisine. So with such versatility in mind, we've developed three different recipes for you to try, all using this master recipe for stuffing a red pepper – but in a salad-y sense.

We recommend serving these either as a significant component to a mezze-type experience or else as the main element to a lunch, supper or dinner by simply adding a side or two (browse our salad section in particular for anything you think you would fancy alongside it). It's also hard to resist some fresh crusty bread or our freshly baked flatbread (page 322) alongside.

The pepper acts almost like a bowl for the filling, with generally 1 pepper (i.e. 2 stuffed halves) allocated per person as a main element to a dish or just 1 half-pepper if it's going to be part of a meal. Use your judgement, also considering the size of the peppers – we've based these recipes on medium-large peppers, so if yours are quite small, you might want to vary the portion size accordingly, perhaps serving 3 halves per portion as a main.

○ red peppers (as many as you would like – see the note above)
○ olive oil
○ salt and freshly ground black pepper

Preheat the oven to 180°C. Using a small knife, cut the peppers in half from their stalk to their base. Remove the seeds, trying your best to keep as much pepper as possible (we often leave the stalk intact – it looks like real food that way!). They need to resemble a small bowl to hold in their filling, so removing as little pepper from each half helps to keep their shape.

Place the peppers in a bowl, drizzle with some oil and sprinkle some seasoning over, rubbing them around in the bowl so they are well covered. Place the peppers on a baking tray in a single layer and drizzle with more olive oil, salt and pepper. Cook in the oven for 8–10 minutes, just enough to soften the pepper but not cook it all the way through – you want it to be tender while retaining its structure, as opposed to collapsing. Leave in for longer if you feel it's necessary. Remove from the oven and set aside as you prepare the relevant filling from the following pages.

❈ Roast red peppers stuffed with smashed chickpeas, tomatoes and roast garlic yogurt

This is just addictive. Make plenty of the filling if you fancy, as it would work well as a salad in its own right.

SERVES 4 AS A MAIN ALONGSIDE SOME GRAINS AND/OR SALAD LEAVES

- 2 red peppers
- 200g dried chickpeas (see page 359 for cooking instructions) or 1 x 400g tin of chickpeas, drained and rinsed
- 1 tsp ground cumin
- 1 tsp ground coriander
- 1 tsp smoked or sweet paprika
- salt and freshly ground black pepper
- extra virgin olive oil
- 20g fresh coriander, chopped
- 3 tbsp tahini
- 4 small handfuls of rocket
- 2 plum tomatoes, cut into small dice
- 2 pickled chillies (page 334), sliced (optional)
- salad leaves or cooked grains, to serve

For the roast garlic yogurt:
- 4 tbsp thick Greek yogurt
- 2 tbsp roast garlic (page 348)
- juice of ½ lemon

Roast the peppers as per the master recipe on page 229. Leave your oven on at 180°C after roasting the peppers, as you will need to roast the chickpeas too.

Place the well-drained chickpeas in a large bowl with the spices and some salt and pepper, then drizzle with olive oil. Place in a roasting tin and roast in the oven for 20–30 minutes, until golden and crisp around the edges, tossing about halfway through. Remove from the oven and allow to cool a little, then add to a large bowl with the chopped coriander, tahini and seasoning. Bash it all together with a wooden spoon – the texture should be quite loose – and leave to the side.

To make the roast garlic yogurt, mix the yogurt, roast garlic, lemon juice and seasoning together in a small bowl. Mix well and taste, adjusting to get it delicious!

To serve, place a handful of rocket in the base of each roasted red pepper half and fill each with the chickpea mixture. Top with some chopped tomatoes and a drizzle of the roast garlic yogurt. Finish with some sliced pickled chillies, if using, and serve on a bed of salad leaves or cooked grains.

❀ Roast red peppers stuffed with peas, mint, spinach and feta

A really refreshing salad that's still somewhat substantial.

SERVES 4 AS THE MAIN ELEMENT TO A MEAL

- 2 red peppers
- 50g peas
- 50g baby spinach leaves, finely sliced
- 20g fresh mint, finely sliced
- 150g feta cheese
- zest of 1 lemon
- salt and freshly ground black pepper
- 2 tbsp dukkah (page 337)

Roast the peppers as per the master recipe on page 229.

Bring a pot of water to the boil with 1 teaspoon of salt. Add the peas and bring back to the boil, then drain as soon as it boils again. Drain and cool the peas immediately under cold running water.

Place half the peas in a bowl and mash them roughly, then mix in the remaining whole peas with the shredded spinach and mint. Crumble in the feta cheese and lemon zest and mix lightly to bring it all together. Taste and adjust the seasoning, being careful with the salt due to the innate saltiness of the feta cheese.

Spoon the mixture into the roasted red pepper halves and place on your serving dish. Finish the peppers with a generous mound of dukkah and serve.

TIPS AND TRICKS

» I love a little chilli with peas, so if you want to add some chilli flakes or sliced fresh chilli to the filling mix, I would thoroughly approve.
» The feta could happily be replaced with ricotta here, but you may need to do a bit more work with the seasoning at the end, given the difference in flavour of the two cheeses.
» Some finely chopped lovage would be another worthwhile addition here. Two or three sprigs should be enough, chopping the stalks very finely and the leaves slightly rougher.

✸ Roast red peppers stuffed with a tabbouleh filling

Tabbouleh is commonly thought of as a bulghur wheat salad, when in actual fact it's more like a parsley salad with a little bulghur added. This recipe needs a good amount of flat-leaf parsley, so try to get your hands on the big bunches rather than the small packets in the supermarket. For an alternative to this version of tabbouleh, see our recipe for pearl barley tabbouleh on page 171, which would work equally well as a filling here.

SERVES 4 AS THE MAIN ELEMENT TO A MEAL

- 2 red peppers
- 100g bulghur wheat (medium grain)
- extra virgin olive oil
- 2 ripe tomatoes (the best quality you can find), chopped into small dice
- ½ tsp ground cumin
- ½ tsp ground coriander
- ½ tsp ground cinnamon
- salt and freshly ground black pepper
- 50g fresh flat-leaf parsley, stalks very finely chopped and leaves roughly chopped
- 20g fresh mint, leaves very finely chopped
- 4 spring onions, finely sliced at an angle
- juice of ½ lemon
- salad leaves, to serve
- thick Greek yogurt, to serve

Roast the peppers as per the master recipe on page 229.

Rinse the bulghur wheat under cold running water and drain. Bring a pot of water to the boil and add the bulghur. Reduce to a simmer and cook until the bulghur has softened slightly but still maintains a little bite – 8–10 minutes should do it. Drain the bulghur in a sieve and rinse with cold running water to cool. Drain well and stir in a good dash of olive oil.

Add the tomatoes to a bowl with the spices and seasoning, then add the bulghur, parsley, mint and spring onions and mix well. Finish by adding the lemon juice and a good dash of olive oil and give it a final mix. Taste and adjust the flavouring with more lemon, seasoning and spices as needed.

To serve, fill the roasted red pepper halves with the tabbouleh mix and serve on a bed of salad leaves. A spoon of thick Greek yogurt would be lovely here with a final sprinkle of herbs on top.

❋ Tangy lamb hotpot with vegetables and bulghur wheat

When it comes to savoury food, there is a strong tradition for Moroccan food to be on the sweeter side. For example, b'stilla, one of their classic dishes served at weddings, is a chicken (or pigeon) pie heavily dusted with cinnamon and sugar. I prefer for things to be on the tangy end of sweetness, so we use tamarind for this recipe. This is more commonly used in South-East Asian cuisine but it works perfectly here. Pomegranate molasses would work equally well.

SERVES 4

- olive oil
- 1 large onion, medium dice
- ½ head of celery, medium dice
- 400g diced lamb
- 1 tbsp ground cumin
- 1 tsp ground cinnamon
- 1 tsp ground turmeric
- 2 carrots, cut into bite-sized pieces
- 2 tbsp tamarind paste (see the tips and tricks for an alternative)
- 400g pumpkin or butternut squash, unpeeled and cut into large cubes (3cm)
- 50–100g prunes

For the bulghur wheat:
- 250g bulghur wheat
- juice of ½ lemon
- 1 tbsp honey
- 1 tbsp pomegranate molasses
- 4 tbsp extra virgin olive oil
- 50g chopped fresh herbs (parsley and/or coriander)

Preheat the oven to 160°C. Heat a large saucepan or casserole over a medium heat and add some oil. Add the onion and celery and sauté for 10–15 minutes, until they soften. Remove from the pot, then raise the heat to medium-high. Add the lamb and cook until it's nicely browned all over. Add the spices, then add back the vegetables you removed. Stir in the carrots and tamarind paste (dispersing it in a little boiling water first), then add enough water to just cover the meat. Cover with a lid and bring to a simmer, then transfer to the oven and cook for 1 hour. Alternatively, you could continue to cook the hotpot on the hob at a gentle simmer for about the same amount of time. >>

After the first hour has elapsed, add the chopped pumpkin or squash and a little more water if needed. Cook for a further 30 minutes, then add the prunes, check the liquid and cook for 30 minutes more.

To check if the hotpot is ready, look for the following signs. The lamb should be very tender and soft, as should the squash and carrot. The liquid should have nicely reduced into a thick sauce and it should coat the other ingredients when mixed. Use these guidelines to gauge if it needs a little more cooking time. If everything is cooked but the sauce is too watery, drain it off and reduce on the stove in a wide pan, then add it back into the pot. To finish, taste and adjust the seasoning.

Place the bulghur wheat in a pot and cover with water. Bring the water to the boil and cook for around 15 minutes, until the bulghur is cooked but retains a slight bite.

To make the vinaigrette, place the lemon juice, honey and pomegranate molasses in a bowl and gradually add the oil while whisking constantly. Add to the warm bulghur with three-quarters of the chopped fresh herbs, reserving about a quarter of the herbs for serving at the end.

To serve, place some of the bulghur in a large, wide bowl with a generous spoonful of the hotpot on the side, spooning the delicious sauce over the meat. Finish by sprinkling the remaining herbs over the dish.

TIPS AND TRICKS

» We always leave the skin on when cooking squash or pumpkin. It adds texture and a lot of flavour, so don't bother peeling it.
» Pomegranate molasses and tamarind are quite similar. They both have a rich, concentrated, sharply sour taste. It is really worth trying to locate some, as they are both a great store cupboard staple. Any good supermarket or Middle Eastern shop will stock it. But if you can't find any, a good squeeze of lemon juice and 1 tablespoon of honey could work just as well.

❊ Jonathan's tagine of hake and fennel with samphire and couscous

Every time I eat fish I always end up asking myself, 'Why don't I eat more fish?', particularly after having this fish dish.

Jonathan, one of our chefs, developed this dish for our autumn evening menu, but it would work well at any time of the year. This is a wonderfully fragrant dish that is actually quite easy to make and can be easily bulked up for a larger group. This might not be a tagine in the purest sense, but it fits in well with that style of food.

SERVES 4

- olive oil
- 2 red peppers (or a mix of colours), deseeded, halved and each half cut lengthways into 3 wedges
- 1 medium bulb of fennel (about 200g), topped and tailed and cut lengthways into 2cm-thick slices
- 1 medium red onion, finely diced
- 3–4 celery sticks (about 140g), finely diced
- 4 garlic cloves, chopped
- 50–100g okra, topped (optional)
- 4 fresh hake fillets
- 1 x 400g tin of chopped tomatoes
- 2 tsp cumin seeds, toasted and roughly ground (see page 352)
- 2 tsp caraway seeds, toasted and finely ground
- 1 tsp smoked or sweet paprika (not hot!)
- ½ tsp ground allspice
- salt and freshly ground black pepper
- juice of 1 lemon

To serve:
- samphire (optional)
- fresh coriander and/or flat-leaf parsley, stalks finely chopped and leaves roughly chopped
- 1 dessertspoon finely diced preserved lemon (skin only) (page 331 or shop-bought) (optional)
- wedding couscous (page 270) or brown rice
- lemon or lime wedges (optional)

First off, get your sauce on the go. In a large saucepan, heat up enough oil to barely cover the bottom of the pan, then add the peppers, fennel, onion, celery and garlic. Press enough baking parchment over the surface of the vegetables to cover them, then pop the lid on and leave on a medium-low heat for 20 minutes or so, stirring occasionally and adding the okra after about 10 minutes, if using. You will know when the vegetables are adequately cooked by testing some between your

fingers – they should be soft without any real crunch, except for the fennel, which ideally should retain a little more texture (but it's not a big issue if this isn't the case for you!).

While that's all happening, prepare the hake. We leave the skin on when serving because it's perfectly edible and is less work. Trim the fillets so they are each of an even size, feeling the flesh to pull out any bones. Keep any off-cuts to one side, as these will be added to the base sauce later.

When your vegetables are adequately sweated, add the chopped tomatoes, spices, a little salt and pepper and any fleshy off-cuts from the hake. Bring to a gentle simmer and cook for 15–20 minutes, uncovered so the sauce will thicken, stirring occasionally. The sauce will have reduced to a thicker, pasta sauce-like consistency and shouldn't be too runny. At this stage, take the pan off the heat and taste, adjusting the flavouring with lemon, seasoning or a little more spice. You're aiming for a nice, fragrant sauce, so keep at it until it's delicious! Keep the sauce piping hot.

Around this time, preheat the oven to 180°C. Next prepare your samphire, if using, by bringing a pot of water to the boil and adding the samphire for 1 minute (no salt needed, as samphire is naturally quite salty). Drain the samphire in a sieve and rinse with hot water from a pot or your kettle. Shake the samphire well and pop into a bowl, tossing with a dash of olive oil and coarsely ground black pepper.

To cook the hake, put a frying pan on a medium-high heat and add a dash of oil once it's hot. Add 1 or 2 hake fillets, skin side down, and fry for 2 minutes to get the skin lovely and crisp. Remove to a plate lined with kitchen paper and repeat for the remaining hake.

Pour the piping hot sauce into a large, wide baking dish and place the fillets on top, skin side up. Pop into the oven for 10–12 minutes.

To serve, either plate up individual portions or, as I always prefer, finish the dish in the baking tray and serve at the table. To finish, scatter the warm samphire on top along with a decent sprinkle of the chopped herbs and the finely diced preserved lemon, if using. Bring to the table and serve in bowls with a big bowl of wedding couscous or brown rice, perhaps with some lemon or lime wedges at the table for people to squeeze over.

» Try the same technique with other fish, such as cod, plaice, salmon or even a mixture.
» The base sauce can be made well ahead of time and kept in the fridge – in fact, it's one of those sauces that will be better after being left for a day or two.
» As you know from other recipes in this book, we are big fans of batch cooking, so you are welcome to make a much bigger batch of the sauce and freeze it. Then, when you want to make this dish again, just defrost your sauce and reheat it and then you've only got the fish and couscous to worry about!

✸ Itzi's stew of cod with pepper and fennel seed

Our dear friend Itzi, who has become quite the blogger (organising-chaosblog.com), gave me this recipe with the promise that it would be delicious *and* healthy. She wasn't wrong. Here is her take on things:

> *We eat loads of fish in our house. Not because it's good for you, but because we love it. In fact, my youngest boy will not eat chicken or turkey, rarely beef, but he loves crab, mackerel, cod, hake … I'm actually proud of that, to be perfectly honest. I love this recipe because it's both comforting and fresh. I love the warmth that the fennel seeds give and the sweetness of the pepper and it nearly transforms itself into a stew, but it's also incredibly fresh with the cod. It's very much comfort food for us.*

There – I couldn't have said it better myself. Thanks, Itzi!

SERVES A HUNGRY FAMILY OF 4

- o olive oil
- o 3 peppers (I like a mix, so maybe 2 ramiro peppers and 1 yellow one, but it's up to you), deseeded and finely chopped
- o 2 red onions, finely chopped
- o 2 garlic cloves, finely chopped
- o 2 tbsp fennel seeds
- o 1 small glass of white wine (Spanish ideally!)
- o 1 x 400g tin of chopped tomatoes
- o salt and freshly ground black pepper
- o 4 x 100–120g cod fillets
- o 100g baby spinach leaves
- o squeeze of lemon (optional)
- o wedding couscous (page 270) or crusty bread, to serve

For the gremolata topping:
- o 50g fresh parsley, stalks very finely chopped and leaves chopped medium-fine
- o 2 garlic cloves, finely chopped
- o zest and juice of ½ lemon

Start by placing a heavy-bottomed pan over a medium heat. It's better to use a wider one rather than a tall one so that all the fish will cook evenly at the end. And since we are being picky about pots, you might also prefer one that can be brought to the table to serve from. Add 2 tablespoons of olive oil to the pot along with the peppers, onions and garlic. Cover and reduce the heat to medium-low and cook the vegetables for 10–15 minutes, until they're nice and soft (cook for longer if they haven't got that far after 15 minutes), then stir in the fennel seeds. >>

Uncover and add the white wine, then turn up the heat a little to unstick all the sweetness from the onions and peppers that might have got stuck on the bottom of the pan. Add the tinned tomatoes and season with salt and pepper. Stir and let it cook, simmering away on a medium heat, for about 8 more minutes for all the loveliness to mix together properly.

While that magic is happening, make the gremolata by mixing together the parsley, garlic and lemon zest and juice.

Add the cod fillets on top of the vegetables and cover the pot with a lid. After about 8 minutes, check that the fish is cooked through by testing that one is hot all the way through and the flesh is turning opaque. Don't let it cook too long, though, or the fish will get rubbery and tough. Remove the fish from the pan and keep warm.

At this point add the spinach to the sauce and stir it through. Taste and adjust the seasoning if needed, adding more salt, pepper or even a dash of lemon if needed, and it's ready to eat! If you feel it's too runny, simply turn up the heat, stirring regularly, until it reduces to desired consistency.

If bringing to the table, add the cod back on top of the stew and sprinkle the gremolata over the dish. Otherwise, if plating individually, spoon big portions of the sauce into warmed wide bowls and top each one with a fish fillet. Finish with a spoonful of the zesty gremolata and maybe a light drizzle of extra virgin olive oil. We recommend serving this with couscous, rice or even just some fresh crusty bread and a glass of Spanish white wine.

✸ Baharat lamb cutlets with roast red onion

'Baharat' means spices. Unfortunately, a lot of time when people hear the word 'spicy', they think of chilli and pepper and things that give food a lot of heat. However, 'spicy' for me means 'lots of flavour', and this is a great example of that. We use a mix of fragrant spices that work wonderfully with this simply handled lamb cutlet.

A rub like this would also work well for a shoulder of lamb or even chicken and beef. The recipe benefits from leaving the lamb to marinate, so try to leave it overnight if possible but even 2–4 hours will be fine.

We serve this as a main course on our evening menu, accompanied by wedding couscous (page 270) and our vegetables with bright spiced butter (page 262). This dish works exceptionally well as part of a sharing supper accompanied by a few different side salads and perhaps a small bowl of harira soup (page 144). These cutlets will be as delicious warm as they would be piping hot.

SERVES 4–6

- 12 lamb cutlets or chops (3 per person for a main, 2 for mezze)
- 4 garlic cloves, crushed to a paste
- 2 red onions, halved across their equator
- olive oil
- 1 tbsp muscovado sugar
- salt and freshly ground black pepper
- 1 tbsp sumac (optional)

For the spice mix:
- 2½ tbsp cardamom
- 1½ tbsp coriander seeds
- 1 tbsp peppercorns (black, pink or a mix)
- ½ tbsp cloves
- 2 tsp cumin seeds
- ½ tsp allspice
- 2 tsp ground cinnamon

For the rosemary salsa verde:
- 20g fresh parsley
- 20g fresh rosemary
- 2 garlic cloves, minced
- zest and juice of 1 lemon
- 50ml extra virgin olive oil, plus extra for drizzling

To serve:
- 1 handful of salad leaves per person dressed with pomegranate molasses dressing (page 199) or lemon dressing (page 179)
- seeds of ½ pomegranate (optional) (page 354)
- wedding couscous (page 270), Aleppine potatoes (page 253) or pearl barley with kale and tomato (page 260)

To make the spice mix, combine all the spices except the cinnamon and grind in a pestle and mortar or a small spice grinder until finely ground, then stir in the cinnamon.

To prepare the lamb cutlets, simply remove any extra fat or overlapping skin that's on the bone or around the meat, trimming it nicely. Smear the garlic paste over the lamb, then add the spice mix – the garlic paste adds flavour as well as allowing the spices to stick better to the meat. It's essential to let the lamb rest and marinate, so ideally leave the cutlets in the fridge for at least 2 hours, but overnight is best.

To make the salsa verde, you have two options. You can chop the herbs very finely and mix them with the minced garlic and lemon zest in a small bowl, then slowly add the lemon juice and oil, whisking all the time. Or you can place the herbs and garlic in a small food processor and roughly blitz (or use a blending stick), then add the lemon zest and juice and slowly drizzle in the oil to create your desired consistency.

When you're ready to cook, remove the lamb from the fridge and allow it to come to room temperature. Preheat the oven to 180°C and heat a griddle pan (or a frying pan if you don't have a griddle pan) over a high heat.

Gently rub each cut side of the onions with a little oil, then place them on the griddle pan, cut side down, for 6–8 minutes, until they have taken on a nice charred colour. Remove from the grill and place on a roasting tray. Sprinkle the onions with a little more oil and the muscovado sugar, seasoning and a pinch of sumac, if using. Roast in the oven for 20–25 minutes, until soft. Leave your oven on for the final stage of cooking the lamb.

To cook the lamb, preheat the griddle pan on your highest heat again. Place the cutlets on the griddle, resisting the temptation to move them for a good 2–3 minutes, until nicely formed sear marks appear. Turn and continue to cook for another 3 minutes, then place the lamb on a tray and cook in the hot oven for 3 minutes. This method will keep the lamb very moist and rare. If you prefer to eat your lamb more well done, see the cooking times in the tips and tricks.

To serve as a main, arrange 3 cutlets per person on a warmed plate, garnished with the roasted red onions and a drizzle of the rosemary salsa verde. Or arrange the cutlets on a platter and serve at the table alongside a simple leaf salad with pomegranate molasses or a light lemon dressing and some pomegranate seeds, if using. For something more substantial, try the wedding couscous on page 270, our delicious Aleppine potatoes on page 253 or the pearl barley with kale and tomato on page 260.

TIPS AND TRICKS

Cooking temperatures for the lamb cutlets:

» *Medium-rare:* Char each side for 2–3 minutes and 5 minutes in a hot oven.
» *Medium:* Char each side for 2–3 minutes and 8 minutes in a hot oven
» *Medium-well:* Char each side for 2–3 minutes and 10 minutes in a hot oven.
» *Well done:* Char each side for 2–3 minutes and 12 minutes in a hot oven.

❀ Roast chicken wings with dipping sauces and herbs

Chicken wings are a bit of a secret shame for me. They are an addictive snack to have any evening, but I generally feel quite guilty about them, as they are too often deep-fried and served with a very buttery, oily and surprisingly sugary sauce. So we decided to have a go at making them just a little healthier without compromising on flavour. The fact that they eliminate a lot of that guilty feeling just adds so much more to the experience! This is actually one of the dishes I'm most proud of. I hope you will see why when you taste it.

These are very easy to make, and with the yogurt and herbs they are really quite a delight and far better for you than the typical wing, so please do make them as suggested below, with the sauces recommended, for the full effect.

SERVES 2–3 PEOPLE AS A SUBSTANTIAL MEAL
WITH SOME SALAD OR 4 AS A DECENT STARTER

- 1kg chicken wings
- 3 garlic cloves, crushed
- juice of ½ lemon
- 2 tsp ground cumin
- 2 tsp sweet or smoked paprika
- 1 tsp ground turmeric
- 1 tsp olive oil
- salt and freshly ground black pepper

To serve:
- 100g in total mixed soft fresh herbs (a mixture of at least 3 or ideally all of the following: coriander, flat-leaf parsley, mint, lovage and/or dill)
- 6 dessertspoons thick Greek yogurt
- squeeze of lemon
- 4–5 tbsp hot sauce (see page 330 for our recipe or use Tabasco or any hot sauce that takes your fancy)

When buying your wings, they are often sold as a full joint with the wing tip attached. If you get them like this, it's very easy to prepare them as follows. Straighten out the wing and just cut down through the joint or 'elbow' – it should be easy enough to cut through. On the wing section, trim off the wing tip.

Next, marinate your chicken wings by placing them in a big bowl with half the crushed garlic and the lemon juice, cumin, paprika, turmeric, oil and some seasoning. Toss them around well and leave to marinate for at least 1 hour or several hours or overnight if you have the time (for a longer marinade, pop them in the fridge, covered). When ready, preheat the oven to 180°C. Tip the wings out onto a lined roasting tin in a single layer and pop in the oven for 20 minutes.

While that's all happening, prepare your herbs by chopping the stalks *very* finely (except the mint) and placing them in a bowl, then chop the leaves *quite* finely and add them to the bowl too. (If you fancy it, some very finely chopped fresh chilli and/or very finely diced red onion would be sensational added to this mix.)

Make your yogurt dipping sauce by folding the remaining garlic purée, seasoning and a dash of lemon juice into the yogurt – don't overmix. Taste and adjust any of the components as you feel necessary. It should be lovely and creamy while also having a nice punch of lemon and garlic to it.

Take the chicken wings out of the oven and turn up the heat to 220°C. Toss them in a decent amount of the hot sauce and return to the oven for the final blast to get them nicely browned and a little crisp and charred on the outside – 5–10 minutes should do it. You can do this under a very hot grill or on a hot frying pan if you prefer, turning once they are nicely browned and repeating on the other side.

To serve, put the yogurt sauce in a bowl with a dash of hot sauce stirred through it. Put the finely chopped herbs in a separate bowl. Serve these on the side, dipping the wings into the yogurt and then the herbs as you eat! Having more hot sauce available on the side too would be appreciated by some people, I'm sure. Serve with finger bowls of warm water with a slice of lemon in each and a good few napkins, and wash down with some crisp white wine or a cold beer.

TIPS AND TRICKS

This recipe can be played around with as you wish – consider trying the following:
» Dress the wings with a little honey and dried chilli flakes instead of the hot sauce before the final blast in the oven.
» Try serving with a little bowl of our dukkah (page 340) instead of or alongside the herbs.
» Make a more classic dipping sauce by mashing some blue cheese into the yogurt and proceeding as described above.

SIDES AND BITES

We've designed a number of side dishes for you to enjoy
as an accompaniment to the mains we've set out on
the previous pages. Again, mix and match to see what
suits you, what you are in the mood for and what you
feel might work best with your meal – there really is no
wrong answer!

✸ Aleppine potatoes

This dish is based ever so loosely on a bite to eat I had one sunny evening in Aleppo, Syria, the most wonderful of cities as it was then, before all the upheaval of the past few years. The dish was essentially potatoes dipped in various spices and eaten alongside some fresh greens and wonderful olive oil. I set out the original version for you to try in the tips and tricks section, but the version I've included in the main recipe is our own twist on things, tying together those wonderful spices with the Irish love of roast potatoes!

SERVES 4

- olive oil
- 500g baby potatoes, cut into bite-sized dice
- salt and freshly ground black pepper
- 1 tsp sweet or smoked paprika
- 1 tsp hot paprika or cayenne pepper
- 1 tsp dried thyme
- 1 tsp ground cumin
- 1 tsp ground coriander
- 50g mixed soft fresh herbs (parsley, lovage, coriander and/or dill), stalks very finely chopped and leaves roughly chopped
- 1 bunch of spring onions, thinly sliced at an angle
- zest of 1 lemon
- 2 garlic cloves, crushed
- lemon dressing (page 179)

Preheat the oven to 180°C. Place a large roasting tin in the oven with a good-glug of oil to heat up. Dry the potatoes quickly with a clean tea towel and season well with salt and pepper. Toss the seasoned potatoes in the hot oil and place in the oven for 15 minutes. Give the potatoes a good shake and return them to the oven for another 10–15 minutes, until completely tender.

Meanwhile, mix together the smoked paprika, hot paprika, dried thyme, ground cumin and ground coriander with some seasoning in a bowl. Mix the herbs, spring onions and lemon zest together in a separate bowl.

After the potatoes have cooked fully, remove them from the oven and sprinkle on the spice mix and a spoonful of the crushed garlic paste and mix very well. Return to the oven for a final 10 minutes. >>

When serving, toss the potatoes in the lemon dressing and top with plenty of the chopped herbs and spring onion mix. Delicious served piping hot or warm.

TIPS AND TRICKS

» We also serve a rendition of these with a rich tomato and red pepper sauce (page 321) and a zesty smoked aubergine yogurt (page 338), which we call our Middle Eastern bravas.

» The original version of this that I encountered in Aleppo involved boiled baby potatoes, halved, served warm on a plate alongside a tiny bowl of olive oil and the spices put in little mounds or separate bowls. You would dip the potato in the oil and then into one or several of the spices, season and eat with some leaves or herbs. So wonderfully simple and worth trying for a very easy nibble alongside some smoked fish or grilled meat, perhaps adding some steamed tenderstem broccoli and a glass of wine for an easy supper.

✿ Middle Eastern mashed potato

We felt we couldn't have a cookbook without a mashed potato recipe so we came up with this, inspired by some common ingredients you will find us using a lot in this book. They're great served as a light supper with a fried egg on top of a big spoonful of the warm mash, drizzled with some hot sauce (page 330), crumbled feta cheese and chopped fresh herbs, or some cooked kale stirred through.

SERVES 4

- 1kg potatoes
- 10g fresh parsley or dill, chopped
- 1 garlic clove, crushed
- zest of ½ lemon
- 1 tbsp Greek or natural yogurt
- 1 tbsp olive oil
- 1½ tsp ground cumin
- 1 tsp ground coriander
- salt and freshly ground black pepper

Wash and peel the potatoes. Place them in a large pot with 1 teaspoon of salt and cover with water. Put the potatoes on to boil, covered, then reduce the heat and simmer for 15–20 minutes, just until the potatoes have softened. Drain off the water and leave the potatoes to steam dry in the hot pot, then mash well and add all the other ingredients. Taste as you go, adding more of each if you prefer until these are delicious!

❈ Green beans with tarator

Tarator is a style of sauce used in Middle Eastern cooking using ground nuts, generally mixed with yogurt or tahini and other ingredients. This really quite excited me when I first came across the concept. This side works well with vegetables and with fish.

SERVES 4

- 60g stale bread, crusts removed
- 70g whole almonds (skinned or unskinned is fine)
- 2 garlic cloves, minced
- 2 tbsp lemon juice
- 60ml olive oil, plus extra for drizzling over the beans
- 60g natural yogurt
- salt and freshly ground black pepper
- 200–250g green beans
- lemon wedges, to serve
- chopped fresh herbs, to serve

To make the tarator, first soak the stale bread in just enough water to wet it. Leave it for about 10 minutes.

Grind the almonds in a small food processor until they are finely ground. Squeeze the bread dry and add it to the food processor along with the minced garlic and lemon juice. Whizz together with the almonds, gradually adding the oil to form a paste. Scrape this out and put in a bowl, then fold through the yogurt. Taste and ensure you're happy with the flavour, adding more lemon, garlic, seasoning or yogurt to make it delicious.

To cook the green beans, bring a large pan of salted water to the boil and drop in the beans. Cook in the boiling water for a maximum of 3 minutes. Quickly remove from the water and drain well. Toss in a bowl with a little seasoning and a tiny dash of olive oil.

Serve immediately in a shallow bowl or spread out over a platter with a generous spoonful of the tarator, a wedge of lemon and some fresh herbs.

TIPS AND TRICKS

» Try other nuts – especially walnut – if you fancy.
» Tarator would go wonderfully with some baked fish or broccoli in particular.

❀ Baby carrots with lemon tahini yogurt

We love to use the best of the seasons in both cafés, and this dish really reflects that. During the late spring and early summer, we serve this as a fresh, inviting side dish. The combination is so tempting that when we can't get our hands on any baby carrots, we like to use fresh large ones chopped into neat wedges and served the same way.

SERVES 2

- 300g carrots (baby, heirloom or regular carrots)
- olive oil
- 2 tsp cumin seeds, very roughly ground
- salt and freshly ground black pepper
- 1 tbsp za'atar, to serve (optional)
- 1 small bunch of fresh herbs, finely chopped, to serve (optional)

For the lemon tahini yogurt:
- juice of ½ lemon
- 3 tbsp natural yogurt
- 2 tbsp water
- 1 tbsp tahini
- 1 garlic clove, minced (optional)

Preheat the oven to 180°C. If using baby carrots in this recipe, simply wash them well but gently and trim the tops. If using 'adult' carrots, simply wash them, cut the tops off, peel and cut into thick wedges.

Drizzle the carrots in a little olive oil and season with the cumin and some salt and pepper. Place on a large baking tray in a single layer and cook in the oven for 15–20 minutes. The carrots are done when they are fully cooked but still retain a little bite. If they are a bit too al dente for you, leave them in the oven a little longer.

To make the lemon tahini yogurt, put all the ingredients in a small bowl and whisk to a runny consistency, adding a little more water if it's too thick. Taste and adjust the seasoning, adding more lemon, tahini, salt or pepper. (A little minced garlic would work extremely well here too.)

Divide the carrots between individual small serving plates or put them on one big platter. Drizzle generously with the lemon tahini yogurt and a good sprinkle of za'atar or the chopped herbs (or both!). Enjoy hot or at room temperature.

TIPS AND TRICKS

» This recipe would work equally well with beetroot wedges, either instead of or in addition to the carrots.

» *Green beans with tarator*
» *Carrots with lemon tahini yogurt*

❋ Pearl barley with kale and tomato

This dish is somewhat inspired by my love of tabbouleh. During one winter, I found myself wondering how on earth I could turn the concept of tabbouleh, a fresh, zingy salad, into a warming winter dish. Well, here's an attempt that is clearly inspired by tabbouleh, but is very much its own thing! This is delicious as a warming side dish (though it's also fine served at room temperature) to accompany some meat or fish or to have as part of a mezze lunch or supper.

SERVES 4–6

- 200g pearl barley
- salt and freshly ground black pepper
- olive oil
- 100–150g kale
- zest and juice of 1 lemon
- 1 x 400g tin of chopped tomatoes
- 2 tsp ground cumin
- 1½ tsp paprika
- pinch of caster sugar (optional)

First cook the pearl barley by rinsing it in a colander, then putting it in a medium pot, topped up with water to about twice its own volume. Add a good pinch of salt and bring to the boil, covered, then reduce the heat and simmer for 20–30 minutes, until it's cooked but still has a bouncy bite to it. Drain well, toss in a dash of olive oil and put to one side.

While the barley is cooking, you can get on with preparing your kale and the sauce. Remove the central rib/stalk from the kale and discard it, then roll up the leaves like a cigar and slice them as finely as you can. Put in a large bowl with a good dash of olive oil, the juice of half a lemon and some seasoning. Toss well and let it sit. (If you fancy, half a clove of minced garlic would be a treat here too.)

To make the sauce, simply put your tomatoes in a small pot and bring to a simmer to reduce to a reasonably thick liquid that's similar in consistency to a pasta sauce. Add the spices and cook for a few more minutes. Taste and adjust the seasoning, adding salt, pepper, sugar and lemon as needed to get a punchy sauce that's full of flavour.

To bring the dish together, add the drained warm pearl barley to your bowl of kale together with the warm tomato sauce and the lemon zest. Mix everything up and adjust the flavour with lemon, spice, sugar or seasoning as needed. Serve hot or warm.

» To make this more substantial, some cooked chickpeas (200–250g, drained and rinsed if tinned) added to the tomato sauce as it's simmering would bulk things up considerably.

» To make this into a lovely simple supper, serve a nice piece of grilled or baked fish on top (salmon would be particularly pleasing) or serve this as a side to our baharat lamb cutlets on page 245.

❋ Vegetables with bright spiced butter

This is such a simple side dish – we serve it alongside all of our main dishes on our evening menu. I'm proud that people seem to love our mains, but we are often so surprised at the enthusiasm that this dish gets! We call it 'bright spiced butter' because it has such a lovely, bright flavour to it. Serve this alongside any main course, really, or as part of a mezze selection.

You will have extra butter, but you can leave it in the fridge quite happily for several days, well covered, or even freeze it in ice cube trays to use when needed down the line. Further uses are suggested in the tips and tricks.

SERVES 4

- 200–250g tenderstem broccoli, cut into bite-sized pieces
- 200–250g green beans, topped and tailed
- 200–250g mangetout, any rough ends trimmed

For the spiced butter:
- 225g butter, softened
- ½ small red onion or ¼ large red onion, very finely diced
- 4 garlic cloves, minced
- 1 tbsp finely diced preserved lemon (page 331 or shop-bought) or the zest and juice of 1 lemon
- 1 tsp chilli flakes or ½ fresh red chilli, deseeded and finely diced (optional)
- salt and freshly ground black pepper

First prepare your butter. Place the softened butter in a large bowl and simply bring everything together. Be generous with some freshly ground pepper too (coarsely ground is best). Taste and adjust the flavours, adding more garlic, lemon and seasoning if needed. You're looking for a really punchy butter full of bright flavours, so don't be timid!

Bring a large pot of water to the boil with 1 teaspoon of salt, then add the broccoli. Cook for 2 minutes, uncovered, then add the beans and mangetout. Bring back up to the boil, then immediately drain well, shaking through a colander. (This can all be done ahead of time – just drop the veg into cold water when it's cooked to cool it quickly. Drain and put to one side, then when ready to use, just blanch it in a pot of boiling water for 2 minutes and drain well.)

Toss the warm vegetables in a few dessertspoons of the spiced butter in a large bowl. Ideally you want the butter to be softly melted over the vegetables as opposed to fully melted and pooled in the bottom of the dish. Bring to the table to serve.

» Throwing some frozen or fresh peas in with the mangetout would be a nice addition.

» We often serve this butter with some charred broccoli and fennel. We blanch the broccoli as above and drain it really well, then griddle it for a few minutes on a super hot griddle pan to get those lovely charred marks and that unique flavour. To prepare the fennel, we trim it, wash it well and cut the fennel into thick enough wedges and roast it off, tossed in a little oil and seasoning, for about 20 minutes at 180°C. We then char these too. To bring it together, we toss the warm vegetables in the bright butter and serve as above (the addition of the chilli works particularly well here).

» Other uses for the butter include a spoonful of it put on a hot steak or baked or grilled fish just as you are serving it; stir it through mashed potato instead of regular butter; smear it over fresh crusty baguette or bread and place in an oven at 180°C for a few minutes; or toss some cooked spaghetti in the butter with mashed anchovies, lots of chopped fresh parsley and toasted breadcrumbs.

❁ Baked sweet potato, chickpea and coriander falafel

I should say that these are perhaps a distant relative of the authentic falafel. Inspired by a visit to a wonderful vegetarian restaurant in Melbourne, these are great as a starter or as part of a mezze or to serve alongside a salad for a light lunch or supper.

Since these are baked, they retain a healthy buzz. Add to that buzz by serving them warm in a Baby Gem lettuce leaf, enjoying the fresh crunch of the lettuce against the warm softness of the falafel. Just note that if you use plain flour instead of gram flour, these delights will lose their gluten-free status!

MAKES 12–14 FALAFEL (2 SUBSTANTIAL STARTERS)

- 100g dried chickpeas, cooked (see page 359) or ½ x 400g tin of chickpeas, drained and rinsed
- 2 medium sweet potatoes (350–400g), scrubbed
- 30g gram flour or plain flour (see note above)
- 20g fresh coriander, finely chopped
- 20g fresh mint, finely chopped
- 1 garlic clove, minced
- ½ red chilli, deseeded and very finely chopped
- zest and juice of ½ lemon
- 1 tsp ground cumin
- 1 tsp ground coriander
- squeeze of lemon (optional)

To serve:
- 1 head of Baby Gem lettuce, broken into individual leaves
- roast red pepper dressing (page 173) or lemon tahini dressing (page 208)
- lime wedges (optional)

Preheat the oven to 180°C. First cook the dried chickpeas according to our method on page 359. Mash the cooked, drained chickpeas roughly (you want these to add a degree of texture to the finished dish).

Place the sweet potatoes on a baking tray and bake in the oven for 30–45 minutes (or more if needed). They are done when the flesh is fully soft all the way through (skewer it with a knife to check). Leave to one side to cool while you prepare the other ingredients. >>

When the potatoes are cool enough to handle, scoop the flesh out of the sweet potatoes into a large bowl (or peel the potatoes – whichever is easier). Mash it with a fork, then add in all the other ingredients, mixing until well combined. Taste and adjust the seasoning – it should be a punchy enough mix that's full of flavour, so adjust with herbs, chilli, garlic, seasoning or lemon as you judge necessary.

Using 2 spoons to shape the falafel, spoon the mix into balls (or use your hands, wetting them regularly so the mix doesn't stick to your fingers too much). The balls should be about the shape of a walnut, perhaps slightly oblong. Spread out on a baking tray lined with non-stick baking paper so they aren't touching each other.

Bake for 10 minutes, then turn up the temperature to 220°C and cook for 5 minutes more. This will create a reasonably dry, almost crunchy exterior with a soft, warm centre.

Serve on a Baby Gem lettuce leaf with a generous dash of one of the dressings over each falafel, or even just a quick squeeze of lime on top. These are lovely served piping hot but they're still good after sitting for a while if you prefer.

TIPS AND TRICKS

» The dressings are well worth serving with these, as then you've got such a party in your mouth between the warm falafel, the cool creaminess of the dressing and the fresh crunch of the Baby Gem lettuce.
» You could add a little very finely diced preserved lemon to the falafel mix for an extra dimension.
» You could replace the sweet potato with an equal amount of carrot or squash, chopped and roasted until fully soft.
» You can leave out the chickpeas if you prefer, but we like it as it adds some extra texture.
» If you like a really good crunch to your falafel (which is how traditional falafels are), then after baking these, give them a quick shallow fry in very hot oil to crisp the outside even further.
» You could make these a lot smaller to serve as canapés, perhaps on top of a thick slice of cucumber, but reduce the initial cooking time by 3 minutes.
» You could cook a lot of these in advance and then just reheat to order in a hot oven for about 5 minutes – easy peasy!
» Our zhoug (page 340) goes really well as a dressing for this too.

❀ Marinated olives

Such an easy dish to have as a nibble with a glass of wine, these really
are worth the little effort required. The quality of your olives will be
very important here, so use the best you can find and always use whole
olives.

MAKES 200G

- 100g whole Kalamata olives
- 100g whole giant green olives
- 1 tbsp fennel seeds, toasted (see page 352)
- ½ preserved lemon (page 331 or shop-bought), skin only,
  very finely diced (optional)
- 1 tsp crushed garlic
- 1 tsp dried thyme
- ½ tsp chilli flakes
- salt and freshly ground black pepper
- extra virgin olive oil

Remove the olives from their brine and place them in a large container
with the remaining ingredients and mix well. Pour in enough oil to
cover the olives, then cover the container. Allow to marinate overnight –
in the fridge is no harm.

These olives keep for 2 weeks in the fridge, but try to bring them up to
room temperature before serving.

TIPS AND TRICKS

» We serve these in the cafés with wine in the evenings alongside some
  of our spiced roasted chickpeas (see our recipe for falafel crumb
  on page 329 – follow the instructions but don't blitz the roasted
  chickpeas at the end).
» If you don't have preserved lemon, some slices of lemon rind will
  help here, but it's very much worth using preserved lemon if you can
  manage it.

❀ Wedding couscous

Inspired by a recipe from Greg Malouf, a wonderful Australian chef, this is a really delicious way to eat couscous, which is too often considered to be a bland carb. We've taken inspiration from his recipe but added some extra elements with the caramelised onions and the lentils, which elevate the couscous to a far more substantial experience.

SERVES 4

- o 100g green or brown lentils
- o 300g couscous
- o 2 tsp ground turmeric
- o salt and freshly ground black pepper
- o extra virgin olive oil
- o 350ml boiling water
- o 100g caramelised onions (page 346)
- o 50g fresh herbs, chopped
- o 30g dried fruit (currants, sultanas, cranberries)
- o 30g almonds, toasted and chopped (see page 352)
- o zest and juice of ½ lemon or orange
- o 20–30g edible flowers (such as marigolds or nasturtiums), to garnish (optional, but worth it!)

Pop the lentils into a pot and cover with at least 3cm of water. Bring to a simmer and cook for 15–20 minutes, until they are soft but still holding their shape. Drain well.

Place the couscous in a large shallow container. Add the turmeric, seasoning and a good drizzle of olive oil. Mix well, ensuring all the couscous is well seasoned and covered in the oil. Pour over the boiling water and give it a good mix with a large spoon. Cover the couscous with cling film and leave to rest for 10 minutes or so, giving it a good stir midway through with a fork so it breaks up nicely rather than forming clumps. When it's done, use your fingers or a fork to fluff up the couscous again and to make sure all the water has been absorbed.

At this point, add all the other ingredients to the couscous. Place in a large serving bowl and drizzle with the lemon juice. Taste and adjust the seasoning, then garnish with the edible flowers and serve.

TIPS AND TRICKS

» To make this more of a salad dish in its own right, add 100g cooked chickpeas and double the amount of herbs as well as perhaps increasing the lemon element by half again. Some finely diced celery would also give it a nice crunch. Or you could go so far as adding some roast carrot slices to bulk it up even further.

» To make it a bit more interesting, stir 1–2 tablespoons of harissa (page 325) into the water before pouring that over the couscous.
» Some pomegranate seeds scattered over it all would be a juicy and beautiful addition too.

❀ Making a mezze

Mezze is a word derived from the Persian word for 'to taste'. For people unfamiliar with mezze, it's perhaps best explained as Middle Eastern tapas in that it involves a similar concept of lots of individual dishes for tasting.

Mezze is a meal best enjoyed with a group of people. As we've said elsewhere in this book, nothing can add more to an enjoyable meal experience than sharing it. Pass those bowls around, try everything and share!

Our entire evening menu in Brother Hubbard is devoted to a mezze experience. While I am very proud that people enjoy our food, they also often comment about their enjoyment of the shared meal experience.

However, there is a warning: making a mezze can be a lot more work than a simple meat-and-two-veg dinner. Unfortunately, no pain, no gain! But if you're willing to put in the effort, it really is worth it. Get one or two people into the kitchen to help you – it will be a lot of fun. And be clever: make extra of a few dishes and you can graze from it for a few lunches or suppers over the subsequent days.

Now, in terms of building your mezze, here are a few thoughts to bear in mind:
» Go for dishes using a variety of ingredients, colours and textures.
» Get the balance right between meat, vegetable and 'carby' dishes so that ultimately you've got a balanced, nutritious meal.
» Get the balance right between hot, warm and cold dishes.
» Get some salads in there for sure.
» Some nibbly bits are excellent for sharing.
» Think about your prep: try to include some dishes that can be made well in advance (particularly your salads and sides) so that you can make any hot dishes just before serving.

Here are some ideas for a casual enough mezze meal:
» Hummus with crudités (see pages 155–159 for our hummus recipes)
» Greek cucumber salad (page 190)
» Beef koftas (page 216)
» Tortilla (page 117)
» Simple green salad
» Wedding couscous (page 270)

Here are some ideas for putting your mezze together for a special occasion. It would involve a busy but fun day in the kitchen (you would need to be up for it, but it would be worth it!):

» Marinated olives (page 269)
» Sweet potato falafel (page 266)
» One of our hummus recipes (see pages 155–159) with flatbread (page 322)
» Roast chicken wings (page 249)
» Roast cauliflower florets (page 173)
» Greek cucumber salad (page 190)
» Middle Eastern slaw (page 176)
» Wedding couscous (page 270)
» Baharat lamb cutlets (page 245)
» Hake tagine (page 238)
» Vegetables with bright spiced butter (page 262)

Now there's some food for thought!

✵ Any Time of the Day

TREATS

We've included the treats section as part of the 'any time of the day' chapter as this seems to be how it is. In the café, it's actually not so unusual for someone to come in and order a brownie for breakfast or a scone at five in the evening.

Most of our treats tend to be slightly on the less indulgent end of the spectrum – we've a lower-sugar, lower-excess approach to all our food. While this is a lot harder to achieve when it comes to treats, we do try. The amazing part of making your own treats is the purity of what you are doing: as you will see, overall there are relatively few ingredients and what you do use is very pure. So even though you're indulging, you'll still feel that you've done yourself some good compared to some of the other options out there.

The thing I love most about food is actually cooking for other people. The act of creation devoted to someone else – creating and cooking something for others that they will enjoy while nourishing them too – is a joy. This is especially the case when it comes to treats, a bright spot in anyone's day, made all the more unique and special because it was made by you for someone you care about. So please have a go at some or all of the recipes listed here and make someone's day – in doing so, it may well also make your own!

✿ Brownies – the basic, classic recipe

Our brownies have always got a great reaction. One food critic who was in likened eating them to that famous scene in *When Harry Met Sally*. Much experimenting before we opened helped us get the right outcome, as did a very valuable chat with my dear friend Darragh, being the brownie obsessive that he is.

Brownies are one of those things that are regarded as simple, but beware! In such simplicity lies the risk of getting it catastrophically wrong. Maybe that's a bit extreme, but in my book (literally!), a cakey brownie is a spoiled brownie (where that happens, see the tips and tricks – I've some ideas for a rescue plan). You're aiming for a reasonably crunchy, hard top and a soft, moist, velvety middle, even practically melting if you so desire.

We do the basic version, and sometimes I think this is the best – it's just about the brownie and the extreme chocolatey-ness of it. But over time we've evolved a number of variations using this basic brownie recipe as the foundation for ever-higher brownie greatness!

As with all recipes, the quality of your ingredients will have a profound impact on the outcome, so be sure to source good-quality chocolate and cocoa in order to score higher, ahem, brownie points with your audience.

MAKES 20–25 BROWNIES

- 225g chocolate (the closer to 70% cocoa solids, the better)
- 275g butter, softened, plus extra for greasing
- 340g caster sugar
- 4 eggs
- 75g good-quality cocoa powder
- 70g plain flour
- 1 tsp salt
- ½ tsp baking powder

For this recipe, we use a 31cm x 21cm Swiss roll tin approximately 4cm deep. This is the standard tray we use for any of the tray-baked recipes in this book. If you don't have a tray this size, use something as close as possible to those dimensions. A different size will affect the depth of the brownie mix in the tray, which will influence the time it takes to bake the brownie. A deeper brownie will take longer and a shallower one will take less time – see how we judge when a brownie is done in the recipe below and simply apply that judgement to your brownies.

Preheat your oven to 170°C. Brush a 31cm x 21cm baking tray with a little melted butter and press in a rectangle of non-stick baking paper so that it comes a little over the sides of the tray on all sides.

When you melt your chocolate, you want it to be just melted rather than piping hot. We do this in a metal bowl set over a pot of boiling water, making sure the bottom of the bowl doesn't touch the water, stirring gently from time to time and resisting the temptation to dip a finger in! A quick visit to the microwave will work too – on a medium setting, heat the chocolate for 1 minute, stir, heat again for 1 minute, and so on until the chocolate is fully melted.

While that's happening, get your butter and sugar into a mixing bowl and cream together until very well combined. A mixer does this perfectly, but so does a wooden spoon and a bit of elbow grease. Next, mix in your eggs two at a time, making sure they are well incorporated before adding the next two. Keep mixing until the egg, sugar and butter become one – there should be no runniness to this but rather a soft, fudgy mass. Add the melted chocolate to the bowl, scraping down the sides to get every last bit of this brown magic into your mix. Mix gently until well combined with the other ingredients – it should look a little like a heavy mousse at this stage.

Now add in your mixed dry ingredients all at once – the cocoa, flour, salt and baking powder. Fold in carefully until everything is well combined into one cohesive mix. Don't be alarmed if it feels like a stiff enough mix – that's fine.

Turn this into your lined tray. Using a spatula, spoon or palette knife, spread the mix evenly so that it covers the entire tray (I tend to build it up a little more in each corner). Pop in the oven on the middle shelf and leave to do its thing for 25 minutes or so. You will see it all melt down first and then it will rise a little (it will sink down again once it's cooled). Test after 20 minutes and monitor at 5- to 10-minute intervals after that. It could take up to 40 minutes, depending on your oven.

Here's the test to know when the brownies are done: take the tray out of the oven gently, closing the door immediately to maintain the heat. Give the tray a little shake. There should be a noticeable wobble in the middle of the brownie – a wobble as opposed to outright runniness. The wobbly bit should just be around the very centre. If it's too wobbly, pop it back in the oven and check it again after 5–10 minutes, depending on how far away from the perfect wobble you felt it was! >>

Once you're happy with your brownie and its wobbliness, take it out of the oven and let it cool on a wire rack. It can't be cut until it's thoroughly cooled or it will just be a mess (I learned this the hard, delicious way). As these are very rich, we recommend cutting them into small 5cm squares.

TIPS AND TRICKS

» The brownie holds up well – if you leave it out at room temperature, covered, it will last for 2–3 days in a near-perfect state (sorry, there's no excuse to eat it all at once!). This brownie also freezes remarkably well if put in a sealed container.

» If you end up overcooking your brownie, it will still be delicious but it will have more of a cakey quality than it should. I suppose this is why it's not called chocolate cake, but a lot of brownie-bakers out there don't seem to realise this. But if you do overdo it, just be sure to serve it with some whipped cream or ice cream and perhaps some melted chocolate ganache over it too. Break it up into a bowl, mix 150g melted chocolate with 75ml cream and pour this over the 'cake', gently tossing everything together with a spatula or wooden spoon and serving in a bowl with ice cream or whipped cream. A raspberry jam sauce (just heat some jam with a splash of water) and whipped cream would also be a delicious way to rescue the brownie. Or if you don't want to go to all that trouble, serving it gently warmed will also help reduce the dry-cakey experience.

» If you overbake your brownie, the most important thing is to remember that the next time you bake them, leave it for less time. Cooking can be quite iterative as you get to know your recipes, your equipment and your ingredients. Every time we cook something we learn something for the next time, so feel free to write some notes in the margin beside this recipe to make sure you don't make the same mistake twice!

❂ Salted caramel brownies

Salted caramel is such an easy thing to make. In essence what you're doing is making a really sugary solution and then evaporating most of the liquid so that you can 'cook' and caramelise the sugar, then you add cream and butter to give it that soft caramel texture and smoothness with a little bit of salt added to get that unique sweet–savoury experience. This holds quite well, so there's no harm in making a double batch (or more) – just follow the same technique with the bulked-up ingredients. This works sensationally with ice cream, as a cake topping or even smeared generously over a rich tea or digestive biscuit.

MAKES 20–25 BROWNIES

- 1 batch of brownies (page 276)
- 150ml boiling water
- 300g caster sugar
- 150g butter, cut into cubes
- 150ml cream (or about 150ml crème fraîche)
- 1½ tsp sea salt flakes (or more to taste) – we like Irish Atlantic Sea Salt or Maldon
- whipped cream or ice cream, to serve

While your brownies are baking, get on with making the salted caramel. Bring the water to the boil in a clean, wide pan, then add all of the sugar. Stir to dissolve the sugar and then bring back to the boil. Keep it at a rapid boil, paying reasonably close attention to it as the liquid reduces.

Dip a pastry brush in water and use it to brush down the sides of the pan if you see any sugar sticking to it or crystallising there. We do this so that the sugar won't burn on the side of the pan, which could potentially cause the caramel to taste burnt.

After a while, you will see the liquid becoming very thick and then it will start to turn light golden brown. Reduce the heat and swirl the pan gently. When the contents of the pan have turned an even golden brown (a little darker is fine too, but not too dark or it will burn and taste bitter), remove from the heat. Add your butter and cream and stir vigorously until well combined. A metal whisk is ideal for this – if it lumps up, return to a medium heat and whisk until all the lumps disappear. Put to one side to cool.

Once cooled, sprinkle half the salt flakes over, stir well and give it a little taste. You want that nice balance between the sweet with just a touch of saltiness. Add more salt if you think it's necessary. >>

To make the salted caramel brownie, simply put a generous dollop of the cooled salted caramel on top of the basic brownie and a very light sprinkle of salt flakes. Serve with whipped cream or ice cream.

TIPS AND TRICKS

» Before the brownie goes into the oven, you can put a spoonful of the salted caramel into the centre of where each portion will be cut and swirl it in. Personally, I prefer it as a topping as opposed to being baked into the brownies, as I find the contrast stands out better as a topping.

❈ Tahini and honey brownies with figs and walnuts

Tahini works sensationally here with the chocolate, the walnuts and figs, turning this into one of the most interesting brownies you will ever encounter!

MAKES 20–25 BROWNIES

- 1 batch of unbaked brownies (page 276)
- 200g walnuts, chopped, plus extra for sprinkling on top
- 6 tbsp tahini or peanut butter
- 2 tbsp honey, plus extra for drizzling on top
- 1 dessertspoon boiling water
- 60–80g dried figs, dried apricots or dried cranberries, roughly chopped (leave the cranberries whole if using)

Make your basic brownie recipe as per the instructions on page 276, adding in the chopped walnuts when folding in the dry ingredients along with half of the dried fruit. Spread out in the baking tray and put to one side.

Put the tahini into a bowl with the honey and boiling water and whisk furiously. You should end up with a thick, smooth mix, but add a dash more boiling water if you feel it needs it. Set aside one-third of this mix.

With 2 large spoons, place dollops of the tahini mix onto the unbaked brownie at even intervals. Take the end of the spoon and gently swirl each dollop of the tahini mix within the brownie to marble it somewhat, but not too much, as you want a contrast. You should end up using about half of the tahini mix for this stage, leaving the rest for later.

Bake as per the master recipe instructions. Once they are baked and cooled, cut your brownies into portions. Using 2 spoons, place a dollop of the remaining tahini mix on top of each one. Drizzle over a little honey to finish and scatter with the remaining chopped fruit and some extra walnuts.

❈ White chocolate, raspberry and rose brownies

These can really be quite beautiful and a light touch with the rose will lead to a magnificent, nuanced experience.

MAKES 20–25 BROWNIES

- 1 batch of unbaked brownies (page 276)
- 350g white chocolate, broken into chunks
- 250g raspberries (frozen are fine here)
- 75ml cream
- 1–2 tsp rosewater
- dried rose petals, to decorate (optional)

Make the basic brownie recipe (page 276) to the stage where it's put in the baking tray (before baking!). Push 100g of the white chocolate chunks into the mix, distributing them evenly throughout the entire tray. Do the same with the raspberries, but don't fully press them in – let them sit more on top. If using fresh raspberries, hold a handful back for decorating at the end.

Bake the brownies as per the master recipe and get on with making the white chocolate and rose ganache. Place the remaining 250g white chocolate in a glass or metal bowl set over a small pot of simmering water and stir until it has just melted. Remove from the heat and whisk in the cream. Add ½ teaspoon of the rosewater, whisking it in well.

Taste the ganache – it should have a decent hint of rose to it as well as the sweetness of the white chocolate. If not, add a tiny dash more of the rosewater, stir well and taste again. Add any more rosewater *very* gradually until you're happy with the flavour. Put to one side.

Once your brownies are baked and cooled, cut them into portions. Put a generous dollop of the ganache on each one and finish with some raspberries and dried rose petals, if using, dotted over it just before serving.

TIPS AND TRICKS

» Dried rose petals over the finished brownie just before serving look sensational if you want to make this extra special!

✵ Baci

The Italian word for kisses, these are a gluten-free wonder. I often describe them as a chocolatey cousin of the amaretti biscuit. I first came across these in Loafer Bread in Melbourne, where one of my jobs on a Monday was to get the mix for these ready for the week ahead. It was always a messy but fun beginning to my week.

This is our version of baci. We started making them on Valentine's weekend in the cafés and they were a massive success. They are a relatively small bite but quite filling, so they're perfect to serve with a coffee or as after-dinner treats. They hold amazingly well in an airtight container, so make plenty! And they are always well appreciated as a gift.

MAKES 16–20

- ○ 150g hazelnuts
- ○ 300g caster sugar
- ○ 150g ground almonds
- ○ 80g cocoa powder
- ○ 2 tbsp honey
- ○ 2 tbsp brandy or amaretto (optional)
- ○ 250g egg whites (about 10 egg whites)

Toast the hazelnuts on a hot dry pan or in an oven set to 180°C for 8–10 minutes. They are done when the skins (if present) come off easily and the nuts have turned a light brown. If the nuts do have skins, rub them off in a clean tea towel. Blitz the toasted, skinned nuts in a food processor to a fine grind, being careful not to over-blitz.

Place all the dry ingredients in a large bowl and mix to combine, then add the honey and brandy or amaretto, if using, and stir well.

Briefly whisk the egg whites just to break them up without whisking them to a froth. Add half of the egg white to the dry ingredients and mix well to combine. The mixture should just about come together and hold its shape, so add more of the egg whites if you need to. You may not need to add all of it. The mixture should be one big mass that's still quite dry but fully combined with no loose crumbs of the dry mix, like the consistency of a firm mashed potato.

Line a baking tray with non-stick baking paper. To shape the baci, use 2 large spoons (like tablespoons or dessertspoons) to spoon neat mounds of the dough onto the lined tray, spaced well apart. Leave the baci out for a few hours or so (or even overnight) so that the outside sets somewhat. This allows the air to form a hard crust on the outside of the treat while leaving the inside moist and soft.

When ready to bake, preheat your oven to 180°C. Bake the baci for exactly 14 minutes. Remove from the oven and allow to cool before devouring. Store in an airtight container for 3–4 days.

TIPS AND TRICKS

» This is the part where you can get creative. The baci are a great treat just as they are, but to make them extra special, melt some dark, white or milk chocolate, whichever you prefer, and drizzle it over the baci. Or you could use the white chocolate and rose ganache topping we use for our brownies on page 283. Or try topping them with some crushed hazelnuts or pistachios, praline (page 341) or freeze-dried raspberries, or experiment with your own ideas.
» If your mix is too wet, the baci won't hold their shape and will bake into flatter-style cookies. Don't worry – they will still be delicious, just make a note in the margin for next time as to where you went wrong.

❀ Flourless citrus and coconut cake

This is based on a recipe in one of my favourite books, *The New Book of Middle Eastern Food* by Claudia Roden. It's well worth looking up. I've read it like a novel, as it's not only full of wonderful recipes, but also the history and stories behind those recipes.

This is an amazing but simple cake, lovely, soft and moist. It also just so happens to be gluten-free and dairy-free (though if you make the ganache topping, make sure your white chocolate is gluten-free). We make these as individual cupcakes.

MAKES 12 INDIVIDUAL CAKES

- o 2 oranges
- o 1 lemon
- o 360g caster sugar
- o 130g coconut flour (or desiccated coconut blitzed to a fine powder)
- o 100g fine polenta
- o 85g ground almonds
- o 50g desiccated coconut
- o 5 eggs, whisked well
- o 2 tsp orange blossom water (optional)
- o 1 tsp baking powder (gluten-free if you want the recipe to be gluten-free)
- o sunflower oil, for greasing
- o Greek yogurt or crème fraîche, to serve

For the white chocolate and coconut ganache:
- o 200ml coconut milk
- o 200g white chocolate, roughly chopped
- o toasted coconut flakes (page 151), to decorate

First you need to boil your oranges and lemon, so put them in a pot, cover them with water and pop a lid on. Bring to the boil and simmer for 40–60 minutes, checking occasionally to make sure they remain just covered with water. Once they are completely soft, drain off the water and leave to cool.

Once they are cool enough to handle, cut the tips off each piece of fruit, then cut in half and remove the seeds. They should be a soft, pulpy mess inside. Place the fruit pulp and skins in a bowl and purée in a food processor or using a stick blender. You should have a fairly smooth purée. If doing by hand, put into a saucepan and go hell for leather with a potato masher – don't worry if it isn't a perfectly smooth purée, as a little chunkiness is no harm. >>

At this stage, preheat your oven to 180°C. Put the purée in a big mixing bowl or the bowl of a stand mixer. Add all of the other ingredients and mix until everything is fully combined.

If using a silicone cupcake mould, brush each individual cup with a little sunflower oil. If using a metal tin, do the same or use paper cases. Spoon the batter into each cup until it's just shy of the top by about 5mm.

Pop in the oven, then immediately turn it down to 170°C and bake for 40 minutes. The cupcakes are done when you stick a clean skewer, cocktail stick or knife in the centre and it comes out clean, without any batter stuck to it. If they're not yet at that point, pop them back into the oven and check again after 5–8 minutes. Leave to cool.

While the cakes are baking, you can make the white chocolate and coconut ganache. Heat the coconut milk in a small saucepan. When it's near the boiling point, remove the pan from the heat and add the roughly chopped white chocolate. Stir well until the chocolate is fully melted, then leave to cool.

Spoon the cooled ganache over the top of the cooled cupcakes, decorate with toasted coconut flakes and serve with a little Greek yogurt or crème fraîche.

Stored at room temperature in an airtight container or tin, these will remain absolutely perfect for 4–5 days. In fact, the flavours come out even better after a day.

TIPS AND TRICKS

» The orange blossom water isn't absolutely necessary, but it does give it that extra fragrant orangey kick.
» You could use a chocolate ganache (melt 50g dark chocolate with 50ml cream in a pot set over a medium heat) instead of the white chocolate and coconut ganache and decorate with the cakes with some toasted chopped almonds.
» Here's a great idea to make life easier down the line: boil multiple quantities of the fruit in a bigger pot, weigh once drained and blend to a purée, then divide the total weight by the number of multiples of the fruit for the recipe that you've cooked and freeze in batches. The next time you want to make this cake, just defrost a batch.

❀ Catherine's super power bars

Our dear Catherine, tired one day of making our very laborious superseed slice, experimented with an alternative treat that ticks the same boxes but with a lot less effort. It was an immediate success – almost overwhelmingly so. The people of Cavan, her hometown, are still talking about it to this day. (I should point out that Catherine works very hard – especially when fuelled by one of her super power bars!) A great snack on the go or for a lunchbox, these keep in an airtight container for up to a week.

MAKES ABOUT 20 BARS

- 200g porridge oats
- 200g quinoa (red is lovely)
- 300g peanut butter
- 200g honey
- 2 tbsp sunflower oil
- 100g currants
- 50g dried cranberries
- 50g coconut flakes

Preheat your oven to 180°C. Line a 31cm x 21cm baking tray with non-stick baking paper.

Place the oats and quinoa on a baking tray and toast in the oven for 10–15 minutes, stirring them halfway through, until the oats are lightly golden.

Melt the peanut butter, honey and oil together over a low heat in a small saucepan.

Place the currants, cranberries and coconut flakes in a large bowl and add the melted peanut butter mixture. Finally, add in the toasted oats and quinoa and mix well to combine.

Scrape the mixture onto the tray and flatten it out so that it evenly fills the tray, pressing the mix down well, especially into the corners. Cover with another layer of baking paper and allow to cool, then refrigerate for 2–3 hours, until firm.

When set, cut into slices or bars and store in an airtight container for up to a week. >>

» If you want to make these vegan, replace the honey with date molasses or even barley malt.

» This base recipe is really versatile, so don't be shy trying to use your own mixture of fruits, nuts and seeds to develop your own super bar! Toast any nuts and seeds you might have and add them in along with any other dried fruit (chopped if necessary) that's lurking in your cupboard.

Anzac biscuits

I first came across these during my time in Australia. A big tradition there is to make these on Anzac Day – they were originally sent over to troops abroad, as the biscuits seemed to hold and travel well. These are chewy, oaty wonders and a real delight with a cup of tea mid-morning. I've added a few tips on how to adapt them to make them even better!

MAKES 12–14 BISCUITS

- 75g rolled oats
- 75g caster sugar
- 60g desiccated coconut
- 55g plain flour
- 50g butter
- 2 tbsp boiling water
- 1 tbsp honey
- 1 level tsp bicarbonate of soda

Preheat your oven to 180°C. Line a baking tray with non-stick baking paper. Weigh out the oats, sugar, coconut and flour in a large bowl.

Melt the butter in a small saucepan, then add the boiling water and honey. Remove from the heat and add the bicarbonate of soda. This will cause the mix to fizz slightly. Stir the butter mixture into the dry ingredients and combine well.

Roll a dessertspoonful of the mixture into a little ball (about 35–40g in weight) and place on the lined baking tray about 2.5cm apart to allow for spreading.

Bake in the oven for 15 minutes, until the biscuits have turned a deep golden brown colour. If your oven gives off an uneven heat, turn the tray halfway through the baking time.

Leave to cool and firm up. Keep in an airtight container and enjoy throughout the week.

TIPS AND TRICKS

» To make these extra special, try adding 40g roughly chopped dried cranberries to the mix and drizzle with a little melted white chocolate when they've cooled after baking.
» Alternatively, drizzle some melted dark chocolate over them and scatter with some diced crystallised ginger for an extra hit of spicy deliciousness.

❋ Walnut and orange blossom baklava

Baklava bought in shops can often taste old and dull and pales in comparison to a fresh, homemade version. It's often a revelation when people try a homemade version and it always gets a great response when we serve it as part of our dessert platter for our Middle East Feast.

MAKES 10–12 PORTIONS (OR 20–25 MINI BAKLAVA)

- 125g butter
- 125g walnuts
- 50g icing sugar
- zest of 2 oranges
- 2 tsp ground cinnamon
- 1 tsp ground cardamom
- 1 packet of filo pastry (20 sheets)

For the syrup:
- 250g caster sugar
- 250ml water
- zest of 2 oranges or 1 tsp orange blossom water

Preheat your oven to 170°C. Melt the butter gently and set aside. Roughly chop the walnuts until it resembles gravel, then mix in a bowl with the icing sugar, orange zest, cinnamon and cardamom.

Brush a 21cm x 31cm baking tin with some of the melted butter. To build the baklava, start by placing one layer of filo in the base of the tin. Brush with melted butter and add another layer of filo. Continue this process until you have used 10 sheets of the filo pastry.

After you've made 10 layers, add a layer of the walnut, sugar and spice mixture, using all of the mix to form the layer. The baklava doesn't need much of this mixture, but it should be an even layer 2–3cm thick all the way across the tin.

Now make the cap by adding the next sheet of filo and brushing with butter. Repeat until another 10 layers are completed, finishing with a last layer of butter.

Carefully cut the baklava into a neat diagonal or square pattern in the tin before baking – a small serrated knife is best for this job. You want to end up with diamonds or squares about 3cm long on each of its 4 sides.

Place in the oven and cook for 30 minutes, then increase the heat to 200°C and bake for another 8–10 minutes, until it's light golden on top. >>

(If you have a fan oven, I recommend putting a wire rack on top of the baklava as it bakes, as oftentimes the fan can blow some of the filo pastry around.)

While the baklava is baking, place the sugar in a small saucepan with the water and the orange zest or orange blossom water. Slowly bring to a simmer, stirring. Continue to simmer until all the sugar has dissolved and the syrup is clear.

As soon as the baklava comes out of the oven, gently but liberally brush with plenty of the orange sugar syrup and then leave to cool. At this stage you may need to redo the original cuts to ease the individual baklava pieces from the tray.

The baklava keeps well if stored in an airtight container. It will be at its best for 3–4 days, but it will be fine for up to a week or more.

TIPS AND TRICKS

» Mix it up by replacing some of the walnuts with roughly chopped hazelnuts, almonds or pistachios to bring the total weight of nuts up to the same amount (125g in total).
» Though not as authentic or traditional, you could add some chopped dried dates, dried figs, dried apricots, dried cranberries or crystallised ginger to the nut filling. Just reduce the nuts by 50g and replace it with 50g of the dried fruit of your choice.

❈ Pear frangipane

This is a delicious, gluten-free tray bake that can evolve with the seasons. Apple and plum also work well here, and I reckon whole strawberries would too – and rhubarb, of course!

MAKES 9 SLICES

- 225g butter, softened
- 225g caster sugar
- 3 eggs
- 250g ground almonds
- 75g rice flour (or plain flour if you don't need it to be gluten-free)
- 1½ tsp gluten-free baking powder (or regular if you don't need it to be gluten-free)
- 1 tsp ground cinnamon
- Greek yogurt or vanilla ice cream, to serve

For the poached pears:
- 5 pears, neither overly firm nor overly ripe
- 500g caster sugar
- 1 litre water
- 1 cinnamon stick
- 1 star anise
- juice of ½ lemon

Preheat your oven to 190°C. Line a 21cm x 31cm baking tray with non-stick baking paper.

Peel and core the pears, then cut in half lengthways from top to tail. Place the 500g caster sugar and the water in a wide pot and heat, stirring regularly, until the sugar has dissolved. Add the pears along with the cinnamon stick, star anise and lemon juice (throw the squeezed lemon half in too) and simmer with the lid on for 10–15 minutes, until the pears are decently tender. Remove from the syrup so they don't overcook, as you need them to retain their shape. When cool, remove the spices and lemon from the syrup and allow the syrup to continue to cool for later.

To make the sponge, cream the butter and sugar together until light and fluffy. Add the rest of the ingredients except the pears and syrup and mix together thoroughly until everything is combined. Alternatively, you can make the sponge quite quickly in a food processor, but be careful not to overmix – a few pulses of the blade is perfect, just until the batter is combined. >>

Carefully tip the cake batter into the lined tray. Use the back of a spoon to spread the batter evenly in the tin, making sure to reach all the corners. Position the pears on top of the batter so that each slice or square of cake will contain a pear, then press down lightly. Depending on how you do this, you might have one pear half left over – cook's treat! Or see the tips and tricks below for some ideas.

Bake in the oven for 40 minutes, until the cake has risen and is golden brown. To check if the cake is ready to come out, pierce a skewer or small knife into the centre of the sponge. If the skewer comes out clean, the cake is ready. If there is still some batter clinging to it, leave it in for 5–10 minutes longer and check again. When cooked, remove from the oven and allow to cool completely.

To finish, gently brush the cooled cake generously with some of the reserved sugar syrup and cut into even squares. We serve this cake with some thick Greek yogurt on the side – the sharpness of the yogurt works amazingly well here – but some soft vanilla ice cream would be a worthwhile accompaniment too.

This cake will keep for 5–6 days in the fridge, uncut, but try to take it out and let it come up to room temperature before serving.

TIPS AND TRICKS

» You will have some syrup left over. This can be refrigerated for up to 1 month and used to poach more pears or any other fruit. It would also be delicious drizzled over baklava, replacing the orange syrup on page 295, or as the glaze for our scrolls on page 59.
» I recommend making extra poached pears. These would work sensationally diced up for breakfast with some Greek yogurt, in a bircher muesli (page 22) or served with our semolina pancakes (page 38), replacing the fruit in those recipes with the poached pear instead. Finely diced poached pear would also work well with the foolish mess on the next page instead of the rhubarb. It's also amazing to eat with some of the almond meringue from the foolish mess recipe and plain whipped cream with some toasted chopped almonds sprinkled on top and maybe a drizzle of the poaching syrup. To make extra, simply store the cooled pears in their syrup in the fridge.

❀ My foolish mess

More of a summery dish, this combines two great classics, Eton mess and a fruit fool, into one gorgeous dish. The idea is to make an Eton mess-style dessert, but replace the traditional whipped cream element with a fruity fool. We also add ground almonds to the meringue to make it that little bit more interesting, but you can skip this if you prefer, simply replacing the almonds with half their weight in sugar. However, by adding the almonds you end up with a lovely fool mixed up into the crunchy almond meringue.

We recommend rhubarb, but you can vary the fruit depending on what's in season. Using mashed fresh berries makes life very easy if you fancy, as there is no cooking involved for that step. See the tips and tricks for more ideas.

This is a dish where you can prepare all the individual components ahead of time and then just bring it all together before serving, which literally takes moments. The recipe below looks like a lot of steps are involved, but it's genuinely very easy, reasonably quick and so worth it. It's an absolute joy to make this.

SERVES 4–6

For the meringue:
- 5 super-fresh egg whites (approx. 180g)
- 360g caster sugar
- 75–100g ground almonds

For the fool base:
- 250ml cream
- 50g icing sugar
- 400g rhubarb (1 medium bunch)
- 200g caster sugar
- zest and juice of 1 orange
- 2 tsp ground ginger (optional)

To decorate:
- fresh mint
- toasted almond flakes

Preheat your oven to 90°C. Line a baking tray with non-stick baking paper.

To make the meringue, whisk your egg whites with one-third of the sugar in a very clean, large bowl (or the bowl of a stand mixer) until

stiff peaks form. Add another third of the sugar, whisking well, then repeat with the final third. Finally, gently fold in your ground almonds with a spatula until fully mixed through.

Using a large spoon and a spatula, spread the meringue over the lined tray in one even layer (you could spoon it out into individual dollops of meringue if you prefer). Bake for about 2 hours. The meringue should be fully hard pretty much all the way through – you want it to be a completely crunchy meringue to contrast with the softness of the fool. If it hasn't quite reached this stage, leave it for longer. Be patient!

You can test to see if the meringue is ready by simply poking a knife or your finger through the centre and seeing what it's like in the middle. This is ultimately going to be broken up, so don't worry about inflicting a bit of damage. It should be pretty hard and crunchy all the way through, but a little chewiness isn't the end of the world either. When it's ready, turn off the oven and leave the meringue in the oven to cool in the dry heat.

To make the fool base, place the cream in a large bowl or the bowl of a stand mixer. Sift the icing sugar over the cream and whisk until it's nice and light. It should be a firmer whipped cream as opposed to an extremely soft one, but be careful not to over-whisk, otherwise you'll end up with butter! Refrigerate until ready to serve.

To make the rhubarb, you've got two options: on the hob or in the oven. I've a marginal preference for the oven, but do what suits you best.

To make the rhubarb on the hob, wash the rhubarb well and chop off the leafy tops and the base of the stalks. Cut the stalks into chunks the length of a matchstick. Place in a wide pot or pan with a lid and add the caster sugar, orange zest and juice and the ginger, if using. Place the pan on a medium heat and bring to a simmer. Put the lid on and simmer gently for 10 minutes or so, until it's beginning to get tender. Leave for a few minutes longer if needed, but be careful – you want it to be tender but still holding its shape. I tend to aim for it to be just hitting that point and then I take it off the heat and leave it to cool in the syrup, which lets it cook a little more in the residual heat. If you're worried it will overcook, take out the rhubarb with a slotted spoon and lay it out on a large plate or tray to cool separately from the syrup.

To make the rhubarb in the oven, preheat your oven to 180°C. Wash and prepare the rhubarb as above. Place in a shallow baking dish and add the sugar, orange zest and juice and the ginger, if using. Cover with tin foil and place in the oven for 12–15 minutes. Check the rhubarb after 12 minutes to see if it has begun to soften, applying the same judgement as in the method above. As soon as it's done, remove it from the oven and allow it to cool and further cook in the residual heat of the syrup.

When it's time to assemble the foolish mess, it needs to be served immediately. It can't sit for too long or it will break down, with the cream softening the meringue. While this isn't a disaster and it will still taste delicious, a big part of this experience is the texture contrast of the crunchy against the soft, so it would be a shame to lose that.

Over a large bowl, break up your cooled meringue into rough chunks about the size of a walnut. Let everything fall into the bowl, the big pieces and the small. In a separate bowl, mash half of the rhubarb and some of the syrup with a fork, then fold this thoroughly through the whipped cream. Mix the rhubarb cream with the broken meringue – it should be a mess (literally!) but not overmixed to the point that the meringue has disintegrated.

Bring it to the table in one big bowl and serve, dividing into individual bowls and casually spooning over the remaining rhubarb chunks, some torn fresh mint and some toasted almond flakes if you fancy.

TIPS AND TRICKS

» The meringue can be made in larger batches and stored in an airtight container for 2–3 weeks. It must be a fully cooked, crunchy meringue, however, otherwise it won't hold that crunchiness for as long.
» Throwing some fresh hulled strawberries in with the rhubarb when cooking it is quite delightful. I might leave out the ginger in this case, but that's entirely up to you!
» Outside of rhubarb season, you can simply use fresh berries, half of them mashed up and folded through the cream, or make a berry and rose compote using frozen berries (see page 343) and just use that in place of the rhubarb when bringing the dish together.
» Other alternatives to berries are kiwi or pineapple, chopped into smaller chunks (do not purée these). Pomegranate seeds look sensational sprinkled over this too.
» For extra specialness, scatter some edible flowers such as marigolds, rose petals or nasturtiums over the finished dish. They add a wow factor to make it a real beauty.

❈ Lemon, yogurt and passionfruit cake

This sensational cake is based on a delightful confection made by our dear friends at Loafer Bread in Melbourne. It ticks all the right boxes in terms of moistness and flavour, with all that wonderful syrup soaked into it.

A word of warning, though: this light-crumbed cake does require gentle handling in the making, as it uses whisked egg whites for its airy structure. That's not to deter you – in fact, it has once or twice not baked right for us and it has still been delicious. Our barista Bruno called it 'Grandmother's Cake' to capture the sense that it's okay to make mistakes and end up with something that can still be enjoyed, as it was made with love nonetheless and should still be appreciated.

MAKES 1 X 20CM CAKE

- 170g butter, softened (salted or unsalted is fine)
- 130g caster sugar
- 3 eggs, separated
- zest of 2 lemons
- 3 passionfruit, seeds scraped out
- 1 tsp vanilla extract
- 260g plain flour
- 3½ tsp baking powder
- 230g natural yogurt
- Greek yogurt or crème fraîche, to serve

For the passionfuit syrup:
- 50g caster sugar
- 75ml water
- zest and juice of 1 lemon
- 2 passionfruit, seeds scraped out

Preheat your oven to 160°C. Grease a 20cm loose-bottomed cake tin with some of the softened butter (use a pastry brush or a piece of kitchen paper to rub it in), then sprinkle with flour and toss it around until the entire interior surface is covered. Turn the tin upside down and give it a gentle tap to get rid of any excess flour. Cut out a circle of non-stick baking paper to line the bottom of the tin.

Cream your butter and sugar together until soft and a little fluffy. A mixer is perfect, but there's no harm in having a workout if doing it by hand in a large bowl with a wooden spoon. Add the egg yolks, lemon zest, passionfruit seeds and the vanilla, mixing thoroughly so that you end up with a nice soft paste. >>

Sift the flour and baking powder together in a separate bowl. Fold one-third of the yogurt through the butter and sugar mix, then fold in one-third of the flour. Alternate folding in each of the remaining thirds of the yogurt and flour, making sure not to overmix but still ensuring everything is well incorporated.

Whisk the egg whites in a separate clean, dry bowl until they form soft peaks. Add one-third of the whisked egg white to the batter, being careful not to overwork it but rather folding it in gently until it is just incorporated. Repeat in two more steps.

Scrape the batter gently into the tin. You need to be careful with all these steps in order to ensure you don't knock the air out of the cake by being heavy handed with the fragile egg whites. Level the batter with a spatula or palette knife. In fact, it's no harm to push it towards the sides, leaving a marginal depression or dent in the middle of the tin as you want the cake to be pretty flat and even when it comes out.

Pop into your oven (gently!) and bake for 40–50 minutes. Check after 35 minutes by quickly opening the oven door and giving the cake a quick, gentle shake – it's done when there's not much of a wobble in the middle. If it's near that point, take it out and do the skewer test: if it's not quite set and/or the skewer doesn't come out clean after being inserted into the middle of the cake, put it back in and check again in 6–8 minutes. Only take it out when it's done, and it's done when it passes the skewer test. After all, who doesn't get upset when their cake collapses? Remove from the oven to cool in the tin.

While the cake is baking and cooling, make your passionfruit syrup. Put the sugar in a small saucepan with the water. Bring to a simmer, then add the lemon zest and juice and the passionfruit seeds. Simmer gently for a further 4 minutes and put aside.

When the cake has cooled, leaving it in the tin, pierce the cake repeatedly with a skewer, making about 20 incisions deep into the cake, all over the top. Spoon one-third of the syrup over the cake and wait a few minutes, until it has all soaked in, then spoon over another third, wait again, then spoon over the final third after another few minutes.

Let the cake sit like that for 1 hour, then take it out of the tin, cut into slices and serve with Greek yogurt or crème fraîche. It holds well for 2–3 days if stored in an airtight tin at room temperature.

» Cakes can be a lot of work, and this one is no exception – it does require a bit more time than some other cake recipes. Happily, not only is it worth it, but you can scale it up if you've a few cake tins. Make double or treble the recipe, dividing it evenly between your cake tins and bake off. If you let them cool fully and then wrap them thoroughly directly in the tin, these cakes will freeze perfectly. When ready to serve, simply defrost them and then skewer and douse in the hot syrup (it's important that the syrup is hot) as per the final steps of the recipe.

» You can leave out the passionfruit entirely and add 50–80g poppy seeds to the cake instead.

» Replacing the lemon zest and juice with orange in the batter and the syrup would also work quite well.

❁ Friands

My sister-in-law, Angie, hailing all the way from New Zealand, introduced me to friands a number of years ago and I haven't looked back since. Often called financiers in Europe, these are popping up on more and more café menus across the land. Not only are they easy to make, but they are really quite delicious and hold well for several days. Plus you can make any number of variations to the recipe – see some of ours on the next page.

MAKES 12–14 FRIANDS

- ○ 240g egg whites (about 10 egg whites)
- ○ 300g icing sugar
- ○ 100g plain flour
- ○ 1 tsp baking powder
- ○ ½ tsp ground star anise, cinnamon, fennel or nutmeg (optional but wonderful)
- ○ 180g ground almonds
- ○ 220g butter, melted

Flavour variations:
- ○ see the options on the next page

Preheat your oven to 180°C. For this recipe, you can use a tray of individual rectangular moulds 9cm long by 2.5cm wide or round muffin tin moulds 7cm in diameter and 4cm deep. Prepare the tins or moulds by brushing them generously with some melted butter and dusting very lightly with plain flour. It's critical this is done thoroughly or the cakes might stick to the tin/mould when you try to remove them.

Place the egg whites in a large, clean, dry bowl and whisk gently until loosened and frothy – you're just aiming to break down and froth up the egg white, but not so much that it forms soft or stiff peaks, like for a meringue.

Sift the icing sugar, flour, baking powder and star anise (or alternative spice, if using) together, then add to the ground almonds in a large bowl. Make a well in the centre and pour in the frothy egg white foam and stir lightly to form a soft batter. Pour in the melted butter and mix well to combine. At this stage you can fold in your optional ingredients.

Divide the batter evenly between the tins and bake in the oven for 35 minutes. The cakes are done when a sharp knife or metal skewer inserted into the centre comes out clean and the cakes themselves are a light golden brown colour. Leave to cool well before removing from the tin or mould.

Raspberry and white chocolate friands

In the café, we add some fresh raspberries and chopped white chocolate to the mix before baking and then top with a white chocolate and rose ganache and some freeze-dried or fresh raspberries when serving. You'll need 1 punnet of raspberries and 100g white chocolate. Follow the master recipe but press 2–3 raspberries and a few chunks of white chocolate into each cake. To decorate, make a batch of the white chocolate ganache on page 283 and hold back one raspberry for topping each cake.

Blackcurrant and lemon friands

Follow the master recipe, adding 8–10 blackcurrants per cake and some lemon zest, then brush with some lemon sugar syrup when they come out of the oven. To make the lemon sugar syrup, bring the zest and juice of 1 lemon to the boil with 100g caster sugar and 50ml water, then reduce down by a third to form a nice syrup. Allow to cool before brushing over the cakes.

Blackberry and orange friands

Add 2–3 blackberries per cake and some grated orange zest. An orange sugar syrup would work well here – just replace the lemon zest and juice with orange from the blackcurrant and lemon recipe.

Brown butter, lemon and thyme friands

Place the butter required in the master recipe into a pan and place on the heat to melt. Add some picked thyme or lemon thyme leaves. Brown the butter as per our instructions on page 356, then add this as per the butter in the master recipe along with the zest of 1 lemon and finish as described above. The friand will be a little darker than usual and have a slightly nuttier taste. Make the lemon syrup as described in the blackcurrant and lemon variation, but add the leaves from 2 sprigs of thyme. Drizzle the finished cakes with the syrup and decorate with some thyme flowers.

DRINKS

We've shared just a few of our homemade drinks here
for you to enjoy. Though these are a little more indulgent
(especially the Prosecco cocktails), as with a lot of what
we do, we tend to have a lighter hand with the sweetness
so proceed with caution in concocting these potions,
remembering that you can always add more but it's very
difficult to take something out once it's added. Please
use these as a starting point to experiment!

❀ Brother Hubbard's hot chocolate

When the barista chatted to the baker, this is what we ended up with! A casual chat between myself and our dear barista, Bruno, led to this meeting of minds – a really rich hot chocolate that actually tastes of chocolate. We serve this in a deconstructed fashion in the cafés. Not only is it more fun, but it also allows you to control how chocolatey or milky you like yours to be. We've noticed that orders tend to come in clusters – once one person orders it, those seated nearby inevitably order it too.

SERVES 2

For the ganache:
○ 50ml single cream
○ 50g good-quality chocolate (ideally at least 55% cocoa solids)

For the milk:
○ 300ml milk
○ 2 heaped tsp cocoa powder
○ 2 tsp dark brown sugar
○ pinch of salt (optional)

Make your ganache by heating the cream almost to the boiling point in a little saucepan. Remove from the heat and add the chocolate, stirring well to make sure it's fully melted. You should have a rich, smooth ganache. Set aside.

Put your milk in a separate pot and bring to a simmer. Whisk in the cocoa and sugar and remove from the heat just as it's coming to the boil.

To serve, warm your mugs with hot water first. Put in a generous amount of the ganache – about 2 tablespoons in each mug – and top up with the hot cocoa milk. Stir well and taste, adding more chocolate or a little more sugar until it's perfect for you.

If you're making this for a few people, heat up a jug and fill it with the ganache. Add the cocoa milk to another large heated jug and then allow people to make the hot chocolate themselves in their own warm mugs. >>

Mocha

To make this into a mocha with an added caffeine kick, add one or two shots of espresso to the ganache in each mug and stir well before adding the hot cocoa milk.

Hot chocolate with salted caramel

If you love salted caramel, why not add a good tablespoon into your hot chocolate? Mix it in when adding the hot milk. The sugar overload is surely outweighed by the deliciousness of it all. See page 279 for our salted caramel recipe.

Festive hot chocolate

At Christmastime, we make this festive by adding a little ground nutmeg and cinnamon (and a touch of ground cloves too if desired) along with the cocoa in the milk. We serve finely ground praline on the side for people to sprinkle over their drink when it's made – it's best enjoyed by eating it with a spoon off the top before it sinks!) See page 341 for our praline recipe.

TIPS AND TRICKS

» We are sticklers for the mugs and jugs being warm! The milk should be piping hot to compensate for the ganache being a little cooler.

» For extra frothy hot chocolate at home, bring your cocoa-sugar-milk mix almost to the boil, then pour into a warmed clean French press (cafetière). Push the filter up and down very rapidly to foam the milk. Do this vigorously for about a minute, then proceed with bringing the drink together as outlined above.

» The chocolate ganache itself will happily keep in the fridge for several weeks – the cream is 'cooked', so it won't spoil as quickly. You'll need to soften it up to use, however, with a quick visit to the microwave or in a saucepan set over a gentle heat.

» My dear James insists a pinch of salt added to the milk makes all the difference, and I'm inclined to agree with him.

❁ Iced Moroccan mint tea

Refreshing on a warm day, on its own or with a meal, our version aims to be lighter and certainly less sweet than what you might encounter elsewhere. In my view, this makes it a drink focused on refreshment.

- green tea, as required
- 2 large bunches of fresh mint
- sugar or honey, as required (see below)
- lemon juice, to taste
- ice cubes, to serve
- lemon slices, to garnish

First off, brew your green tea. The usual rule of thumb is to brew by adding about 2 grams of green tea to every 150ml of hot water (using a pot of water just off the boil). So if you want 600ml of tea, use about 8 grams of tea leaves. Leave to infuse for 1–3 minutes, depending on how strong you like your brew and depending on the particular tea you're using.

Once brewed, pour the tea through a strainer and add a good bunch of fresh mint – be generous. Leave to cool, then put into the fridge to chill for several hours.

Make your sugar syrup by mixing equal parts water to caster sugar and bringing to the boil in a saucepan. Depending on how much tea you've brewed, 30 grams of each will probably do it – anything left over will hold for a long time in the fridge for the next time you make this drink (or use it as a sweetener for some of our other homemade drinks). If you prefer not to use sugar, you can make a honey syrup in the same way, simply substituting the honey for the sugar. Leave to cool.

Once the tea and sugar syrup have chilled adequately, you can make the iced tea. Add the green tea to a large jug or pot, removing the mint. Add a decent dash of lemon juice and some sugar syrup to taste, as well as a generous amount of chilled water. Taste, adjusting to get the flavour just right – it should be light and refreshing, and in my opinion, not overly sweet. You will need to play around with it a bit to get it to your liking.

Now take one large mug of the drink and purée this with another generous bunch of fresh mint leaves in a small container using a stick blender or in a large blender. Add this green purée back to the mint tea, stir well and give it a final taste, adjusting as you like.

Serve over ice with some additional sprigs of mint in the glass and maybe a fresh slice of lemon.

TIPS AND TRICKS

» You can store this in the fridge for 3 days, but I recommend skipping the very last stage of puréeing the mint until you're about to serve the drink.
» You might find that the drink is adequately minty from the initial mint infusion without the need for the final element of puréed mint.

❀ Raspberry, apple and rose

Referred to as 'the RAR' by people in the know (i.e. those working in the cafés), this is an extremely refreshing yet fragrant cold drink and a thing of beauty to behold. As with all of our homemade house drinks, a very light hand with sugar is necessary – it shocks me how sweet shop-bought drinks are. Here, you're just adding a little sweetness to the help the natural flavours along.

MAKES 6 LARGE GLASSES

o 50g caster or granulated sugar
o 120g fresh or frozen raspberries (1 small punnet or equivalent)
o 50–75ml fresh apple juice (the best quality you can manage or juice your own!)
o lemon juice, to taste
o rosewater, to taste
o fresh mint sprigs, to garnish
o ice cubes, to serve

First make your sugar syrup: bring 50ml of water to the boil in a small pot and add the sugar. Stir well so the sugar dissolves and set aside to cool.

Next, put your raspberries, apple juice and 500ml water into your blender and whizz for several minutes, until perfectly puréed. If using a stick blender, blend the ingredients together in a jug or large pot. Let it blend for twice as long as you think is necessary. Pour the mix through a very fine sieve into a large jug or pot to strain out the raspberry seeds.

This next bit is entirely up to you – add a decent amount of water, a good squeeze of lemon, the rosewater (½ teaspoon at a time) and a little of the cooled sugar syrup. Bring it together until it tastes right. We like it to be:

» *Light* – well diluted as opposed to being a heavy, syrupy drink. You want it to be refreshing and healthy and you want to be able to drink more than one glass!
» *Not too sweet* – start with just a little sugar syrup, adding more if necessary. This drink should not taste overly sweet.
» *Just a little rosy* – rosewater is a powerful ingredient, so only use a very small amount. Remember, you can always add more but you can't remove it!
» *Nicely acidic* – the lemon is there to give it a nice sharpness that adds to the refreshing experience.

Serve with a sprig of mint over ice in a glass that's chilled from the freezer if you really want to impress. >>

» Frozen raspberries are particularly handy for this recipe, but check the news as there were some scares about using frozen berries a while back. If this is still the case or if you're uncertain, bring them to the boil in a little pot, barely covered with water, and use this, cooled, as the mix you purée.

» Once the drink is strained and before you add the other ingredients, you can store this as a fresh cordial for a few days in the fridge.

» You didn't hear it from us, but you can use the base cordial to make an amazing cocktail using vodka or gin (we christened it the RARita!). Use the same approach outlined above in terms of getting the balance of the drink right. You might want to make it somewhat less diluted with water, then add your shot of vodka or gin in each glass and serve over ice.

» If you fancy adding a little fizz, hold off on some of the water and instead add sparkling water to taste.

» If you want an extra special fancy fizz, why not make this into a Prosecco cocktail? See page 318 for how to make our rosita cocktail.

❊ Prosecco, three ways

We tend to go for the crisper, drier varieties of Prosecco with a clean palate. After tasting many of the various Proseccos out there (any excuse, really), we realised we were going for something as close to Champagne as possible without paying a premium price. A dry Cava or French Crémant or even a Sekt from further afield should do the trick. The better the wine, the better the cocktail.

To make your brunch, evening, day – even your life – that little bit extra special, here are a few Prosecco cocktails for you to try.

The orangey mimosa

So, so simple: add one part fresh orange juice (ideally strained) to three parts Prosecco. A tiny drop of orange blossom water gives it an extra orangey fragrance. Depending on the establishment, this can often be made with too much orange juice (it's cheaper!) – we prefer it tasting quite light on the orange. But if you prefer otherwise, adjust the ratio to what you like. As always, tasting is the best way to go here.

The rosita

Blend the following into a purée: a handful of fresh or frozen raspberries with some fresh apple juice, a little lemon juice, a spoonful of honey and a little rosewater to taste, starting with a little and then adding more if needed. Use this as the base for the rosita, adding about three parts Prosecco to one part of this purée, and serve with a sprig of mint in the glass. Be careful, though, as it can sometimes foam up, so add a little Prosecco at a time rather than all at once. Taste and adjust accordingly and maybe add an additional raspberry in the glass when serving.

The Silk Road spritz

Taking us from Iran to Italy, this incorporates two of our favourite things: Prosecco and pomegranate, together at last. Wash one pomegranate and cut it in half along the equator. Deseed one half, then squeeze the other half over a classic citrus press to extract the juice from it (you might need to strain this if any bits fall in). Juice half a lemon and add 1 dessertspoon of honey, mixing well so the lemon dissolves the honey. Add this to the pomegranate juice. To make the drink, add one part of the pomegranate base to three parts Prosecco. Add a teaspoon of pomegranate seeds and a little sprig of mint to each glass.

+ Supporting Recipes

+ Tomato and pepper sauce

This sauce is so versatile that it's well worth making more than one batch – you'll see that we use it a lot throughout this book! See the tips and tricks for lots of ideas.

- 1 red pepper
- 1 yellow pepper
- 1 dessertspoon oil
- 4 fresh tomatoes, diced into 1cm cubes (or 200g tinned chopped tomatoes)
- 1 tsp paprika
- 1 tsp ground cumin
- pinch of caster sugar (optional)

Wash each pepper, cut them in half from stem to tail and remove the seeds and stalk, then cut across into 1cm-thick slices.

Heat the oil in a saucepan set over a medium heat, then add the peppers and cook for 10 minutes with the lid on, until they're soft but not falling apart (you want there to be a slight bite). Add the tomatoes to the pan once the peppers are cooked and cook for a further 5–8 minutes, with the lid off, until the tomatoes are softened and you have a chunky-style sauce (if you are using tinned tomatoes, you might need to cook it for about 5 minutes longer so the sauce reduces). Add your spices and cook for a further 2 minutes. Now taste the sauce, adding more spice, salt, pepper or even a little pinch of sugar if you feel it needs it. It should be a wonderfully rich and flavourful sauce.

Stored in an airtight container, this sauce will keep in the fridge for 4 days or up to 2 months in the freezer.

TIPS AND TRICKS

» This pepper and tomato sauce is incredibly versatile. It's the base for our Turkish eggs menemen (page 55) and our shakshuka baked eggs (page 72), so make a double batch so that you can make one of the other dishes in a jiffy. We also use it with our savoury beghrir pancakes (page 42).
» The sauce is also amazing in an omelette or as a sauce to serve warm alongside our tortilla (page 117) or as the base for Itzi's cod stew (page 242). It could also feature as a nice sauce for pasta, perhaps with some pan-fried chorizo added, on top of a baked potato or to serve alongside any grilled fish or meat.

+ Flatbread

Bread-making was actually what got me into cooking, as a homage to my grandfather who was a master baker way back in his youth. While I may have been trying to revive a family tradition, I'm afraid my granddad would not have encountered this Middle Eastern staple, a simple flatbread. This is perfect with hummus or any manner of dips, a salad or a soup. It's ideal to serve with any meal, really, freshly baked and always served warm.

MAKES 8–10 FLATBREADS

○ 250g strong white flour
○ 2 tsp cumin seeds, toasted and roughly crushed (see page 352)
○ 1 level tsp salt
○ 150ml warm water
○ 10g dried fast action yeast
○ 1 level tsp caster sugar
○ 1 tbsp olive oil, plus extra for brushing

For the topping (any or all of the following):
○ za'atar
○ sumac
○ sesame seeds
○ poppy seeds
○ flaky sea salt

To make the dough, place the flour, crushed cumin seeds and salt in a mixing bowl (if making the bread by hand) or the bowl of a food mixer (if making it by machine). Heat the water so that it's a little warmer than your body temperature. Dissolve the yeast and sugar in a little of the warm water, then add it to the flour along with the oil. Add three-quarters of the remaining warm water and mix well.

Knead the bread by hand or machine. If you are kneading the dough by hand, see our recommended method on page 349. Either way, add more water if the mix is too dry and not forming a springy, elastic dough after a few minutes (see page 351 for a description of what this should be like). Continue kneading for about 8 minutes. It's done when it passes the following test: take a little ball in your fingers and stretch out the dough – if you can get it to the point where a thin 'window' or skin of dough forms that's just about thin enough for you to see light through it, it's ready.

Put a little oil in the bowl you mixed the dough in, then form the dough into a ball and turn the dough over in it to lightly coat it in the oil. >>

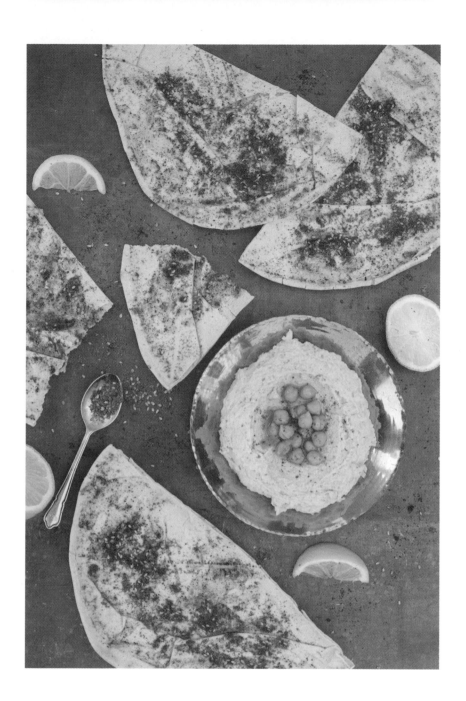

Cover the bowl with a clean damp cloth or some cling film. Set aside in a warm place and leave to rise for 20–30 minutes, until it has doubled in size.

While the dough is rising, preheat your oven to its maximum temperature, which should be about 250°C. The oven needs to be very hot as these flatbreads cook so quickly. You will also need 2 baking trays (or else cook 4 flatbreads at a time, doing 2 batches in total), which should be preheated in the oven.

Divide the dough into 4–5 equal pieces of about 120g each. Roll out each piece into a long oval shape about the size of an oval dinner plate. The dough should get to the thickness of a coin. Repeat for the other dough balls, then cut each oval in half diagonally.

Take the baking trays out of the oven and line with non-stick baking paper. Place each flatbread on the lined baking trays, but avoid them touching. Brush lightly with oil and sprinkle with your toppings, then crumble the salt flakes over. Leave to rest for 5 minutes.

Place in the oven and bake for 5–8 minutes or so. The breads should be light golden and browned on the edges and may even have puffed up. Remove from the oven and cover with a clean towel. Leave to rest for about 5 minutes, but longer is fine too.

TIPS AND TRICKS

» Make a double batch, baking off the bread fresh in batches. It will reheat perfectly in a medium oven for 5 minutes the next day.

+ Harissa

A valuable and versatile addition to any kitchen, this powerful spice condiment gives a punch to so many dishes. Originating from North Africa, it's now becoming more and more popular as a base flavour for many dishes and dressings. As with virtually everything in our kitchen, we make this from scratch. It's not too much work and a little goes a long way, so a batch will keep you going for some time.

One of the most popular ways we use it is folded through crème fraîche with a little lemon juice as a sauce for our poached chicken sandwich. It works well as a dressing base for a potato or couscous salad and we mix it with lemon and olive oil as a soup dressing from time to time. We also use it as a base flavour in our Moroccan zalouk (page 100).

MAKES 1 JAR

- 8 medium red chillies
- 1 medium onion, roughly chopped
- 10 garlic cloves, roughly chopped
- good olive oil
- 1 x 400g tin of chopped tomatoes
- 2 tsp cumin seeds, toasted and ground to a rough powder (see page 352)
- 2 tsp coriander seeds, toasted and ground to a rough powder
- 2 tsp caraway seeds, toasted and ground to a rough powder

Preheat your oven to 190°C. Cut the tops off all the chillies and cut them in half lengthways. Using a teaspoon, scrape the seeds out of half of the chillies. We leave some seeds in for heat, but all of them may be a bit too much! Or you can leave them out altogether if you prefer. Either way, chop the chillies roughly.

Place the chopped chillies in a roasting tray with the onion, garlic and a drizzle of oil. Pop into the oven and roast for about 25 minutes, until the onion, chillies and garlic have browned nicely. Add the tomatoes to the roasting tray and cook for a further 15–20 minutes. Remove the tray from the oven and allow to cool slightly.

Transfer the contents of the tray to a food processor with the toasted ground spices and blitz to a paste. Alternatively, use a hand-held blender in a deep bowl. >>

Store the harissa in a sealed container for up to 3 weeks in the fridge. Cover the harissa with a small amount of good olive oil, which helps preserve the harissa for longer by keeping the air from contacting the paste.

TIPS AND TRICKS

» If you find the harissa too hot, add some tomato purée to the finished paste to dilute the intensity somewhat.
» Such a versatile ingredient – use it to add a spicy kick to soups, sauces and dressings.

+ Eamon's chorizo jam

Eamon says: '*This versatile recipe holds a place very close to my heart. I'm super proud of it, as it combines some of my favourite flavours into such a delectable treat.*' With hints of maple, coffee and a sweet smokiness, it sits proud atop some fried eggs and sourdough for a tasty brunch, it makes enough for 4 rarebits (page 92) or serve in a bowl with some cheese, pickles and flatbread. There are countless ways to serve this versatile creation. How will you eat yours?

SERVES 4–6 AS A STARTER OR NIBBLE WITH SOME BREAD

- 250g cooking chorizo
- 1 medium or large onion (150–200g)
- 2 garlic cloves, crushed
- 50g muscovado sugar
- 50ml espresso coffee
- 2 tbsp cider vinegar
- 1 tbsp maple syrup
- pinch of salt

First let's do some preparation: peel the onion and slice it as finely as you can – the thinner the slice, the quicker it melts when cooked. Chop your chorizo into small bite-sized pieces and measure out the rest of your ingredients.

Heat a saucepan on a medium-high heat – there's no need to add any oil. Add half the chorizo and let its natural fats do the work. Remove when crisp and repeat with the other half. At this stage, remove all but 1 tablespoon of the smoky oil from the pan, turn down the heat and add the onion. Sauté for 10–15 minutes over a low-medium heat, until soft and caramelised. Add the garlic and cook for 5 minutes more.

Add the chorizo back to the pan along with the rest of the ingredients and cook on a medium heat for about 20 minutes, stirring regularly to avoid it sticking to the pan. After the 20 minutes, check the consistency: it should be a glossy, jammy texture. If there is still a lot of liquid, just keep reducing until it's thick.

Allow to cool slightly before digging in. This is best served at room temperature or slightly warm. Store in the fridge for up to 1 week.

TIPS AND TRICKS

» Get the best chorizo you can for this recipe. Better-quality chorizo has more flavour and more natural oils. >>

» You are looking for cooking chorizo, which is less common than the dried variety found in a lot of supermarkets. You can find it in any good deli. We recommend Gubbeen fresh chorizo from County Cork or a good-quality Spanish cooking chorizo.

» I recommend using the strongest coffee you can get your hands on. Fresh espresso is best, but it doesn't need to be hot. If instant is your only option, add an extra spoonful.

+ Falafel crumb

I came up with this one day when trying to see what we could use as a new crunchy crumble to put over salads and soups. It's been a firm favourite ever since.

This recipe does absolutely require dried chickpeas that have been soaked. Tinned chickpeas just won't work here.

- 200g dried chickpeas, soaked overnight (see page 359)
- 1 tbsp lemon juice
- 1 tsp ground cumin
- 1 tsp ground coriander
- 1 tsp sweet or smoked paprika
- dash of olive oil
- pinch of salt

To soak the chickpeas, see page 359 for our recommended method. The next day, when you're ready to cook, preheat your oven to 180°C.

Drain and rinse the soaked chickpeas, making sure you drain them really well. Pat them dry in a clean tea towel, then mix with all the other ingredients in a bowl.

Spread the chickpeas in a single layer in a roasting tray and roast in the oven for 30 minutes. The chickpeas should be crispy – if they aren't, cook them for longer until they reach this stage, turning the oven down to 160°C. When they're done, turn off the oven and let the tray sit in the oven for another 30 minutes so that the chickpeas dry out and crisp up even more.

These are lovely just as they are, but you can also roughly crush or grind them (a food processor is best) to use as a crumble on top of a soup or over a salad to add a really great texture as well as a nice spiced flavour.

TIPS AND TRICKS

» These are a great snack to have with a beer or a glass of wine and maybe some marinated olives (page 269) as a pre-dinner nibble.

+ Brother Hubbard hot sauce

After hours of research, tons of tastings and plenty of chilli-induced injuries, we finally arrived at a hot sauce we are proud to call our own. It's sweet, tart and packs a punch. Toss it with some crispy roast chicken wings (page 249), drizzle on an avocado with a slice of sourdough or serve with some cream cheese and celery for a light snack. This is such a simple recipe that we urge you to make a double batch. It lasts for weeks, but may well be gone within days.

MAKES 1 JAR

- 250g medium red chillies
- drizzle of oil
- 1 carrot, roughly chopped
- 1 onion, roughly chopped
- 6 garlic cloves, roughly chopped
- 500ml cider or white wine vinegar
- 100ml boiling water

Take half of the chillies, chop off the tops and slice the chillies down the middle. Using a teaspoon, scoop out all the seeds and white pith and roughly chop the chillies. For the remaining chillies, cut the tops off and then just chop roughly, seeds, pith and all. Leaving the seeds in half of the chillies will add the nice heat you're looking for.

Heat a medium pot set over a medium heat with a drizzle of oil and add the chopped carrot, onion and garlic. Sauté for 10–15 minutes – do not colour, just soften. Add the chillies to the pot along with the vinegar. Bring to the boil, then reduce the heat and simmer for 10 minutes. Remove from the heat and allow to cool slightly.

Place the vegetables in a food processor or blender. While blitzing, gradually add the boiling water to thin out the sauce and develop the consistency you're looking for. We find that adding the full 100ml of water leaves you with a thick but pourable sauce that's perfect for our purposes. Store in the fridge in an airtight tub or sterilised jar for 2–3 weeks.

TIPS AND TRICKS

» We like to keep some texture to the sauce, but if you like a thinner, more liquid sauce, add a little more water and strain the sauce through a fine mesh sieve to remove most of the solids.

+ Preserved lemons

This wonder ingredient is an absolute must to have in your fridge. A little goes a long way and they add an amazing zing to a dish. If you are not inclined to make these yourself, you can buy a jar of them in any good Middle Eastern shop or well-stocked supermarket.

MAKES 1 X 1 LITRE JAR

- 250g fine sea salt
- 8–10 lemons
- extra freshly squeezed lemon juice, if needed

You'll need a 1 litre glass jar or a medium plastic container of equivalent size, sterilised by putting it in a pot of boiling water for 2 minutes.

First add a layer of salt to the bottom of the sterilised jar or container. Rinse the lemons and scrub them well.

Top and tail each lemon, then cut two-thirds of the way down the lemon in a cross-section. To do this, cut the lemons lengthways in half but not all the way down to the base – leave them connected at the bottom. Then make another cut as if you were about to cut the lemons into quarters, but again, don't cut it all the way through. Gently pull open the lemons and sprinkle well with the salt, inside and out.

After salting, press each lemon quite forcefully into the bottom of the jar or container so that the juices are extracted and rise up to the top of the jar (a metal spoon helps with this step). Repeat with all the lemons and cover the top with more lemon juice if needed and a last handful of salt.

Close with a lid and store in the fridge. The preserved lemons will be ready after about 3 weeks, but do rotate the jar several times over this period.

When using the lemons, remove some from the jar and rinse to remove the salt. Remove the pulp and seeds with a spoon, then thinly slice or dice the lemon rind to use in your chosen recipe. The preserved lemons can be stored in the fridge for up to 6 months. >>

» Throughout this book we suggest using lemon zest more often than not. Ideally you'll want to use unwaxed lemons if you're zesting them, but washing them in hot water or quickly blanching them in boiling water works too.

» These make a great gift if you know anyone who loves cooking Middle Eastern food. They will think of you every time they use the lemons (which will be often).

» Experiment by adding whole spices like coriander seeds, fennel seeds, bay leaves and peppercorns or even sweet spices like cinnamon sticks and cloves.

» For uses of preserved lemons, see our recipes for beetroot and preserved lemon fritters (page 79), mackerel, baby potato, pea and fennel salad (page 182) and Jonathan's tagine of hake and fennel (page 238).

+ Tomato and apple ketchup

Not quite a ketchup but existing somewhere between a red sauce and a brown sauce, this tomato and apple concoction sits amazingly well on our bacon sandwich (page 47) or as an accompaniment to cold meats and cheeses.

A word to the wise: cayenne pepper is an extremely hot spice and can easily overwhelm the taste buds. Use it sparingly to give this sauce a nice mellow heat rather than making it a hot sauce. The flavours will develop a lot more when the sauce has cooled to room temperature or if it's cold from the fridge.

MAKES 1 JAR

- 2 black peppercorns or ½ tsp ground black pepper
- 2 cloves or ½ tsp ground cloves
- 2 allspice berries or ½ tsp ground allspice
- 400g ripe tomatoes, diced, or 1 x 400g tin of chopped tomatoes
- 150g caster sugar
- 110g eating apples, cored and roughly chopped
- 110g onions, chopped
- 110ml cider vinegar
- 1 level tsp salt
- ¼ tsp cayenne pepper

Using a pestle and mortar or a spice grinder, grind the peppercorns, cloves and allspice berries to a fine powder (or use ½ teaspoon of pre-ground versions of each of these spices and mix to combine).

Place all the other ingredients in a large pot and add the spice mix. Bring the mix to the boil, then reduce the heat and simmer for about 10 minutes, stirring regularly. It's ready to come off the heat when the tomatoes have broken up and the apple is nearly mush.

Leave to cool for 4–5 minutes, then liquidise in a blender or food processor. Cool completely, then refrigerate for up to 4 weeks.

+ Pickled green chillies

This recipe was inspired by all those late-night nibbles in the local kebab shop. These are really delicious as part of a mezze or sliced and added to a sandwich.

MAKES 1 X 1 LITRE JAR

- 500g long green cayenne chillies
- 500–800ml white wine or apple cider vinegar, to cover
- 2 tbsp caster sugar
- 1 tbsp yellow mustard seeds
- 2 star anise
- pinch of salt

Wash the chillies, then prick each one three or four times with the tip of a sharp pointed knife or a needle. This allows the pickling vinegar to get in.

Heat the vinegar in a medium pot with the sugar, spices and a pinch of salt. Simmer the liquid for 5 minutes, stirring to dissolve the sugar.

Pack the chillies tightly into a clean plastic container or glass jar. Pour over the hot pickling liquid, making sure the chillies are completely submerged.

These nifty pickles will be ready after 24 hours and will keep for up to 1 month in the fridge.

TIPS AND TRICKS

» Nacho lover? Try these chopped over your favourite nachos with some sour cream, guacamole and salsa.
» This recipe makes a lot of pickles. They last well in the fridge, but if you prefer to make less, simply halve the recipe.

+ Pickled fennel with turmeric

This pickle is so easy, and good for you too. Turmeric is a well-known antioxidant and is anti-inflammatory. Paired with the fennel, this vibrant, subtle pickle adds a splash of colour to salads and works wonderfully with any fish dish.

MAKES 1 JAR

- o 250ml cider vinegar
- o 100ml water
- o 2 tbsp caster sugar
- o 1 tbsp ground turmeric
- o 1 tsp fennel seeds
- o 1 tsp yellow mustard seeds
- o 1–2 fennel bulbs, depending on their size (you want 500g)

Heat all the ingredients except for the fennel in a small pan. Bring to the boil and simmer for a minute or two.

Meanwhile, remove any of the herby fronds from the top of the fennel bulbs (keep them for salads or a soup garnish). Chop the bulb in half and remove the tough core at the bottom. Wash well, then cut into thin slices, ideally 2–3mm thick. A mandolin is ideal for this, but so is a sharp knife along with some care and patience!

Place the fennel in a plastic bowl or container. Pour the hot pickling liquid over the fennel and stir. Cover with cling film and leave to pickle for at least 12 hours, stirring once or twice throughout. Store in an airtight jar in the fridge for up to 1 week.

+ Easy neon pickled onions

We call this neon due to the bright purple colour it takes on. This handy, tasty garnish looks amazing and adds a huge amount of bright flavour to a lot of dishes. Bulk up on this recipe if you fancy so that you can have them to hand as needed.

- 2 medium red onions
- decent pinch of salt
- juice of 2 lemons
- 1 tsp caster sugar

Top and tail the onions, then peel them and cut them in half. Place them cut side down on your chopping board. Using your sharpest knife and your best knife skills, slice the onions into half-moons as thinly as possible. The thinner you can get them, the quicker they pickle and the prettier they look. A mandolin also works perfectly for this. Place the sliced onions in a bowl or Kilner jar and sprinkle with a pinch of salt.

Juice your lemons, then stir in the sugar until it dissolves (the acidic lemon juice will do this easily without needing to heat it). Pour the juice through a strainer over the onion, then leave to pickle overnight. If you're using a bowl, cover it tightly with cling film. If you're using a jar, just cover it with the lid. In reality, they will be decently pickled even after 2 hours or so, but the longer you leave the onion to pickle, the more vibrantly neon pink the colour will be.

Stored in the fridge, this will last for several weeks.

+ Dukkah

This is really handy to have in your store cupboard. We use it on top of hummus and a few of our salads and egg dishes in particular. Dukkah is essentially a mix of toasted nuts and fragrant spices. The recipe below gives a delicious outcome, but feel free to play around with it – add a different nut, toasted sunflower seeds or even some chilli flakes.

MAKES 1 MEDIUM JAR

- 200g hazelnuts
- 15g fennel seeds
- 10g caraway seeds
- 10g cumin seeds
- 10g coriander seeds
- 20g mixed sesame seeds
- 10g dried thyme
- 5g salt

Preheat your oven to 180°C. Place the hazelnuts on a baking tray and roast in the oven for 8 minutes. Remove them from the oven, and while still hot, place them on a clean tea towel and rub them to remove the skins. Set aside while you prepare the spices and discard the skins.

Pop all the seeds except the sesame seeds into a pan. Place the pan on a medium heat and toast the seeds for 7–8 minutes, until lightly done and you can smell the spices in the air. Remove them from the pan straight away. Toast your sesame seeds in the same pan for 3–4 minutes, just until they are lightly toasted, and remove from the pan immediately.

To bring the dukkah together, you can use a small food processor to roughly grind the nuts, then tip them into a large bowl with the sesame seeds. Grind all the toasted spices and the thyme to a coarse powder in a spice grinder, then add to the bowl and mix everything together. Or if making it by hand, chop the nuts to a medium gravel and grind the spices and thyme in a pestle and mortar. Mix everything together in a bowl.

Finish by tasting and adding the salt as needed. The mix should be quite chunky, with larger pieces of hazelnuts and a good texture throughout. Store the dukkah in an airtight container for up to 4 weeks.

+ Smoked aubergine yogurt

The king of soup dressings – and salad dressings, for that matter! This is one dressing I am so proud to call my own invention. It adds a lovely contrast to so many dishes. We use it in our Middle Eastern slaw (page 176) and on our Moroccan zalouk (page 100) in particular, and it works particularly well as a dressing for our harira soup on page 144. It's so tasty that it's worth experimenting with on any number of dishes.

MAKES 1 SMALL BATCH

- 1 aubergine
- 2 garlic cloves, crushed
- juice of 1 lemon
- 200ml Greek yogurt
- 50ml olive oil
- salt and freshly ground black pepper
- pinch of cayenne pepper or paprika (optional)

First prepare the aubergine. If you have a gas hob, lay the aubergine directly over a gas flame and let it 'burn' for several minutes on each side. Alternatively, place it under the grill set to its maximum setting, turning once each side is well burnt. The objective is to get the skin very charred ('smoked') while cooking the inside of the vegetable at the same time. Hold your nerve! The aubergine is done when the outside is very black and charred and the vegetable flesh inside is extremely soft, practically mushy, all the way through. A little pulp or juice may seep out of it, but don't worry. Put in a bowl to one side to cool.

Cut the cooled aubergine in half from top to tail and scoop the flesh out into a bowl. A little bit of the charred skin might make it into the bowl – this will add a nice smoky flavour, but try to avoid too much of this getting in. Mash well with a fork until the aubergine is good and mushy.

Using a spatula or large spoon, fold in the crushed garlic, lemon juice, yogurt and olive oil. Taste and adjust the seasoning, adding more garlic, lemon, yogurt or oil if needed. The dressing will look a little off-white or even grey and should taste slightly smoky with a good hit of lemon and garlic, so be brave with the seasoning. If you feel it needs a little something else, you can add a few pinches of cayenne pepper or paprika.

Keep in a sealed airtight container in the fridge for up to 4 days. It may split slightly, but just stir it up and taste it each time you use it, as you may need to adjust the seasoning or lemon.

+ Zhoug

We use this fragrant, spicy herb paste quite a lot in various dishes (see pages 122 and 266). It works well folded gently through crème fraîche with a dash of lemon to make a lovely creamy dressing or used as a base for an oil dressing by whisking it with lemon and olive oil.

MAKES 1 SMALL JAR

- 50g fresh coriander, including stalks
- 50g fresh parsley, including stalks
- 2 green chillies, deseeded
- 2 garlic cloves, minced
- 3 tbsp extra virgin olive oil
- 3 tbsp water
- ½ tsp ground cumin

Put all the ingredients in a food processor or blender (or use a hand-held blender) and purée for several minutes to form a fine paste or thick sauce. It will have a full-on flavour, but remember that it's going to be eaten alongside lots of other lovely ingredients and probably some bread, so it needs to be good and punchy. With that in mind, taste and adjust the seasoning, adding more chilli, garlic or spices as you see fit.

+ Hazelnut praline

Praline is essentially a toasted nut and caramelised sugar brittle that is ground and used as a sprinkle. It's one of those handy store cupboard items that can spruce up any number of sweet dishes. We use this for our semolina pancakes (page 38) and as a brownie topping, adding a spoonful of melted chocolate on top of a brownie and sprinkling some praline over with a heavy hand. We even serve it with our hot chocolate at Christmas (page 309) and it's perfect for sprinkling over chocolate or vanilla ice cream.

MAKES 1 SMALL JAR

- 100g hazelnuts or nuts of your choice
- 200g caster sugar

If the nuts have their skins on, it's best that they are removed as they can add too much of a bitter taste to a recipe. To do this, simply spread them on a baking tray and roast in a hot oven (200°C) for 8–10 minutes. Remove them from the oven and allow to cool a little. The easiest way to remove the skins is to place the nuts in a clean tea towel and give them a shake and a rub through the towel, then pick out the skinned nuts.

To make the caramel base for the praline, I like to use a non-stick pan as it's easier to clean up later. Place the caster sugar in the pan and place it on a medium heat to melt. Try not to stir the sugar, as it will only cover your spoon in hot caramel, which is quite hard to clean. Please also be aware that you are working with an extremely hot substance as the sugar heats, so be very careful not to get any on your clothes or skin. I find the best way to make a caramel is to gently move and swirl the pan as the sugar is turning into a liquid. The end product should be a golden honey brown, if not a touch deeper in colour than that, and all the sugar should be fully dissolved and liquid. Be patient and keep at it until this stage is reached.

When you do reach this stage, add the nuts and swirl the pan until the nuts are all coated in the caramel.

The next step is to place a piece of non-stick baking paper or a silicone mat flat on your work surface or on a large baking tray. Pour the nut-caramel mix directly onto the sheet in an even and uniform layer. You want it to spread out, but make sure it doesn't pour off the sides. Now simply leave it to cool completely and harden. >>

To finish, blitz it in a food processor and use it to sprinkle on top of your favourite desserts. Stored in an airtight container, it will keep for up to 1 month.

TIPS AND TRICKS

» Try this recipe using other nuts: walnuts, pistachios or almonds would all be particularly good. Leaving the skins on the almonds works well for me, but do roast them first, like you do with the hazelnuts in the above recipe.
» Make this into a spread of sorts by continuing to blitz the praline until a paste is formed, perhaps adding a tablespoon or two of honey while it's blending. This would be sensational as a cake filling, a topping on a brownie or just smeared over a plain biscuit.

+ Berry and rose compote

A very easy and versatile recipe, this compote will hold in the fridge for up to 1 month.

MAKES 1 LARGE JAR

- o 500g frozen mixed berries
- o 200g caster sugar
- o 1 tsp rosewater

Put the berries and sugar into a large pot. Put on a medium heat and slowly cook, stirring regularly until the sugar has dissolved and the compote has slightly thickened. Remove from the heat and leave to cool.

Stir in the rosewater, then taste and add a little more if you feel it needs it. However, please note that whenever you use rosewater, it should not be overpowering – a little goes a long way, as all you ever want is a hint of rose.

TIPS AND TRICKS

» This is great served with our granola and some natural or Greek yogurt (page 27), bircher muesli (page 22) or semolina pancakes (page 38). Or try it with the foolish mess on page 299 instead of the other fruit components.
» This compote would also be delicious warmed up and spooned on top of ice cream as an easy wintertime dessert.

How To

How to sweat onions, celery and garlic

Many of our recipes begin by asking you to sweat a mix of these base vegetables. Here is the recommended method.

Wash, peel and skin (as appropriate) the vegetables in question. Chop as recommended in the recipe. Generally, a medium dice will work for most recipes.

Heat a good dash of oil in a medium or large pot set over a medium heat. The size of the pot will depend on what else will be added to the pot later in the recipe, especially in the case of soup. When the oil is hot, add your vegetables, giving them a good stir in the oil.

Next, take a suitable piece of greaseproof paper or baking parchment and press it over the surface of the vegetables. This allows them to sweat better because the paper traps the steam the vegetables generate. The paper need not be cut exactly – I generally tear off a square that will fit easily over the diameter of the base of the pot and press that over the vegetables, with the excess simply pressed up against the sides of the pot.

Pop a lid on the pot and continue to sweat over a medium heat for 15 minutes or so, until the vegetables are fully tender, stirring every 5 minutes and replacing the paper and lid afterwards. They are done when you can easily mash a bit of onion between your fingers. The objective is to cook them fully without caramelising or browning them, but if that accidentally happens, don't fret – it isn't too big a deal for most recipes and you will know better next time!

How to caramelise onions and garlic

This is a delicious recipe to add to your repertoire, plus caramelised onion pops up in a number of our recipes. And when you are going to the trouble of making one batch, why not make several at the same time? I always recommend making multiple batches at once and either storing it in the fridge for up to 2 weeks or else freezing some. I recommend adding garlic here too, but you can just as easily leave it out.

Prepare 500g of onions by cutting each one in half from top to tail, removing the skins and then cutting the onions into 1cm-thick slices. If using garlic, break up 2 heads of garlic into individual cloves, removing the skins of each clove and trimming the end. Roughly chop.

Heat a wide-bottomed saucepan over a medium-high heat, adding a dash of oil. Once heated, add all of the onions and garlic, give them a good stir and turn the heat down to low-medium. Cook uncovered, as you want the moisture to evaporate so the sugars can caramelise. Stir every 10 minutes and cook until they turn a lovely deep brown colour. This can take up to 45 minutes or so – be patient. If you are making multiple batches of this recipe, you might need to cook them a little longer.

If some of the mix catches a little on the bottom, don't worry – this will add a lot of flavour. To save yourself a lot of time scrubbing and deglazing, just pop a lid on the pot once it's off the heat and let it sit for 10–15 minutes. The glaze should be fully absorbed back into your richly browned onions and garlic.

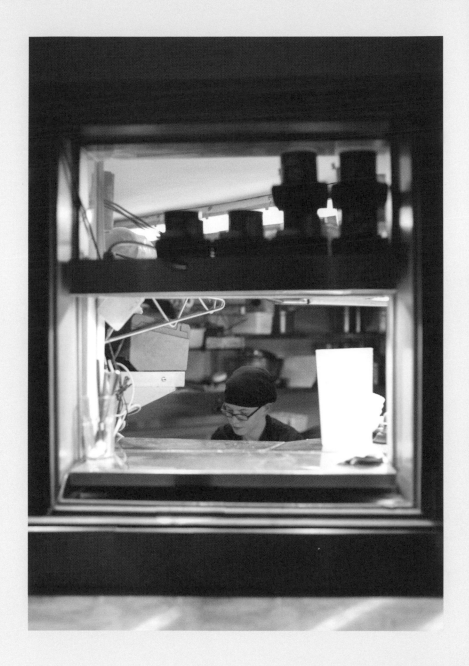

How to roast garlic

Roast garlic is a wonderful ingredient to have to hand – I would go so far as to say that it's invaluable – so I recommend making multiple batches of this recipe. It will hold in the fridge for 2 weeks or so, or put some of the finished paste into an airtight container and freeze it. Not only is it easy to make, but it can add so much depth to so many sauces and dressings.

- 2 heads of garlic
- drizzle of extra virgin olive oil
- salt and freshly ground black pepper

Preheat your oven to 190°C. Cut the top off the garlic bulbs, making sure the tip of each clove has been trimmed off but keep the whole bulb intact (don't worry, though, if individual cloves fall off). You're aiming to make an opening in each clove so that you can squeeze the roasted garlic flesh out at the end – think of it like nature's very own mini-tube of garlic paste!

Place the bulbs in a square of tin foil that will be large enough to encase the bulbs in a little parcel. Drizzle 2 teaspoons of olive oil over the garlic along with 1 tablespoon of water. Wrap the foil around the garlic to create a little parcel, ensuring it is brought together tightly to seal it up. Pop in the oven and roast for 30–40 minutes. The garlic is done when it's lovely and soft, and ideally a little darkened. If it hasn't taken on enough colour, leave it in the oven for an additional 10–15 minutes with the parcel open.

Remove from the oven and allow to cool. When it's cool enough to handle it, squeeze the roasted garlic out of each clove into a small bowl. Using a fork, mash this up to a smooth purée with a little salt and pepper to season. Your roasted garlic is now ready to use! This will hold in the fridge for 2 weeks or you can freeze it in smaller batches.

How to knead dough by hand

A handy technique (no pun intended!) if you don't have a food mixer or if you fancy a workout. Kneading dough by hand is also a very satisfying way of making dough and I recommend doing it the odd time so that you get to understand dough/bread-making a little bit more.

What's the point of kneading dough? You want to bring the flour together with the other ingredients and work the mix so it becomes an elastic, cohesive mass, as this is what will give the finished bready product that springy and airy feel that you want.

By applying a kneading action, you are developing the gluten (a protein in the flour), which allows this elasticity to form. When you have formed the dough, you leave it to rest so the yeast can get to work raising the dough by creating carbon dioxide, lifting and lightening the dough (which also helps to further develop the gluten). By doing all of this, you end up with a dough that can be baked off into a light, airy, springy bread that's delicious to eat. If you didn't go to all this trouble, you would end up with a hard, heavy, dense mass – essentially one giant lump of a cracker.

So first, clear a decent-sized area on your clean countertop and dust it lightly with flour. Keep an open bag of flour within arm's reach for later on.

To bring the dough together, put all the dry ingredients in your recipe (except the yeast) in a large bowl and mix well with your hands so everything is evenly distributed. Take about two-thirds of the warm, wet liquid mix and dissolve the yeast in it, then add this to the dry mix. Using one hand, bring the mix together so that a dough begins to form by simply working the mix to incorporate the wet components into the dry components.

This is where you need to use some judgement – you want the mix to form so it becomes a soft mass. If it's too wet or too dry, you can't knead it effectively. Add more of the liquid if it needs it (you've a third of the liquid put aside) – you may not end up having to use it all. If you've added too much, simply add a little more flour. You want to end up with a cohesive mass of dough that will come away in one lump from the bowl, albeit feeling slightly sticky. Keep mixing the dough in the bowl until it gets to that point. >>

Now take the dough out of the bowl, place it on the floured countertop and knead it. The dough might be a bit sticky at first, but it should become less so by working it. To knead, you are essentially stretching the dough out, pulling it back over itself and repeating. Do this for several minutes – you don't have to kill yourself, but a bit of elbow grease is no harm. Again, you may need to add a little more flour or even a little more liquid if you feel it isn't forming a dough that becomes one soft, springy mass. You might also have to continue sprinkling a little flour over the dough, the countertop or your hands from time to time.

To test when the dough is adequately kneaded, simply take a small piece of it (the size of half a walnut) and stretch it out between your fingers to form a thin sheet – imagine it being the springy base of a trampoline. When this can stretch out enough so that it becomes extremely thin and skin-like without tearing and it's thin enough to see light through it, you're done. If it hasn't reached this point, just continue kneading for a few more minutes and repeat the test. It could take up to 10 minutes to reach this point, so have a wee break if you need it.

When it has passed the test, form the dough into a large ball. Rub some oil over the bowl the dough was originally in and pop the ball of dough back in it. Cover the bowl with cling film or a clean, damp tea towel and set it aside, ideally in a warm place, so the yeast can work its magic. The dough is ready for the next stage, as per your recipe, when it has doubled in size due to the action of the yeast inflating it with the carbon dioxide it has produced.

How to toast nuts, seeds and spices

Toasting nuts, seeds and spices can really bring out the best in them. A quick toasting dramatically improves the flavour as well as adding an improved texture and colour to seeds and nuts.

Overall, when toasting nuts, seeds and spices, I recommend toasting each nut, seed or spice separately. They often toast at different rates, so you want to avoid a pan of mixed spices, for example, where one type is getting burnt while the other is underdone.

To toast nuts (almonds, hazelnuts, etc.) and seeds (sunflower, pumpkin, etc.), heat a dry frying pan over a medium heat for 2 minutes. Add the nuts or seeds and continue to heat, tossing every 10–15 seconds until they are nicely toasted. Cook them like this for anywhere from 2 to 5 minutes in total, until the nuts are lightly toasted, then transfer to a bowl, otherwise the nuts might burn from the residual heat in the pan.

To toast spices (like cumin, coriander, fennel or sesame seeds), put a large, dry pan on a medium heat, then add the seeds, tossing from time to time, until the seeds are nicely toasted. Generally, 1 minute or so should suffice on a hot plate. Remove from the heat and from the pan so that they don't toast too much – you need to be careful here. You want them toasted enough that they start to give off their lovely fragrance, but going too far will destroy this loveliness entirely. So please be watchful!

To grind the toasted spices, a pestle and mortar is the old-school method – but also a bit of hard work if you've a lot to do (and if you are following our recipes, you will have realised we are quite fond of our spices!). Those apothecaries of yore must have had some biceps! You could also buy a hand mill, which cuts out a lot of the work.

However, if you do love spices, it's worth investing in a spice grinder – or you might find that some food processors come with a spice-grinding component. Of course, you could cut out all of this by just buying ground spices, but ultimately it's considered to be far better, and will get the best flavour for your dish, to buy your spices whole and toast and grind them yourself as needed.

How to deseed a pomegranate

We use a lot of pomegranates in our kitchens, as much for their beauty as for their flavour. Here is the best way to get all the seeds out without it taking all day. This is how they have done it for centuries in the Middle East. There is nothing terribly graceful about this, but it's a lot of fun.

Wash your pomegranate and cut it in half across the equator.

Wearing an apron, hold the cut half over a large bowl or container, with the cut side facing down above the open palm of your hand. In your other hand, take a heavy spoon (a large serving spoon or wooden spoon) and with medium force bash the back of the pomegranate. Continue doing this, adjusting the pressure of the bashes so that you are getting the seeds to fall out without breaking up the pomegranate. This is fun, isn't it?

Keep going, moving the 'bash point' all around the back of the pomegranate half until you've knocked out all the seeds. Repeat with the other pomegranate half.

When you're done, pick through the contents of the bowl to remove the odd bit of white flesh that may have fallen in.

How to make brown butter

This is a firm favourite that works incredibly well as a very simple dressing on any soup that involves a creamy component. When you make a brown butter, you are cooking the butter solids in the fat component of the butter so that they caramelise. In doing so, the butter takes on a lovely brown colour as well as a sweet, nutty flavour.

Put 150g butter (or more, as necessary) into a medium-sized saucepan set over a medium heat. Let it melt, then bring it to the boil by turning up the heat. The butter will start to foam up – control the heat so that it stays foaming without rising above the sides of the pan. After a few moments, you will see parts of this foam with little brown specks in it. As soon as you see these, turn off the heat and let the butter sit.

Once the foam has dissipated, the butter should now be speckled with a chocolate-brown colour. If it isn't quite there yet, simply return it to the heat and cook further until this point is reached. When decanting the butter, use a spatula to scrape all the brown bits from the bottom of the pan, as that's where all the flavour is.

The brown butter is now ready to use in your recipes (see pages 138 and 307), or you can use melted brown butter as a dressing for soups or to toss with some broccoli, fennel, Brussels sprouts or roasted carrots or parsnip when serving. Any leftovers will hold in the fridge perfectly for up to a month – just reheat it when you need to use it, stirring well to redistribute the brown sediment throughout the melted butterfat.

How to cook beetroot

The earthy goodness and rich, vibrant colour of beetroot makes it such a unique ingredient to be used in so many dishes. It's up there with the carrot in terms of its versatility when it comes to featuring in sweet and savoury recipes! We use it in several of our recipes, and if it's not to be used raw, here's how we handle it.

Wash your beetroots well to remove any dirt. Trim lightly to remove any straggly roots.

Place on a baking tray with a light splash of water (about 100ml) and cover very tightly with tin foil. Roast in the oven for up to 1 hour (or more) at 160°C, though you may need to increase the cooking time depending on the size of your beets. They are cooked when a skewer or knife slips in easily, indicating they are tender right through to the centre. Leave in for longer if needs be, adding another dash of water if necessary. Since they are so well covered, it's difficult to see how you can take these too far!

When done, leave them to cool. Top and tail them and peel them using gloved hands if you like, but you may be lucky and the skins might just rub off for you. I wash the peeled beetroot to ensure all traces of the skin and its debris are removed. These are now ready to use in your recipes (see pages 106, 134 and 158 for uses).

Alternatively, simply wash, top, tail and peel the fresh beetroot, cut it into even-sized chunks or wedges, toss in a little oil and seasoning and roast in the oven at 180°C for 30–45 minutes (or more), until the wedges are fully tender all the way through.

How to poach an egg

Any talk about poaching eggs is always a controversial discussion. However, after many years of testing various methods, I've found that this method is the most reliable. You will need a small sieve (the size of sieve that will sit over a cup) and a wide, shallow pan (about 5–6cm deep). It's important to use the freshest, best-quality eggs that you can.

Fill your pan to within 2cm of the top with water and bring to the boil. Add a dash of white wine vinegar or lemon juice to help 'set' the egg as soon as it's added to the water.

Once the water is boiling rapidly, turn down the heat until it becomes something more than a simmer but something less than a rapid boil.

Get a bowl or a cup and place the sieve over it. Crack the egg into this and let it sit for about 30 seconds to allow the watery outer layer of the egg white to drain off. Now gently tip the egg into the water by holding the sieve over the pot and sliding it in, trying not to let the sieve touch the water. Repeat for the number of eggs you wish to cook.

Cook the eggs to your liking, but at least until the white is fully set (3–4 minutes) or longer if you like a firm yolk (about 8 minutes).

If you want to cook a lot of poached eggs at once, set a bowl of iced water to one side and add the cooked eggs to this directly from the hot water so that they chill immediately. Do this with all of your eggs. When ready to serve your eggs, refresh them by popping them back into a pot of boiling water for about 1 minute or so – you want them to reheat, not start cooking again. Lift out using a slotted spoon onto some clean kitchen paper, rolling the egg over so it dries, then use in your desired dish.

How to cook dried chickpeas or beans

It would seem that a far more economical and environmentally-friendly way of using chickpeas or beans is to buy them dried and rehydrate and cook them yourself. It takes a little more time, but it's worth it!

Put the dried chickpeas or beans in a large container or pot that's big enough to hold them plus three times their volume of water. Top up with cold water to three times their volume – this is very important. If you're cooking different varieties of beans and chickpeas, soak and cook them separately, as they may not take the same amount of time to cook. Add 1 tablespoon of bicarbonate of soda and 1 tablespoon of salt. These will help the beans to absorb water and they will also help the skins to soften when they cook. Leave for a minimum of 12 hours or overnight, but anything up to 24 hours is perfectly fine.

When ready to cook, drain off all of the water and rinse the beans under cold running water. Put into a large pot and cover with fresh water up to twice their volume. Cover with a lid and bring to the boil, then turn the heat down to a simmer. I recommend adding several bay leaves when boiling the beans. (Don't add salt to the cooking liquid – while it works in your favour when soaking the beans, it will work against you when cooking them, as it risks making the beans tough.)

Cook until the beans or chickpeas are fully cooked, which can take anything from 40 minutes to 3 hours, depending on the type of bean or chickpea. Test by tasting and assessing the texture. They should be fully soft with little or no gritty texture (which you will discover in an undercooked bean) and only slightly firm. You don't want to overcook them or they will all turn mushy.

When you feel they are adequately cooked, drain well. If not using immediately, rinse them under cold running water, drain well and store in the fridge for 2–3 days.

How to cook a ham hock

Ham hock is such a flavourful way of eating ham. It's also incredibly versatile and it goes with virtually any salad. Or for an extra special brunch or supper, use it to make our croque monsieur on page 88.

SERVES 4–6, DEPENDING ON WHAT YOU ARE USING IT FOR

- 4 ham hocks
- dash of oil
- 2 large onions, chopped
- 2 large carrots, chopped
- 10 garlic cloves, roughly chopped
- 400ml white wine
- splash of cider vinegar
- 4 bay leaves
- 3 star anise
- 2 cinnamon sticks
- 300ml apple juice
- 500ml water

First soak the ham hocks overnight to remove some of the salt that was added when preserving the ham. Cover the hocks in water and store in a large, covered container in the fridge. If you don't have time to soak them overnight, put the hocks in a large pot, cover with water, cover the pot with a lid and bring to the boil. Discard this water and repeat once more.

When the hocks are ready to use, heat a good dash of oil in a large pot set over a medium heat. Sweat the onions, carrots and garlic until soft, pressing a sheet of baking parchment over the surface of the vegetables, covering with a lid and stirring every 5 minutes. They should be ready after about 15 minutes. Remove the parchment, then add the wine, cider vinegar, bay leaves, star anise and cinnamon. Turn up the heat to simmer the ingredients until the liquid has reduced by half.

Next add the ham hocks, apple juice and enough of the water to cover the hocks. Bring to the boil, then reduce to a gentle simmer. Cover the hocks with some greaseproof paper, cover the top of the pot tightly with tin foil and then cover this with the lid to create a tight seal so that the hocks can steam in the liquid produced. Leave to cook slowly for 2½–3½ hours. Check occasionally to make sure there is enough liquid in the pot, but always seal it tightly with the tin foil again. The hocks are ready when the bones are falling out of the hocks. Drain and allow the hocks to cool so that they can be handled, then pull the meat from the bones, removing any skin on the outside of the hocks first and discarding any sinew and skin.

Ingredients We Use

Orange blossom water

Orange blossom water is a by-product of the extraction of essential oils from fresh orange blossom flowers. It provides a fragrant element to dishes it's used in, adding the essence or, dare I say, 'spirit' of the orange rather than a full-on orange experience. However, it's quite powerful so please do be careful. A little goes a long way, so use it sparingly. Remember, you can always add more to a dish, but it can be very hard or impossible to take it out.

It's commonly used as a flavouring for baklava mixed with a simple sugar syrup (page 295). We sometimes use it in a salad dressing, but it has the most prominence on our menu in our orange blossom butter (page 66), which we serve with our scones.

You can buy it in any Middle Eastern store, but it's becoming more and more popular in supermarkets too. If you can't source it, a fine orange zest purée will help or you can use orange oil or even an orange liqueur if you're so inclined, but you might have to play around with the quantity you use to get the right intensity.

Rosewater

Rosewater is made by steeping rose petals in water. It's used to flavour food and can be used in perfumery too. One of its most common uses in food is the traditional Turkish delight sweet. Similar to orange blossom water, it's also traditionally mixed with a simple sugar syrup and used to soak a baklava straight from the oven. We use it in our raspberry, apple and rose drink (page 315), berry and rose compote (page 343), rosita Prosecco cocktail (page 318) and the white chocolate and rose topping for our brownies (page 283).

This is becoming a more popular ingredient, so you should find it in a lot of supermarkets and certainly in a Middle Eastern or Asian store. Vanilla extract can work in certain recipes in its place, but it really is a unique flavour, so substitute it with caution.

Pomegranate molasses

Pomegranate molasses is a syrup made from reducing down fresh pomegranate juice so that the sugar caramelises and the liquid evaporates, resulting in a thick, dark red liquid. It's quite a tart syrup and is commonly added to stews and sauces in Middle Eastern cuisine. We use it a lot as a base in salad dressings. It adds a rich, sweet tartness that works extremely well with a little lemon and olive oil. We also use it in our recipes for baharat lamb cutlets (page 245), nectarine and goats' cheese salad (page 199) and in the tips and tricks section of our recipes for yogurt, tahini, honey and nuts (page 36).

Again, most Middle Eastern or Asian shops should stock this as well as a number of larger supermarkets. A substitute might be a little honey and lemon mixed together. Alternatively, tamarind paste works well in providing a certain type of sweet-sour note.

Sumac

Sumac is made from the berries of a sumac tree native to the Middle East and Africa. The berries are picked and then dried before being ground to produce a powder that has a tart, tangy lemon flavour. It was traditionally used when lemon was out of season, but it can be used at any time, as it adds a slightly different note to a dish than an actual lemon. It can be used in rubs and marinades too. We use it in the café as a final flourish sprinkled over a number of our dishes for an added burst of flavour as well as for its beautiful dark red colour, so you will see it suggested as an optional ingredient in many of our recipes.

If you can't get your hands on sumac, an alternative would be some finely grated lemon zest, perhaps mixed with a little ground pepper and a touch of paprika.

Za'atar

Za'atar is a traditional spice mix that's very popular in the Middle East. There are numerous different variations on the mix depending on the locality, but most contain the same staple ingredients of dried thyme, oregano and marjoram, toasted sesame seeds, salt and sumac. Za'atar is also the name for an herb found in the Middle East that's very like oregano. Za'atar can be used as a seasoning for meats and fish and is commonly found sprinkled over hummus. It's also a popular topping for certain breads – we use it on our flatbread (page 322) as well as recommending it on hummus or on our Middle Eastern breakfast plate (page 52).

If you can't source za'atar, a good substitute is dukkah – see our recipe on page 337. It's not quite the same, but it ticks a similar enough box.

Index

Acknowledgements

It has been an amazing adventure writing this book. It allowed me the time to think carefully about the overall approach to our food and, in doing so, I've realised how many people have influenced the food that I love, the food that is in this book. The old adage of 'too many cooks spoil the broth' doesn't apply here: the collaborations I've had with so many wonderful chefs, cooks, editors, photographers, designers and stylists – and so many other folks – has led to a result that I'm so very proud of!

Many thanks in particular, though in no particular order:

To some wonderful and inspirational chefs out there that I've admired so much over the years: Yotam Ottolenghi, Nigel Slater, Claudia Roden, Sam & Sam Clark to name but a few. Sincerely, your contribution to my life has actually been quite profound.

To the *Guardian* newspaper (yes, I'm thanking an entire newspaper) – not only did you introduce me to some wonderful food writing but you are also actually almost wholly responsible for setting me off on my journey by inspiring me with that article, many moons ago, about the psychology of regret, giving me that 'eureka' moment to just go do it, get on with the dream and the adventure.

To Darina and her gang at Ballymaloe, for teaching and inspiring me and supporting our little café over the past number of years. Darina also put me in touch with her son, Isaac, who provided invaluable advice on the business side of producing a cookbook.

To Michelle (Julio, Melbourne) and Andrea (Loafer Bread, Melbourne), who provided such inspiration and education as regards the food I now cook and whose presence and influence, so profound, is felt throughout this book.

To Sadhbh, for daring to dream with me that we could actually write a book and always giving me such wonderful advice, support and, when needed, frank honesty!

To Nicki, Teresa and Ruth, who have been wonderful collaborators in shepherding this book from its very inception right through to the wonderful, beautiful physical reality that you now hold before you.

To Orla, Jane and Leo, who put down a tremendous week with us styling and photographing our food. It was an awful lot of work but also such fun, so thank you for making us look good and for being such a pleasure to work with during such an intense week.

To Graham, for bringing all elements of the book together stylistically in order to make the whole so much greater than the sum of its parts.

To Kristin, my editor, who patiently went through my manuscript, line by line, to make this book read and sound so much better than ever I could have hoped. Each interaction has been sparkling – I'm not sure how many authors look forward to their editor's comments and calls as much as I did.

A special mention to my kitchen teams in Brother Hubbard, my collaborators in the kitchen, who inspire me with their energy and creativity, so much of it reflected in these pages – you all have your influence and presence in so many of our recipes and your names are peppered throughout these pages. Having disappeared for so many weeks to finish this book, I am also deeply grateful to the entire team in our cafes who always keep the ship sailing in my absence.

Eamon is almost as responsible for bringing this cookbook together as I am and his hard work, creative talents, dedication and overall good humour have made this book more exciting and more fun than I ever could have dreamt of – thank you, thank you – it is always a joy cooking and creating together.

I must convey my sincere gratitude to my wonderful James, for his patience, his support, his careful proof reading and his dedicated recipe testing – where would I be without you?

In this book, I've really tried to convey the sense of community that enshrouds Brother Hubbard – there are far too people to thank individually. From our suppliers to our team to our wonderful customers, the influence of that community on what we do and what this book is has been profound. Thank you.